Offbeat Florida: The nature, history, culture, and quirk of the Sunshine State

Neala McCarten

ISBN: 978-0-9973322-4-7

NOTE: Although every effort has been made to provide accurate information, many smaller attractions have limited days and hours which can also vary seasonally. University-based museums may close during school holidays. In addition, hurricane damage has caused closures. Readers are advised to call or check the website (or both) for current information.

Legend for Cover Map Icons

	Flora-Bama Bar and its unique Mullet Toss		Tallahassee has been the capital since 1824		Panhandle is famous for its tupelo honey
	Carrabelle is famous for having the world's smallest police station		Crawfordville and the old Ford graveyard		The Stephen Foster Folk Culture Center State Park
	Cummer Museum of Art and Gardens in Jacksonville		St. Augustine Alligator Farm since 1893		Lubee Bat Conservancy, University of Florida bat house
	Crystal River National Wildlife Refuge is the only refuge created for Florida manatees.		Clydesdales in Dunnellon		Mermaids at Weeki Wachee Springs State Park
	International Speedway track and museum at Daytona Beach		Surfing Santas at Cocoa Beach		Guang Ming Temple is the largest Buddhist temple in Central Florida.
	Havana, FL is known for its cigar heritage		Chihuly art in St. Petersburg		Kennedy Space Center Visitor Complex
	Zora Neale Hurston, a Black American writer and anthropologist, lived in Eatonville and used it in her novels		Dali museum in St. Petersburg		The Florida coast is the final resting place for many wrecked ships
	Sarasota has true circus history, and live performances		Florida still has its beloved drive-in movies		The 205-foot-tall carillon at Bok Tower Gardens
	Navy SEAL museum at Ft. Pierce		Morikami Museum and Japanese Gardens, Delray		Ah-Tah-Thi-Ki museum of Seminole culture and history
	Port Mayaca Polo Club welcomes visitors in Okeechobee		Ted Smallwood's General Store has morphed into a museum in Chokoloskee		Butterfly World is an aviary and raises butterflies for sale in Coconut Creek

Regions of Florida

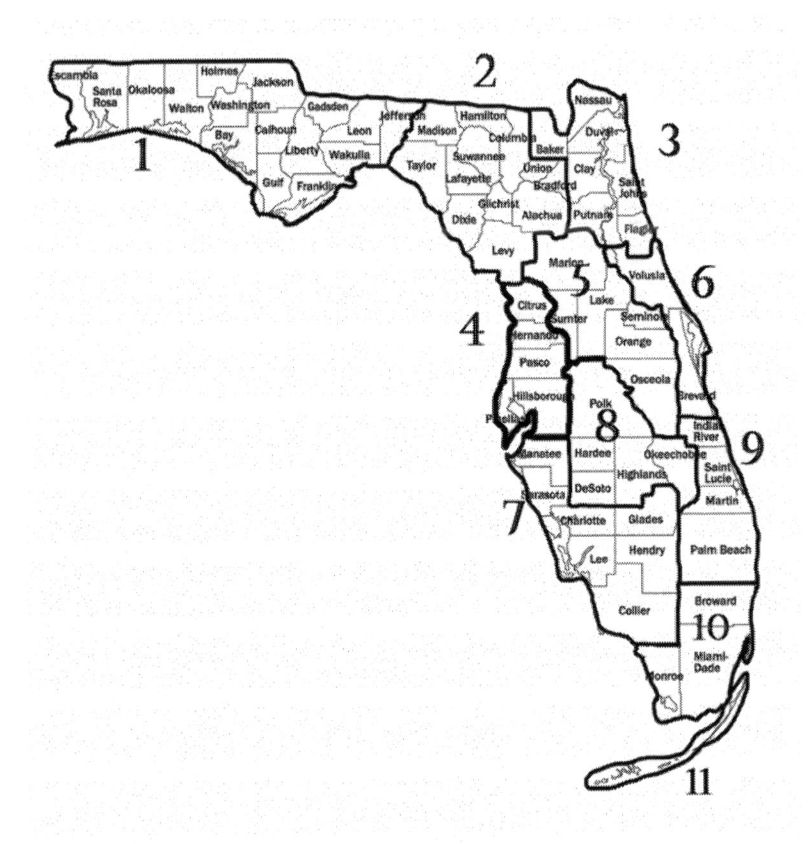

Preface

I never expected to move to Florida. I grew up in New York City where south Florida was a vacation destination, and honestly, I wasn't impressed. It was crowded and hot, especially in the summer. So, when family and friends moved away (and moved to Florida) I opted to go to Albuquerque, New Mexico, a city and a state that I will love forever.

Life, especially my life, often takes unexpected turns and I eventually found myself moving to Florida. Whether I chose Daytona or the Grand Scheme of Things chose it for me I will never know. But I fell in love with Daytona and the central east coast of the Sunshine State.

There are some states that are just not like the others. I suppose most of the states of these United States have something that differentiates them, but there are those that are just a bit more different, in the best sense.

The surprise for me was that Florida is among them. What? Florida? The land of the Mouse? Of people slathered in sunscreen? Of endless highways filled with cars going nowhere?

Go beyond those stereotyped places and suddenly there's wonderful, and sometimes heart-breaking history. There's nature that is barely tamed as well as pleasures and experiences hard to find elsewhere.

Welcome to Florida… the state you only think you know.

Neala McCarten

Table of Contents

Florida: The state you only think you know

Florida is a complicated state, filled with contradictions. It has been regularly ravaged by natural disasters; homes and businesses flattened by hurricanes, crops destroyed by infestations, and freezes. It has a climate so tough that special breeds of cattle and horse evolved to survive, Florida's beloved Crackers. Unrestricted industries have decimated the land and polluted the water but at the same time many are working to save them.

Despite challenges, Florida has managed to thrive, often in unexpected ways. The sophisticated pleasures of large cities draw millions while in smaller towns residents and visitors enjoy the thrills of figure-eight car races, rodeos, and strawberry festivals. Florida has one of the country's best state park systems. Literally award-winning. Up and down the length of the state are parks and gardens filled with beauty, as well as preserves where history is held in stasis against the crumblings of time. Much has been lost to development, but much still remains.

Florida may have culture wars, may be challenged by nature, but it is still here, still vibrant. And, surprisingly offbeat.

Florida history

Life in Florida began long before colonial powers and the give-and-take wars of Spain, France, and England.

Over 12,000 years ago hunter/gather groups lived in an area much wider than Florida is today – the sea level was lower and the land was drier. Over time these groups developed agriculture, and traded across what is now the southeastern United States. They constructed large temple mounds and village complexes. By the time the Spanish arrived in the early 1500s there were multiple native cultures throughout Florida.

Colonial Powers Arrive

But that all began to change with Ponce de Leon's landing in 1513 somewhere between Cape Canaveral and St. Augustine. He called the area La Florida, in honor of Pascua Florida (Feast of the Flowers), Spain's Easter celebration. After sailing around the peninsula, he returned to Spain. He believed there was gold to be found and so he returned. And that's where he made his mistake. Instead of precious metals he found angry Native Americans who fought off the interlopers. Many of the soldiers were killed and de Leon was badly wounded, eventually dying from his injuries.

But that didn't stop others from coming. Panfilo de Narvaez landed in 1528 and got into a war with the native group called the Timucuans whose territory extended across the northeast and central parts of Florida. He ultimately disappeared in a hurricane trying to reach safety in Mexico. Hernando de Soto came in 1539 in his unsuccessful search for gold. His well-equipped landing force didn't help him. There was no gold and in the process of seeking riches (and perhaps in fits of anger as well) he destroyed many of the towns and villages. Eventually he too met his death.

It has been suggested that the Native Americans were initially successful in holding off the Spaniards because of their method of warfare – continually harassing the Spaniards with their superior hunting skills. They could also fire three to four arrows in the time it took for the Spanish soldiers to reload an arquebus or crossbow.

Then, things began to change. The colonial dreams of France and Spain started to take shape. In 1562 the French Protestant Jean Ribault landed, ultimately establishing Fort Caroline at the mouth of the St. Johns River, near present-day Jacksonville. Pedro Menendez de Aviles came a few years later in 1565 and established St. Augustine as a base to protect the galleons carrying the cargo from their colonies in South and Central America, and to maintain domination of Florida.

Jean Ribault was not about to let De Aviles take over his territory. He intended to destroy the Spanish forces at St. Augustine. But it was hurricane season and his ships were carried south and wrecked on the coast of the area that is Daytona Beach and Cape Canaveral. De Aviles retribution was swift and bloody. Almost everyone was killed. Only a few were able to escape to ships and return to France. The women and children who managed to survive went to Havana to fend as best they could.

The inlet where the massacre occurred is called Matanzas -- meaning "slaughter" in Spanish – and is still known as the Matanzas River. Thus Spain, in a true river of blood, took control of Florida for the next 235 years.

Finally established, the Spanish began constructing forts and Catholic missions. Soon their territory extended across north Florida and into South Carolina. The French never returned to Florida, but the British, still colonizing the newly discovered continent, also made attempts into the area. And the Native Americans who had lived in Florida slowly disappeared through death from diseases brought in with the colonists, absorption, and flight.

The British and the Spanish had different approaches to ruling Florida, largely arising from their attitude to slavery, and the Spanish commitment to extending Catholicism to the New

World. Any slave who could escape to Spanish Florida and would agree convert to Catholicism would be freed. The Spanish even constructed a fortified town in 1736 just north of St. Augustine for the former African slaves. Called Gracia Real de Santa Teresa de Mose (pronounced MosA). This would be the first free Black settlement in North America.

The Spanish had a long run, dominating the area until 1763. Then, during the Seven Years' War between Spain and England (1756-1763), Britain captured Havana. This was a major blow to the Spanish who ultimately traded Florida for the return of that city. Thus, the British took back control.

It was now Britain's turn to colonize Florida. One of the most famous land grants (huge swaths of territory given to those who would colonize the land and pay tribute) was given to Andrew Turnbull, a Scottish doctor. His grandiose idea was to create the largest British colony in the America. He named the new colony New Smyrna, in honor of the ancient Greek city of Smyrna on the Aegean coast of Anatolia (which was his wife's birthplace). He eventually persuaded 1,400 colonists to come as indentured servants, the majority from the island of Menorca (the smaller cousin to Minorca). But he greatly oversold the quality of life the newcomers would have. They struggled with disease, hunger, raiding parties, and harsh treatment by overseers. Eventually winning their freedom, the survivors moved north to St. Augustine where they still have a cultural presence. Little is left of his colony but the city of New Smyrna Beach is a popular tourist destination.

Meanwhile, further north Britain was forcing the relocation of Native Americans to make room for White settlers on the fertile land. History records the devastation of the Native American population on their forced marches, and the hardships and deaths they experienced. Ironically, one of the unintended consequences of this forced relocation was the emergence of the Seminole Nation. In the 1770s Creeks from Georgia and Alabama who successfully escaped to Florida were joined by other remaining Native groups as well as escaped slaves to form the Seminoles, a name which is said to mean either *wild people* or *runaway*.

British rule of Florida lasted only until the American Revolution ended their colonial adventure. Although our famous revolution never made it to Florida, it did create economic and political issues for Britain. In a political switch, Spain became an ally of France and helped capture Pensacola from the British in 1781.

With Spain now in charge of parts of Florida, Spanish colonists resumed pouring in lured by land grants. They were joined by refugee settlers from the newly formed United States of America, who didn't participate on the winning side in the Revolutionary War. Finally, Spain's policy of freeing any enslaved person who would convert to the Catholic faith also brought newcomers to the area.

Florida, once again, proved difficult to hold. Decades of war had left Spain financially challenged. The new United States of America didn't want a foreign power sitting so close and the Federal government certainly wanted to keep their own settlers coming into the area. In 1821 Spain formally ceded Florida to the United States.

What to do with the Native Americans

The issue of foreign powers resolved, there was still the problem of the Native Peoples who wanted to keep their land. The new nation decided military action was the solution. In 1818, General Andrew Jackson fought the Seminoles in what would later would be called the First Seminole War.

Initially, many of the Seminole Nation agreed to relocate to the land that became Oklahoma, but not all the Seminoles were convinced this was to their benefit. When federal troops attempted to force those who were reluctant to leave, the Seminoles responded by attacking plantations where the troops were often stationed. They also freed the enslaved men and women, many of whom then joined the Seminole Nation. The fighting became a bloody battle for the soul of Florida and the land itself. This became known as the Second Seminole War (1835–1842). Ultimately, the Seminoles lost and the remaining 200 or 300 men, women, and children retreated to the impenetrable Everglades.

In 1845 Florida became the 27th state entering as a slavery state and joined the Confederacy during the Civil War. Although Florida largely escaped the ravages of that war the former enslaved people did not fare well. Emancipation was a sham, and a system of tenant farmers and sharecroppers was little better. Reconstruction was not for the formerly enslaved.

Capitalism Appears

Meanwhile, seekers of a new life continued to come south, and by the end of the 19th century, Florida was a burgeoning economic powerhouse of cattle-raising and agriculture. Citrus farming became the rage but there was even cigar manufacturing. Exploitation of the state's extensive natural resources – from sponges to phosphate mining began in earnest.

At the dawn of the 20th century railroads opened the interior and southern reaches of the state. Now agriculture, lumber, and a fledgling tourist industry became mainstays of Florida's economy.

Henry Flagler and Henry B. Plant not only constructed

railroads but also hotels to serve the rich vacationers. Land values followed a boom then bust cycle, depending on whether or not a horrific natural disaster had occurred. Central Florida is largely marsh – wetlands frequently or continually inundated with water. The best known, largest, and most crucial is the Everglades. Plant and animal life abound because nutrients are plentiful and the pH is usually neutral. These marshes recharge groundwater supplies and provide water to the streams. This is considered particularly important during periods of drought. But all this was inconvenient if you wanted to create either a farming empire or sprawling housing development.

As the railroads extended south the marshes were drained to create orchards and the resulting crops were shipped north. But, as so many had found, Florida was a land not easily tamed. One cautionary tale comes from the experiences of Hamilton Disston (1844-1896). He bought four million (yes, four million) acres of Florida land in 1881.

It was reportedly the largest land purchase by a single person in world history. His investment spurred growth throughout the state and efforts to drain the Everglades triggered Florida's first land boon. Kissimmee, St. Cloud, Gulfport, and Tarpon Springs were reportedly the result of some of his efforts.

But instead of riches, he lost his proverbial shirt. When he was unable to drain the Kissimmee River flood plain, the surface water around Lake Okeechobee, and the Everglades, he was forced to sell much of his investment at a loss. The parts he did drain destroyed the marsh's ability to recharge the streams and created a drought drying the area north of Lake Okeechobee. If that wasn't enough, devastating freezes crippled production. His empire and his dreams collapsed. Disston eventually returned to his home town of Philadelphia, dying shortly thereafter.

Today with the development of refrigerated air Florida continues to draw tourists and new residents. With a growing awareness of the importance of preserving the resources of the state, if for no other reason than tourism, there is more willingness to moderate the previous headlong rush into terraforming the land.

Visiting the Sunshine State

The long peninsula of Florida is divided into regions, although the divisions can be fluid. For the purposes of this book 11 areas have been identified and numbered, generally from west to east, and north to south. Although using regions to organize the state may suggest that towns in different regions are far apart, in actuality those at the edges can be quite close while towns within the same region can be hours away.

With its burgeoning population centers Florida has numerous metropolitan areas composed of main cities and satellite towns. Some sprawl over two counties, others are limited to one. The convention in this book has been to create an abbreviation for any metropolitan area that contains more than one county. For metropolitan areas that are just one county, travelers should consider all the towns in that one county as convenient for day trips.

A Note on Time Zones

Although most of Florida is in the Eastern Time Zone, much of the Panhandle is in the Central Time Zone -- all of Region 1 and the western end of Region 2. Specifically, the following counties:

- Escambia County
- Santa Rosa County
- Okaloosa County
- Walton County
- Holmes County
- Washington County
- Bay County
- Jackson County (borders Eastern Time)

- Calhoun County (borders Eastern Time)
- Gulf County is split with two time zones. The north side of Gulf County is in the Central Time Zone and the south side along the Gulf Coast is in the Eastern Time Zone.

Region 1 Panhandle: Panama City, Pensacola, and Tallahassee

Northwest Florida is home to barrier islands, maritime forests, historic forts, bayous, and marine habitats. It is sometimes called the Forgotten Coast because it has been (relatively) forgotten by developers.

Apalachicola National Forest is the largest national forest in Florida covering more than a half-million acres of longleaf pine, freshwater springs, rivers, and lakes. Many of the special places to explore are included below, but there's more recreational opportunities included on their website. https://www.fs.usda.gov/attmain/apalachicola/special places

The **Gulf Islands National Seashore** spans both Florida and Mississippi. In the Florida section, the park offers all manner of outdoor activities as well as ranger-led excursions. https://www.nps.gov/guis/planyourvisit/florida.htm

The National Forest Preserves does exactly that – preserves what the Panhandle once was with hundreds of miles of trails and dozens of recreation areas throughout the Ocala, Apalachicola, and Osceola National Forests. https://www.fs.usda.gov/florida/

Scenic Highway 30A is a 24-mile corridor that hugs the Gulf of Mexico with sugar-white sand beaches and rare coastal dune lakes. It is considered a tourist attraction of major proportions. https://friendsofscenic30a.com/

The city of **Tallahassee** and its metro area **(TMA)** encompasses Gadsden, Jefferson, Leon, and Wakulla counties. **Fort Walton Beach (FWB)** includes the town of Destin as well as all of Okaloosa County, and Walton County. **Pensacola (PMA)** has its own metropolitan area including Escambia County and Santa Rosa County. NOTE: Santa Rosa Beach is a community in Walton County and part of the Fort Walton metropolitan area. It is different from Santa Rosa County.

Apalachicola, FL (Franklin County)

This city's Historic District contains hundreds of homes and buildings dating back to the 1830s. Enjoy a self-guided walking tour with a map available from the Chamber of Commerce and Visitor Center at 17 Ave E; Apalachicola, FL 32320; Phone: (850) 653-9419 or download a copy here: https://cdn.floridasforgottencoast.com/cdn-uploads/2017/10/14095542/apalachicola-historic-walking-tour.pdf

Chapman Botanical Garden adjoins the Orman House Historic State Park (See below). Walking trails showcase its beauty. 177 Fifth St; Apalachicola, FL 32320; Phone: (850) 653-1210; https://www.floridastateparks.org/learn/chapman-botanical-gardens

Visit the **John Gorrie Museum** and say "thank you" to the man who invented the ice machine and the principle which also led to the refrigerators, and air-conditioning that we all enjoy today. 46 Sixth St; Apalachicola, FL 32320; Phone: (850) 653-9347; https://www.floridastateparks.org/parks-and-trails/john-gorrie-museum-state-park

Orman House Historic State Park features the antebellum Orman House built in 1838 by Thomas Orman overlooking the Apalachicola River. **Three Soldiers Monument** also onsite honors southern soldiers who served in the Vietnam War. The monument was cast from the original molds of sculptor Frederick Hart's installation at the Vietnam Veterans Memorial in Washington, DC. The monument and the Chapman Botanical Garden are linked by pathways and a parking lot. 177 Fifth St; Apalachicola, Fl 32320; Phone: (850) 653-1209; https://www.floridastateparks.org/parks-and-trails/orman-house-historic-state-park

Blountstown, FL (Calhoun County)

The **Panhandle Pioneer Settlement** is a living history museum with 18 buildings, dating from 1820s to the 1940s. The buildings were moved from locations throughout Calhoun County and now form a farm community within Sam Atkins Park. 19972 SR 71; Blountstown, FL 32424; Phone: (850) 674-2777; http://www.panhandlepioneer.org/

Bristol, FL (Liberty County)

Torreya State Park combines a horticultural rarity and an architectural treasure. The park was named after the extremely rare species of Torreya tree that grows only on the bluffs along the Apalachicola River. The park's hardwood forest provides one of the few fall color displays in Florida. Visitors can also tour the Gregory House built in 1849 by plantation owner Jason Gregory. 2576 NW Torreya Park Rd; Bristol, FL 32321; Phone: (850) 643-2674; https://www.floridastateparks.org/parks-and-trails/torreya-state-park

Bruce, FL (Walton County) (FWB)

The town of Bruce is the home of the **Muscogee Nation of Florida**. The Creek predecessor of the Muscogee Nation of Florida signed 11 treaties with the United States between 1790 and 1833 in which they agreed to relocate from their traditional homelands (which included the states of Georgia, Alabama, and Florida). Those who formed the Muscogee of Florida traveled south to escape the federal government's removal policies. The museum offers a view of life in Bruce from the early 1900s until today. Visitors can enjoy walking trails, and heritage sites including historic buildings and museums. NOTE: Museum is currently under renovation. Call or email for updates. 278 Church Rd; Bruce, FL 32455; Phone: (850) 835-2078; http://www.mnoffl.com;

Carrabelle, FL (Franklin County)

This city is famous for having the world's smallest police station, but it has more to see than the teeny, literally phone booth-sized station.

The police station website says it best: *We still have our "Smallest Police Station in the World" (it's a phone booth) on US 98 at the corner of CR67. The original is now on display in the hallway of the current department between the World War II Museum, and the Police department.*
http://www.carrabellepolice.com/about.html

Camp Gordon Johnston Museum focuses on World War II history and artifacts. It is across the highway from Carrabelle Beach, one of several beaches on which troops practiced amphibious landings. FREE. 1873 Hwy 98 W; Carrabelle, FL 32322; Phone: (850) 697-8575; https://www.campgordonjohnston.com/

Carrabelle Bottle House is a tiny bottle-built house open to visitors who can step inside and peer out through the colorful walls. Next to the tiny structure is a tiny lighthouse. 604 SE Ave F; Carrabelle, FL 32322; Phone: (850) 697-9620; http://carrabelle.org/things-to-do/carrabelle-bottle-house/746/

Now home to the **Carrabelle History Museum**, Carrabelle's original City Hall was constructed in the 1930s and has four rooms filled with its collections. FREE. 106 Ave B, SE; Carrabelle, FL 32322; Phone: (850) 697-2141; http://www.carrabellehistorymuseum.org/

Crooked River Lighthouse was built on its current site in 1895 and restored in 2007. This iron skeleton structure is topped with a circular parapet. There are 128 steps (almost 11 flights) to climb to the top, weather permitting. Indoor exhibits include a historical setting of the early 1900s, examples of beacons, the methods of constructing a skeletal tower lighthouse, and objects of everyday life in the Keeper's Room. FREE with a charge to climb the lighthouse. 1975 Hwy 98 W; Carrabelle, FL 32322; Phone: (850) 697-2732; http://www.crookedriverlighthouse.com/

A quirky story is told to explain the unusual name given to **Tate's Hell State Forest**. Legend has it that a farmer named Cebe Tate went into the swamp in search of a panther that was killing his livestock. Things didn't go as planned and Tate was lost in the swamp for several days and nights, bitten by a snake, and had to drink from the murky waters to slake his thirst. Finally, he came to a clearing near Carrabelle, only living long enough to murmur *My name is Cebe Tate, and I just came from Hell*. The reason to visit, besides the great story behind the name, is its forest of tiny cypress trees. Usually 50-feet tall or more, these mini versions are closer to 6- to 15-feet tall. The culprit is said to be the clay in the soil which stunts their growth. A boardwalk and overlook provide accessible viewing. 290 Airport Rd; Carrabelle, FL 32322; Phone: (850) 697-0010;
http://carrabelle.org/things-to-do/day-trips/dwarf-cypress-stand-in-tates-hell-state-forest/1040/
https://www.fdacs.gov/Forest-Wildfire/Our-Forests/State-Forests/Tate-s-Hell-State-Forest

Chipley, FL (Washington County)

Wondering where Florida's highest waterfall is found? It's in **Falling Waters State Park** surrounded by huge trees and fern-covered sinkholes. A boardwalk trail leads visitors to Florida's highest waterfall at 74 feet. The Falling Waters Sink is a 100-foot-deep, 20-foot-wide cylindrical pit into which flows a small stream that drops 73 feet to the bottom of the sink. 1130 State Park Rd; Chipley, FL 32428; Phone: (850) 638-6130; https://www.floridastateparks.org/parks-and-trails/falling-waters-state-park

Chipley has claim to one rather dubious honor – home of **Kudzu**. Erected in 1967 by Florida Board of Parks and Historic Memorials, likely before its invasive properties were fully understood, the sign says: *Kudzu, brought to this country from Asia as an ornamental, was developed near here in the early part of the Twentieth Century and given to the world as a soil-saving, high-protein forage plant by Mr. and Mrs. C.E. Pleas. The fast-growing, deep-rooted leguminous vine has been widely grown in the United States as a drought-resisting, erosion-controlling plant that compares with alfalfa in pasture and hay-making values.* The plaque can be found at the intersection of West Jackson Avenue (US. 90) and West Boulevard. Learn the history of kudzu at: https://www.invasive.org/biocontrol/25Kudzu.cfm

Seacrest Wolf Preserve offers the opportunity to experience wolves up close. Reservations are required for walking tours through the large two- or three-acre natural wolf habitats. NOTE: There are strict rules about clothing, and photography is not allowed. 3449 Bonnett Pond Rd; Chipley, FL 32428; Phone: (850) 773-2897; https://www.seacrestwolfpreserve.org/

Crawfordville, FL (Wakulla County) (TMA)

It doesn't have a formal name, but the collection is often

called **Harvey's Ford Collection** or the **Old Ford Graveyard**. The names describe exactly what visitors can see and photograph – an assemblage of rusting vintage Ford trucks and cars, arranged in chronological order by owner Pat Harvey. NOTE: About 1/4 mile north of Emmett Whaley Rd on the west side. 4204 Crawfordville Hwy; Crawfordville, FL 32327; https://www.roadsideamerica.com/tip/15949

DeFuniak Springs, FL (Walton County) (FWB)

Climb Florida's tallest mountain... which isn't very high. At 345 feet above sea level **Britton Hill** is the lowest peak in the country. Part of Florida's ancient ridges, it was formed millions of years ago when most of Florida was under water. Today these dune ridges are some of the oldest land forms in Florida. It's located in Lakewood Park. 2759 North County Hwy 285; DeFuniak Springs, FL 32433; Phone: (850) 892-8108; https://www.visitflorida.com/en-us/things-to-do/arts-history/britton-hill-highest-point-florida.html

DeFuniak Springs is home to the historic **Florida Chautauqua Assembly**, a once-gated campus/resort built during the Victorian era. The Chautauqua welcomed visitors to its annual, multi-week assembly from 1885 to 1927. The historic assemblies were revived in 1993 and still continue today as a four-day program with notable or famous keynote speakers, educational breakout sessions, performance teas, evening dinner performances, and exhibits relating to an annual theme. The grounds are mostly intact and the structures are listed on the National Register of Historic Places. Take the **DIY Historic District Tour** starting at 1162 Circle Dr for an overview of the campus/resort grounds and history. Download the walking tour brochure and learn more here: https://www.defuniaksprings.net/1277/Historic-District-Tour The town still hosts a yearly assembly. https://floridachautauquaassembly.org/

Located in historic train depot, **Walton County Heritage Museum** is the county's repository for artifacts, photographs, and documents related to life in Walton County with a focus on 1885-1945. 1140 Circle Dr; DeFuniak Springs, FL 32435; Phone: (850) 951-2127; http://www.waltoncountyheritage.org/

Destin, FL (Okaloosa County) (FWB)

Destin Harbor Boardwalk bustles with bars, restaurants, and shops as well as opportunities to book sea and sky experiences. 102 Harbor Blvd; Destin, FL 32541; Phone: (850) 683-3009; https://www.destinboardwalk.com

Destin History & Fishing Museum features history from the 1830s, with an emphasis on the evolution of the fishing industry from seine boats to party boats. Peruse over 60 local species, plus an outdoor Museum Historic Park Complex with more exhibits. 108 Stahlman Ave; Destin, FL 32541; Phone: (850) 837-6611;
http://www.destinhistoryandfishingmuseum.org/

Eastpoint, FL (Franklin County)

Apalachicola National Estuarine Research Reserve is the second-largest estuarine research reserve system in the country, spanning more than 246,000 acres in Apalachicola Bay. Highlights include exhibits and aquaria, and a coastal walk from the Nature Center to the shoreline. A half-mile of elevated boardwalks surround the Nature Center. FREE. 108 Island Dr (State Road 300); Eastpoint, FL 32328; Phone: (850) 670-7700; https://www.apalachicolareserve.com/

Elgin Air Force Base, FL (Okaloosa County) (FWB)

(See also Valparaiso, FL)

The **Air Force Armament Museum**, adjacent Eglin Air Force Base, displays about 30 different aircraft, along with several hundred pieces of armament. A 32-minute film on the history of Eglin Air Force Base is shown continuously throughout the day. Coming soon will be Quonset huts with the histories of Black soldiers. FREE. 100 Museum Dr; Elgin AFB, FL 32542; Phone: (850) 882-4062; http://www.afarmamentmuseum.com/

Fort Walton Beach, FL (Okaloosa County) (FWB)

Emerald Coast Science Center features hands-on science from dinosaurs to robotics. There's even a mini-makers lab. Their rescued and donated animal exhibits include everything from snakes to parakeets. 31 SW Memorial Pkwy; Fort Walton Beach, FL 32548; Phone: (850) 664-1261; https://www.ecscience.org/

Heritage Park & Cultural Center conveniently groups several of the attractions of Fort Walton in one location. **Fort Walton Mound** was built as a ceremonial and political center by the Mound Builder Culture between 800-1400 AD. This is one of three surviving mound complexes in the Panhandle; the others are Tallahassee's Letchworth-Love Mounds Archaeological State Park, and the Lake Jackson Mounds Archaeological State Park. The on-site museum depicts 12,000 years of Native American living and includes collections of prehistoric ceramics. **Garnier Post Office Museum** interprets items from the early postal era of this county covering the years 1918 to 1956. The two-room **Camp Walton Schoolhouse** covers educational history from 1911 to the 1930s. 139 Miracle Strip Pkwy SE; Fort Walton Beach, FL 32548; Phone: (850) 833-9595; https://www.fwb.org/parksrec/page/heritage-park-cultural-center

Havana, FL (Gadsden County) (TMA)

Named after Havana, Cuba for its high-quality tobacco growing and cigar making, the tobacco farming is gone, but the town still invites visitors to explore its antiques, furniture design centers, boutiques, shops, and cafes. NOTE: Almost everything in Havana is closed Mondays and Tuesdays.

Havana History & Heritage Society Shade Tobacco Museum interprets the history of the town, its tobacco heritage, and more with 14 exhibits and several videos. Limited hours. 204 Second St NW; Havana, FL 32333; Phone: (850) 270-7315; https://www.facebook.com/havanahistoryheritage/

Marianna, FL (Jackson County)

Bellamy Bridge Heritage Trail is a one-half mile multi-use trail with access to historic Bellamy Bridge, built in 1914. The bridge and the trail are rumored to be haunted. 4057 Hwy 162; Marianna, FL; https://bellamybridge.org/

Chipola River Paddling Trail begins at the bridge on State Road 166 in Marianna and flows over 50 miles through river swamps and hardwood forests. https://www.paddleflorida.net/chipola-river-paddle.htm

Florida Caverns State Park offers 45-minute cave tours of limestone stalactites, stalagmites, soda straws, flowstones, and draperies. This is the only state park in Florida where visitors can take a guided tour through a large cave system. A self-guided museum is located upstairs in the visitor center. The scenic Chipola River winds through the park. 3345 Caverns Rd; Marianna FL 32446; Phone: (850) 482-1228; https://www.floridastateparks.org/parks-and-trails/florida-caverns-state-park

Built in the 1890s and significantly remodeled in 1910 the historic **Russ House** is considered a beautiful Classical Revival/Queen Anne home, and is now the visitor center for Jackson County. Guided tours are available daily during regular business hours. FREE. 4318 Lafayette St; Marianna, FL 32446; Phone: (850) 482-8061; https://visitjacksoncountyfla.com/play/culture-heritage/historic-joseph-w-russ-house/

If you want to take a break and grab some ice cream, **Southern Craft Creamery** makes its ice cream from the milk of its own dairy cows and uses local ingredients for flavors. Private tours by appointment only. 2884 Jefferson St; Marianna, FL 32446; Phone: (850) 372-4958; https://www.southerncraftcreamery.com/

Milton, FL (Santa Rosa County) (PMA)

Southern Raceway is a family-owned raceway with a short racing season. 9359 Nichols Lake Rd; Milton, FL 32583; Phone: (850) 623-2333; https://southernraceway.com/

West Florida Railroad Museum occupies the L&N Milton combination freight and passenger depot that was built in 1907-09 (on the site of the original 1882 depot). Although open Wednesday through Saturday, the best days to visit are said to be Friday and Saturday. NOTE: They recommend email as the preferred form of contact: conductor@wfrm.org; 5003 Henry St; Milton, FL 32570; https://www.wfrm.org

Monticello, FL (Jefferson County) (TMA)

Golden Acres Ranch, just outside of town, combines raising sheep and goats, farm tours, and jelly-making from the native Mayhaw trees on the property. Mayhaw look a bit like cranberry and are fruity and tart. They grow in moist soil in river and creek bottoms. 704 Barnes Rd; Monticello, FL 32344; Phone: (850) 242-3747; https://goldenacresranchflorida.com/

The **Monticello Historic District** encompasses twenty-seven city blocks of buildings built before 1930. The circa 1890 opera house is still in use today. https://www.visitflorida.com/en-us/cities/monticello.html

Panacea, FL (Wakulla County) (TMA)

The town was first called Smith Springs after the mineral waters and their curative properties. Then, in 1893 a group of Bostonians purchased the land and preferring a more evocative name, called the town Panacea, after the goddess of universal remedy. The town thrived until the Depression and a hurricane in 1928. The springs were mostly abandoned. If you wish to explore the ruins, stop by the Wakulla Visitor Center at 1505 Coastal Hwy; Panacea, FL 32346 for more information. The town holds the Blue Crab Festival the first Saturday each May. More information at: http://www.bluecrabfest.com/.

Gulf Specimen Marine Laboratory specializes in small marine creatures – seahorses, hermit crabs, spiny box fish, electric rays, and red and white spotted calico crabs. They have both *Looking* and *Touching* tanks. Something a bit unexpected is the story of Jake and Blinky, crocodiles who fought to the death and are now immortalized as fiberglass models. 222 Clark Dr; Panacea, FL 32346; Phone: (850) 984-5297; https://gulfspecimen.org/

Panama City and Panama City Beach, FL (Bay County)

Situated in the geographic center of Northwest Florida, Panama City is the largest city between Pensacola and

Tallahassee. Panama City is a separate entity from Panama City Beach, although they are only a few miles apart.

Panama City, FL

This more urban enclave boasts a downtown with an arts and theater district, entertainment hub, shopping district, and local colleges as well as its St. Andrews historic district. http://historicstandrews.com

Panama City Center for the Arts offers changing exhibits in each of its galleries, over 30 exhibitions a year. FREE. 19 E Fourth St; Panama City, FL 32401; Phone: (850) 640-3670; https://www.pccenterforthearts.com/

Panama City Publishing Museum contains more than 70 major historical items, including original printing presses and office furnishings, photos, newspapers, and documents produced by the paper's publisher (and the city's founding father) George Mortimer West. In 2008 the City of Panama City bought the building, restored it, and opened it as a museum. Enjoy a guided walking tour of the historic district that starts at the museum. 1134 Beck Ave; Panama City, FL 32401; Phone: (850) 872-7208; https://historicstandrews.com/museum/

Science and Discovery Center of Northwest Florida is a children's museum highlighting interactive science and natural history, plus play areas, live reptiles, and a nature trail. 308 Airport Rd; Panama City, FL 32405; Phone: (850) 769-6128; http://www.scienceanddiscoverycenter.org/

Panama City Beach, FL

Panama City Beach is located about 10 miles away on the Atlantic Ocean.

Gulf World Marine Park provides daily shows and exhibits, as well as interactive programs with a variety of animal species. 15412 Front Beach Rd; Panama City Beach, FL 32413; Phone: (850) 234-5271; https://gulfworldmarinepark.com/

Man in the Sea Museum is dedicated to preserving the history of diving with exhibits and a large collection of antique diving equipment. Visitors will also be able to see SEALAB-I, the United States Navy's first underwater living facility. 17314 Panama City Beach Pkwy; Panama City Beach, FL 32413; Phone: (850) 235-4101; https://maninthesea.org

St. Andrews State Park is at the far eastern edge of Panama City Beach. With the Gulf of Mexico on one side and St. Andrews Bay on the other the park is known for its outdoor opportunities. There are trails and wildlife, as well as fishing from several piers. Rent a bicycle, canoe, or a kayak. For those interested in exploring Shell Island, there is a shuttle that regularly runs from the mainland to the island. Call to reserve a spot, and to ensure service during the winter season. 4607 State Park Ln; Panama City Beach, FL 32408; Phone: (850) 708-6100; https://www.visitpanamacitybeach.com/things-to-do/parks/st-andrews-state-park/

WonderWorks, in its distinctive upside-down building, combines education and entertainment with over 100 interactive exhibits. Explore the hurricane shack, play a game of Mindball, design and ride your own roller-coaster, play virtual sports, climb the indoor ropes course, or compete in a game of laser-tag. This is one of two Florida locations for the science-focused indoor amusement park chain. The other WonderWorks is in Orlando. 9910 Front Beach Rd, Panama City Beach, FL 32407; Phone: (850) 249-7000; https://www.wonderworksonline.com/panama-city-beach/

ZooWorld Zoological and Botanical Conservatory Zoo focuses on conservation with over 260 animals plus programs and shows. NOTE: Extra cost for several of the animal interactions. 9008 Front Beach Rd; Panama City Beach, FL 32407; Phone: (850) 230-1243; https://zooworldpcb.com/

Pensacola, FL (Escambia County) (PMA)

Often referred to as The City of Five Flags, Pensacola has changed ownership several times. Spanish, French, British, Confederate, and American flags have all flown over the city.

Pensacola was also an important early center of blues, ragtime, vaudeville, and jazz activity, and developed into a regional cornerstone of the *chitlin' circuit* in later years. In fact, it's one of only two cities in Florida that are recognized as part of the famed Mississippi Blues Trail. https://msbluestrail.org/blues-trail-markers/pensacola-blues. The other is Tallahassee.

"Chappie" James Museum showcases the life of Daniel "Chappie" James, a fighter pilot in the US Air Force who became the first Black officer in the history of the United States military to attain the rank of four-star general. 1606 Dr. Martin Luther King Jr Dr; Pensacola, FL 32503; Phone: (850) 542-4721; https://www.chappiejamesmuseum.org

Cryptologic Command Display protects historic naval cryptologic documents, equipment, artifacts, and photographs. Visitors without a valid Department of Defense ID card (active or retired military) **must** obtain a pass from the Visitor's Center located in Building 777, just inside the Naval Air Station main entrance on Navy Boulevard. NOTE: The list of required documents and information can be found: https://usncva.org/cryptologic-command-display.html

Destination Archaeology Resource Center describes the

Florida archaeological sites that you can visit, both on land and underwater. There are exhibits, events, and programs throughout the year. FREE. NOTE: The website provides information on archaeological sites across the state. 207 E Main St; Pensacola, FL 32502; Phone: (850) 595-0050 ext. 108; https://destinationarchaeology.org/exhibits

Fort Barrancas (Fort San Carlos de Barrancas) is a United States military fort and National Historic Landmark within the Naval Air Station Pensacola. The bluff (or barrancas) overlooking the entrance to the bay was considered of such strategic importance that the Army Corps of Engineers built Fort Barrancas over the ruins of previous forts built by the Spanish, French, and British. The visitor center offers indoor exhibits about the history of the area. 3182 Taylor Rd; Pensacola, FL 32508; Phone: (850) 455-5167; https://www.nps.gov/guis/learn/historyculture/fort-barrancas.htm; https://www.nps.gov/guis/planyourvisit/fort-barrancas-area.htm

Completed in 1834 to defend Pensacola Bay and its naval yard, **Fort Pickens** is the largest of Pensacola's four forts and offers visitors the opportunity to explore its tunnels and cannons. Indoor exhibits focus on the natural environment, wildlife, and history of the Fort Pickens area. 1400 Fort Pickens Rd; Pensacola Beach, FL 32561; Phone: (850) 934-2600; https://www.nps.gov/guis/planyourvisit/fort-pickens-area.htm

Over the course of its history, the land that is now Pensacola has been occupied by the British, the Spanish, the French, the Confederacy, and (finally) the United States. **Historic Pensacola Village** illuminates the city's story through furnished period houses and archaeological sites including the oldest church in Florida still on its original foundation. Eleven of Pensacola's most historic attractions are included and are open to the public. NOTE: Paid parking is available at Tarragona and Church Street. Free on-street parking may be found in the area however only two hours in the same space is currently permitted. 120 Church St; Pensacola, FL 32502; Phone: (850) 595-5985; http://historicpensacola.org/plan-your-visit/museums-properties/

National Naval Aviation Museum displays 150 restored aircraft, including rare and one-of-a-kind flying machines, vintage uniforms, as well as dioramas depicting World War I Western Front, and Main Street USA in 1943. Movies, flight simulators, and Blue Angels 4D Experience are also available. Check the site for the schedule of the Blue Angels practice sessions. West Gate off Blue Angel Parkway. 1878 S Blue Angel Pkwy; Pensacola, FL 32508; Phone: (850) 452-3604; https://www.navalaviationmuseum.org/

Pensacola Museum of Art displays selections from its permanent collection as well as special time-limited exhibits. 407 S Jefferson St; Pensacola, FL 32502; Phone: (850) 432-6247; https://www.pensacolamuseum.org/

The 11-mile **Pensacola Scenic Bluffs Highway** shadows the Escambia River and Bay through miles of wetlands where US 90 meets the Escambia River. https://floridascenichighways.com/our-byways/panhandle-region/pensacola-scenic-bluffs/

University of West Florida Archaeology Institute showcases exhibits on the archaeology of Northwest Florida, as well as Escambia and Santa Rosa counties. The artifacts cover Prehistoric Native American, Colonial, Early American, and Victorian eras and are displayed in the exhibit area of the Archaeology Institute. FREE. 11000 University Pkwy; Bldg 89; Pensacola, FL 32514; Phone: (850) 474-3015;

https://uwf.edu/cassh/community-outreach/archaeology-institute/museums/

Veterans Memorial Park and Wall South is a collection of memorials to the American revolution, Korean War, WWI, WWII, and War on Terror. Its *Wall South* is currently the only permanent replica of the Washington DC National Vietnam Memorial. 200 S 10th Ave; Pensacola, FL 32502; Phone: (850) 434-6119; https://veteransmemorialparkpensacola.org/Home

Perdido Key, FL (Escambia County) (PMA)

Connected by bridges on the east to Pensacola (Florida) and on the west to Orange Beach (Alabama), Perdido Key is often said be on the Flora-Bama border. It’s a popular vacation spot with opportunities for sports both in and above the water.

Perdido Key is home to the famous **Flora-Bama Bar** and its unique Mullet Toss with contestants competing to see who can throw dead mullet further over the state line of Florida and into Alabama. Three days of events and parties surround the Toss, usually held in April. 17401 Perdido Key Dr; Perdido Key, FL 32507; Phone: (850) 492-0611; http://www.florabama.com

Port St. Joe, FL (Gulf County)

(See also Panama City, FL)

Cape San Blas Light is a skeletal tower with eight cast iron legs that support the watch room and lantern. The Cape San Blas Lighthouse, two Keepers Quarters', and Oil Shed have been relocated to George Core Park and are open to the public. 200 Miss Zola's Dr; Port St Joe, FL 32456; Phone: (850) 229-8261; https://www.facebook.com/Cape-San-Blas-Lighthouse-116302328410959

Florida's first constitution was drafted in the short-lived town of St. Joseph, which was selected over Tallahassee to host Florida's first State Constitution Convention. **Constitution Convention Museum** commemorates the work of the 56 territorial delegates who drafted Florida's first constitution in 1838. Visitors can take a self-guided tour through displays and exhibits of the era. Artifacts from the original settlement in St. Joseph are displayed. A replicated convention hall takes visitors into delegates' debates through life-size, audio-animated mannequins. 2201 Centennial Dr; Port St Joe, FL 32456; Phone: (850) 229-8029; https://www.floridastateparks.org/parks-and-trails/constitution-convention-museum-state-park

Forgotten Coast Sea Turtle Center has interactive experiences to connect with local sea turtles and coastal habitats. You can also sign up to do their sunrise patrol along the beach. No phone number is available, contact via email at: sjpturtlepatrol@gmail.com
1001 10th St; Port St Joe, FL 32456; http://www.floridacc.org

Santa Rosa Beach, FL (Walton County) (FWB)

Eden Gardens State Park offers the renovated 1897 Wesley House with white columns and a wrap-around porch. Visitors can take a guided tour of the Wesley House, meander through the blooming ornamental gardens (in flower during the winter and spring), as well as fish off the dock in Tucker Bayou. 181 Eden Gardens Rd; Santa Rosa Beach, FL 32459; Phone: (850) 267-8320; https://www.floridastateparks.org/parks-and-trails/eden-gardens-state-park

Topsail Hill Preserve State Park is named for its white quartz beaches and its spectacular dunes, which rise like a ship's sails over beaches and the waters of the Gulf of Mexico. Canoe, kayak, or paddleboard on Campbell Lake, an almost

100-acre coastal freshwater dune lake surrounded by ancient coastal dunes and maritime forest. 7525 W County Hwy 30A; Santa Rosa Beach, FL 32459; Phone: (850) 267-8330; https://www.floridastateparks.org/parks-and-trails/topsail-hill-preserve-state-park

Seaside, FL (Walton County) (FWB)

This resort community is an example of late-20th-century New Urbanist design of walkable neighborhoods, and environmentally friendly life-style. It is most famous, however, for being the location for the very quirky film *The Truman Show*. For more information on the movie see: https://en.wikipedia.org/wiki/The_Truman_Show

St. George Island, FL (Franklin County)

Cape St. George Lighthouse and Museum is a 72-foot-high brick lighthouse on a barrier island off the coast near Eastpoint. FREE. NOTE: There is fee to climb the lighthouse. 2B East Gulf Beach Dr; St. George Island, FL 32328; Phone: (850) 927-7745; https://www.stgeorgelight.org/

Dr. Julian G. Bruce St. George Island State Park offers nature trails on the bay side with undeveloped beaches on the gulf. 1900 E Gulf Beach Dr; St. George Island, FL 32328; Phone: (850) 927-2111; https://www.floridastateparks.org/parks-and-trails/dr-julian-g-bruce-st-george-island-state-park

St. Marks, FL (Wakulla County) (TMA)

Florida's first railroad built in St. Marks in 1836 is now a popular bicycle and equestrian trail. **The Tallahassee-St. Marks Historic Railroad State Trail** runs about 20 miles from Florida's capital city to the coastal community of St. Marks, and it offers multiple entry spots. https://www.floridastateparks.org/parks-and-trails/tallahassee-st-marks-historic-railroad-state-trail

The historic **St. Marks Lighthouse**, located in the **St. Marks National Wildlife Refuge**, is the second oldest lighthouse in Florida. The keeper's house is open for tours. 1255 Lighthouse Rd; St. Marks, FL 32355; Phone: (850) 625-9121; https://www.fws.gov/refuge/St_Marks/

The museum at **San Marcos de Apalache Historic State Park** displays pottery and tools unearthed near the original fort. Interpretive displays explain its history, and an 18-minute video recounts the days of the Spanish, English, American, and Confederate forces that once occupied the site. A self-guided interpretive trail is open to visitors and guided tours are available. 148 Old Fort Rd; St. Marks, FL 32355; Phone: (850) 925-6216; https://www.floridastateparks.org/parks-and-trails/san-marcos-de-apalache-historic-state-park

Tallahassee, FL (Leon County) (TMA)

This city has served as the capital since 1824 when the area was a US Territory. Today Tallahassee hosts colleges and universities and offers visitors both outdoor and indoor attractions. The city is one of only two that are included on the famed Mississippi Blues Trail: https://msbluestrail.org/blues-trail-markers/mississippi-to-florida. The other city is Pensacola. Some of the city's Civil Rights history is depicted on the corner of East Jefferson St and Monroe St. Sixteen terrazzo panels relate the story of the city's bus boycott of 1956, and the lunch counter sit-in demonstrations of 1960-1963. https://visittallahassee.com/partners/tallahassee-leon-county-civil-rights-heritage-walk/

22nd Floor Capitol Gallery on the top floor of Florida's Capitol building showcases Florida artists in the gallery space and throughout the Capitol Complex. FREE. 400 S Monroe St; Tallahassee, FL 32399; Phone: (850) 245-6490; https://dos.myflorida.com/cultural/programs/exhibitions/

Alfred B. Maclay Gardens State Park boasts a picturesque brick walkway, a secret garden, reflection pool, walled garden, and hundreds of camellias and azaleas. Peak blooming season is from January through April, and during that time guided tours are often offered on Saturdays and Sundays. Pick up a self-guided Gardens Walking Tour brochure at the ranger station. 3540 Thomasville Rd; Tallahassee, FL 32309; Phone: (850) 487-4556; https://www.floridastateparks.org/MaclayGardens

Bellevue Plantation at Tallahassee Museum was once the plantation home of a French princess (by marriage) but Catherine Murat was also the owner its enslaved people. Both the lives of the plantation owners and the enslaved workers are explored through the onsite buildings. 3945 Museum Dr; Tallahassee FL 32310; Phone: (850) 575-8684; https://tallahasseemuseum.org/explore-the-museum/bellevue-plantation/

Guided and self-guided tours of the Florida's **Capitol** are available through the Welcome Center. Reservations are suggested for tours during the legislative session (March and April). FREE. 402 S Monroe St; Tallahassee, FL 32399; Phone: (850) 488-6167; http://myfloridacapitol.com

Florida Historic Capitol Museum is in the original capitol, restored to its 1902 appearance. Visitors can follow the Self-Guided Civil Rights Tour of sites in the building where some of the state's important events in the Black civil rights struggles took place. In addition, there are two floors focused on broader Florida's political history. FREE. 400 S Monroe St; Tallahassee, FL 32399; Phone: (850) 487-1902; http://flhistoriccapitol.gov/

FSU Museum of Fine Arts offers special exhibitions as well as diverse permanent collections. FREE. 530 W Call St; Tallahassee, FL 32306; Phone: (850) 644-6836; https://mofa.fsu.edu/

Goodwood Museum & Gardens was originally a 1,600-acre cotton plantation and the current 20-acre site still contains the main house, plus 20 structures dating from 1835 to 1925. The main house features original family furnishings, porcelain, textiles, glassware, and art. The grounds are FREE but there is a charge to enter the house. 1600 Miccosukee Rd; Tallahassee, FL 32308; Phone: (850) 877-4202; https://www.goodwoodmuseum.org/

Public tours of the **Governor's Mansion** are available at specific times during the year, and by special appointment. Tours are 30 minutes long and include the five state rooms plus the outdoor Manatee Sculpture Courtyard. Parking is available directly across the street. Contact the Mansion for upcoming tour calendar. FREE. 700 N Adams St; Tallahassee, FL 32303; Phone: (850) 717-9345; https://www.floridagovernorsmansion.com/schedule_a_tour

The Grove is considered one of the best-preserved antebellum residences in Florida and an excellent example of Greek Revival architecture. The museum illuminates critical moments of history. FREE. NOTE: Open Wednesday through Saturday. 902 N Monroe St; Tallahassee, FL 32301; Phone: (850) 363-5688; https://thegrovemuseum.com

John Gilmore Riley Center & Museum for African American History & Culture explores the time of

Reconstruction after the Civil War and the cultural heritage of the historic Black American Smokey Hollow community. 419 E Jefferson St; Tallahassee, FL 32301; Phone: (850) 681-7881; http://rileymuseum.org

Knott House Museum was constructed in 1843, probably by George Proctor, a free Black builder. Attorney Thomas Hagner and his bride Catherine Gamble became the home's first residents the following year. FREE. 301 E Park Ave; Tallahassee, FL 32301; Phone: (850) 922-2459; https://museumoffloridahistory.com/about/the-knott-house-museum/

Lake Jackson Mounds State Park was an early Native American political and ceremonial center with a complex of six temple mounds, and one possible burial mound. These earthen mounds were constructed during the Mississippian Period. In addition to the mounds, the complex included a large village, central plaza, and surrounding farmsteads. Artifacts recovered during excavations of Lake Jackson mounds show the cultural, religious, and trade connections between the people of Lake Jackson and mound complexes throughout the Southeast. Two of the Temple Mounds can be viewed by the public. 3600 Indian Mounds Rd; Tallahassee, FL 32303; Phone: (850) 487-7989; https://www.floridastateparks.org/parks-and-trails/lake-jackson-mounds-archaeological-state-park

Leon Sinks Geological Area, part of Apalachicola National Forest, offers visitors something unique – one of the most extensive underwater cave systems in the world. Hiking trails, boardwalks, and interpretative signs help visitors explore and understand the phenomena. 2564 Wildflower Rd; Tallahassee, FL 32305; Phone: (850) 643-2282; https://www.fs.usda.gov/recarea/apalachicola/recarea/?recid=75300

Letchworth-Love Mounds Archaeological State Park is believed to include Florida's tallest ceremonial mound, likely built between 1,100 and 1,800 years ago. Several smaller mounds are nearby. 4500 Sunray Rd S; Tallahassee, FL 32309; Phone: (850) 487-7989; https://www.floridastateparks.org/parks-and-trails/letchworth-love-mounds-archaeological-state-park

Lewis Spring House is best known for being one of only two pod-shaped houses designed by Frank Lloyd Wright, featuring concentric and intersecting circles. Tours are scheduled through their website. 3117 Okeeheepkee Rd; Tallahassee, FL 32303; https://www.preservespringhouse.org/

Meek-Eaton Black Archives presents special exhibits from the over 5,000 manuscripts, rare books, journals, magazines, maps, newspapers, and photographs. The center is one of ten Black archives in the United States and is one of the largest in the Southeast. FREE. Florida A&M University; 445 Gamble St; Tallahassee, FL 32307; Phone: (850) 599-3020; https://www.famu.edu/academics/libraries/meek-eaton-black-archives-research-center-and-museum/index.php

Mission San Luis de Apalachee was a Spanish Franciscan mission built in 1633, and the site reconstructs the Apalachee Indian and Spanish community that disappeared three centuries ago. Costumed interpreters reproduce daily life. 2100 W Tennessee St; Tallahassee, FL 32304; Phone: (850) 245-6406; http://www.missionsanluis.org/

Museum of Florida History offers exhibits and artifacts covering Florida's history and prehistory from prehistoric animals, Native peoples and cultures, through territorial expansion, statehood, and modern development. Plus, wrecked Spanish fleets and a recreated steamboat. FREE. R A Gray

Building; 500 S Bronough St; Tallahassee, FL 32399; Phone: (850) 245-6400; https://museumoffloridahistory.com/

National High Magnetic Field Laboratory is the largest magnetic research facility in the world and houses some of the world's most powerful magnets. Monthly tours are available at its Tallahassee location. FREE. There are additional tour options at their Gainesville, FL location (See below). NOTE: Closed toe shoes are required. 1800 E Paul Dirac Dr; Tallahassee, FL 32310; https://nationalmaglab.org/news-events/events/for-community/public-tours

Tallahassee Automobile Museum displays more than 130 rare autos including an 1894 Duryea, 1931 Duesenberg, as well as the Tucker, and Batmobiles. Plus, antique boat motors, musical instruments, Native American artifacts, sports memorabilia, motorcycles, and pedal cars. 6800 Mahan Dr; Tallahassee, FL 32308; Phone: (850) 942-0137; https://tacm.com

Tallahassee Museum is set amid 52 acres with exhibits of native wildlife, nature trails, historic exhibits, and even zip lines and aerial adventure courses. The museum is also home to 14 historic buildings. Jim Gary's Twentieth Century Dinosaurs features vividly colored dinosaurs sculpted from recycled car parts. 3945 Museum Dr; Tallahassee, FL 32310; Phone: (850) 575-8684; https://tallahasseemuseum.org/

Valparaiso, FL (Okaloosa County) (FWB)

(See also Elgin Air Force Base, FL)

Heritage Museum of Northwest Florida preserves regional history through artifacts, textiles, and documents. 115 Westview Ave; Valparaiso, FL 32580; Phone: (850) 678-2615; https://heritage-museum.org/

Vernon, FL (Washington County)

Built in 1857, **Moss Hill United Methodist Church** was constructed of pine heartwood lumber which produces a sticky resin. The result was the construction materials actually captured the hand, finger, and foot prints of those handling it. The building itself is usually closed but the grounds and cemetery at Moss Hill are open to the public. A marker in front of the historic church provides information on the structure, and the cemetery contains the graves of many early settlers of Washington County. FREE. Corner of Vernon and Greenhead Rds; Vernon, FL 32462; Phone: (850) 638-6013; https://www.exploresouthernhistory.com/mosshill1.html

Wakulla Springs, FL (Wakulla County) (TMA)

Edward Ball Wakulla Springs State Park is home to one of the world's largest and deepest freshwater springs. Visitors can take guided boat tours, hike and bike the trails, and even choose to stay at the 1930s Spanish style lodge. Visitors are invited to appreciate its period furniture, original elevators, as well as colorful painted ceilings that depict wildlife, and Old Florida scenes. 465 Wakulla Park Dr; Wakulla Springs, FL 32327; Phone: (850) 561-7276; https://www.floridastateparks.org/WakullaSprings

Wausau, FL (Washington County)

If possums are your thing, this tiny town should be on your radar. It's home to the **Possum Monument.** Unveiled in 1982, the inscription reads: *Erected in grateful recognition of the role the North American possum, a magnificent survivor of the marsupial family pre-dating the ages of the mastodon and the dinosaur, has played in furnishing both food and fur for the early settlers and their successors.* The 1982 session of the

Florida Legislature further recognized the possum by passing a joint resolution proclaiming the first Saturday in August as *Possum Day.* You can visit the monument any time, but Possum Day is celebrated with special events. Find it on SR 77.
https://www.exploresouthernhistory.com/possummonument.html

Wewahitchka, FL (Gulf County)

(See also Panama City, FL)

The Panhandle is famous for its tupelo honey from the white tupelo gum tree found in the swampy areas of north Florida. It's considered the best honey produced, often with prices to match. And it is delicious. Check out the yearly festival held in May. http://www.tupelohoneyfestival.com/

Dead Lakes is a destination for fisher folks, photographers, and nature lovers. The environment reportedly formed when the Apalachicola River's sand bars blocked the Chipola River. The resulting high water killed thousands of trees in the floodplain, leaving a graveyard of bottom-heavy cypress skeletons, stumps, and knees. The only way to see, photograph, or fish is by boat.
https://myfwc.com/fishing/freshwater/sites-forecasts/nw/dead-lake/

FOCUS ON: Cypress Knees

The puzzling structure found above the roots of a cypress tree is called by the odd name *cypress knees*. Although it's not clear what they do, these knees are generally seen on trees growing in swamps.

One possible function is that they provide oxygen to the roots that are growing in the low oxygen waters typical of a swamp. But, swamp-based cypress whose knees were removed continued to thrive. Another suggestion is that they provide structural buttressed support and stabilization. Lowland or swamp-grown cypresses found in flooded or flood-prone areas tend to be buttressed and *kneed.*

What is known is that the height of the knee seems to be determined by the average depth of the water and the density of the surrounding soil.

At one time there was a roadside attraction devoted to these puzzling protrusions. Gaskins Cypress Knee Museum was located in Palmdale, but little of it is left.

Even when there's no tupelo honey festival, you can still visit **Smiley Honey** to learn about tupelo honey, and perhaps buy some. They advise calling to make sure they are open, because "*we are sometimes closed for one reason or another (like delivering honey, visiting with beekeepers, or maybe even fishing).*" 163 Bozeman Cir; Wewahitchka, FL 32465; Phone: (850) 639-5672; https://www.smileyhoney.com

Region 2 North Central Florida: Gainesville and the Off Shore Islands

North Central Florida is world-renowned for its fresh water springs and rivers but it's also known for cave diving and bat watching.

Visitors to this part of the state will want to explore the **Old Florida Heritage Highway** starting just south of Gainesville along US. 441. Highlights include the Cross Creek home of Marjorie Kinnan Rawlings, historic Paynes Prairie State Preserve, and the town of Micanopy.
https://floridascenichighways.com/our-byways/northern-region/old-florida-heritage-highway/

The area also encompasses the **Florida Black Bear National Scenic Highway** corridor along SR 40 and SR 19 which is the backbone of a network of scenic roads and interpretive trails.
http://floridablackbearscenicbyway.org/

The **Gainesville** Metropolitan Area (**GMA**) includes the counties of Alachua, Levy, and Gilchrist, and their associated cities of Cross Creek, Micanopy, Newberry listed below. Although Ocala is less than an hour away from Gainesville, these cities are in different counties and different regions (See Region Five below).

Cedar Key, FL (Levy County) (GMA)

This cluster of islands off the west coast could be the clam center of the state. You can even take a boat tour of the offshore clam farms.

Cedar Key Museum State Park features shell and artifact collections, as well as intricate dioramas spanning from prehistoric times to the early 1900s. You can learn the story of Cedar Key and the people who lived in the area, opening a window into Florida's history and ways of life that have all but vanished. 12231 SW 166 Ct; Cedar Key FL 32625; Phone: (352) 543-5350; https://www.floridastateparks.org/parks-and-trails/cedar-key-museum-state-park

Southern Cross Sea Farms describes itself as "one of the largest producers of hard-shell clams in the state of Florida." NOTE: Tours are currently suspended. Check the website or call for updates. 12170 SR 24; Cedar Key, FL 32625; Phone: (352) 543-5980; http://www.clambiz.com

FOCUS ON: Florida's Beloved Manatees

If a state can be in love, then Florida is in love with these peaceful grass-eating mammals. The West Indian manatee, also known as the North American manatee and sometimes as sea cows because of their diet of sea grass, lives in mostly shallow coastal areas, including rivers and estuaries. But within that classification mitochondrial DNA patterns (genetic material inherited only from the mother) indicate that there's a distinct group that makes Florida its home.

Considered to be a threatened species, its vulnerability is not from predators but from careless humans in boats, and changes in the environment that threaten its food supply. Almost all manatees carry scars from boat strike collisions with watercraft. Manatees can hear boats, but often do not have enough time to get out of the way of an approaching boat. A boat going at a slower speed gives the manatee more time to react and move to safety.

Entanglements, ingestion of debris, pollution that poisons their food supply, habitat loss, and harmful algae blooms are also reducing the population.

Manatee watchers look for these truly gentle giants all year long, but in winter the manatee often congregate in the warmer water of the springs, and in the water outflow of power plants making them easier to see. As mammals they must surface regularly to breathe and careful observers may spot their noses poking out of the water as they take a breath.

https://en.wikipedia.org/wiki/West_Indian_manatee
https://www.savethemanatee.org/manatees/facts/

Chiefland, FL (Levy County) (GMA)

Manatee Springs State Park is both a top place for spotting manatees, and one of Florida's first-magnitude springs, releasing an astounding 100 million gallons of water daily. Rangers conduct guided walks. 11650 NW 115 St; Chiefland, FL 32626; Phone: (352) 493-6072; https://www.floridastateparks.org/parks-and-trails/manatee-springs-state-park

Cross Creek, FL (Alachua County) (GMA)

Marjorie Kinnan Rawlings Historic State Park is the former homestead of Pulitzer Prize-winning Florida author Marjorie Kinnan Rawlings, and straight out of Old Florida. Rawlings wrote *The Yearling* as well as other works in her Cracker style home and farm. The house has been restored and is preserved as it was when she lived there. Guided tours are available. 18700 S CR 325; Cross Creek, FL 32640; Phone: (352) 466-3672;

https://www.floridastateparks.org/parks-and-trails/marjorie-kinnan-rawlings-historic-state-park

FOCUS ON: The Origin of Florida Crackers

Controversy swirls around anything related to Florida Crackers. Some see it as a designation for the hardy early Florida settlers, others as a racial epithet for bigoted Whites of the south, with room for everything in between.

Most origin stories highlight of the word's beginnings from the cracking sound made by their braided leather whips, 10 to 12 feet long. The sound could be heard for miles, and became a form of code used by cowboys (also called Crackers, or Cracker Cowboys).

Although using Cracker to refer to people can be controversial, using it to refer to livestock is a compliment. Cracker livestock is hardy and tough. They originated from the 1521 cattle and horses brought by Spanish explorer Juan Ponce de Leon. That failed mission left them free to roam over the land. Subject to bugs, heat, drought, floods, and humidity, the cattle and horses evolved to be tougher than the environment and became known as Cracker cattle, and Cracker horses. They were a good match for the hardiness of the pioneer families.

When these folks built their wood-frame houses, the architectural style became known as Cracker houses. Metal hip roofs collected rainwater; wide, shaded porches cooled the interior; raised floors kept it dry during flooding; and open straight central hallways from the front to the back of the home maximized the breezes. The design is sometimes called shotgun hallways or a dog-trot/dog-legged design. As a plus, cracks between flooring were said to made sweeping easier.

These families would bring their cattle to market, and one of the routes used was called the Florida Cracker Trail. It runs between east of Bradenton and Fort Pierce, a total distance of approximately 120 miles.

An annual Cracker Trail ride is generally held the last full week in February. The ride ends with a parade through downtown Ft. Pierce. More information at: https://floridacrackertrail.org/

Fort White, FL (Columbia County)

Known for its tubing, **Ichetucknee Springs State Park's** eight major crystal-clear springs come together to create the six-mile Ichetucknee River. Within the park, **Blue Hole Spring** leads to a cave system that experienced divers can explore. Use a mask and fins on the surface to see the turtles and fish who make the Blue Hole their home. NOTE: You must be cave/cavern scuba certified to venture into the cave system. 12087 SW US 27; Fort White, FL 32038; Phone: (386) 497-4690; https://www.floridastateparks.org/parks-and-trails/ichetucknee-springs-state-park

Gainesville, FL (Alachua County) (GMA)

Gainesville has two bat-centric locations – Lubee Bat Conservancy, and the University of Florida bat house. Another treat at the University of Florida is their carillon performances usually held during fall and spring semesters. The UF Carillon Studio Concert Series is performed by students. https://arts.ufl.edu/sites/carillon-studio/welcome/

Bluefield Estate Winery specializes in blueberry wines, and muscadine grape wines. They also have the standard varietals with a fruity twist. 22 NE CR 234, Gainesville, FL 32641; Phone: (352) 337-2544; https://www.facebook.com/BluefieldEstateWinery

Cade Museum for Creativity and Invention was named after Dr. James Robert Cade, the lead inventor of Gatorade. The goals are to encourage visitors to think like an inventor, actually meet inventors and entrepreneurs, and become an inventor. NOTE: Open Thursday through Sunday. 811 S Main St; Gainesville, FL 32601; Phone: (352) 371-8001; https://www.cademuseum.org

Devil's Millhopper Geological Park surrounds a bowl-shaped cavity 120 feet deep leading down to a miniature rain forest. Within the limestone sinkhole are fossilized shark teeth, marine shells, and the remains of extinct land animals. Visitors can learn more about the sinkhole through interpretive displays and appreciate the view of more than 100 feet of exposed geologic strata (rock layers). The further down you go, the older the rocks. 4732 Millhopper Rd; Gainesville, FL 32653; Phone: (352) 955-2008; https://www.floridastateparks.org/parks-and-trails/devils-millhopper-geological-state-park

On the campus of University of Florida, **Florida Museum of Natural History** is the state's official natural history museum. FREE. NOTE: There is a charge for special exhibits including **Butterfly Rainforest** which features hundreds of free-flying butterflies, and birds from around the world. 3215 Hull Rd; Gainesville, FL 32611; Phone: (352) 846-2000; https://www.floridamuseum.ufl.edu

For something unusual, take a walk through the solar system with the **Gainesville Solar Walk**. Scaled at four billion to one

(yes, that was billion), start your tour at NW 8th Ave. The path spans almost a mile with each planet honored with its own monument and plaque.
https://www.alachuaastronomyclub.org/solarwalk.html

Kanapaha Botanical Gardens shelters 24 major collections visitors can admire along a 1 ½ mile paved walkway. These include the state's largest public display of bamboo, and the largest herb garden in the Southeast. 4700 SW 58th Dr; Gainesville, FL 32608; Phone: (352) 372-4981
https://kanapaha.org

Lubee Bat Conservancy is home to over 200 bats, and saves and protects both the bats and their habitats. Guided tours are available but reservations must be made in advance. The conservancy also creates special events and festivals. 1309 NW 192nd Ave; Gainesville, FL 32609; Phone: (352) 485-1250; https://www.lubee.org/

Matheson History Museum interprets local and Florida history in an 1867 house. Visitors can peruse 20,000 historic Florida postcards from every county in the state, 1,500 Florida stereoview cards, illustrations of Florida from Frank Leslie's Illustrated Newspaper and Harper's Weekly newspaper, and the Bone Photograph Collection of photographs taken by local professional photographer Elmer Bone from the 1920s to the 1950s. 513 E University Ave; Gainesville, FL 32601; Phone: (352) 378-2280; https://mathesonmuseum.org

National High Magnetic Field Laboratory has a primary location in Tallahassee (with monthly tours) but also offers weekday tours of its High B/T Facility in Gainesville, FL where it conducts *challenging experiments at the combined extremes of sub-mK temperatures and high magnetic fields.* NOTE: Advanced appointments are recommended especially since the facility will be closed to tours during sensitive experiments. University of Florida at Gainesville; 1800 E Paul Dirac Dr; Tallahassee, FL 32310; Phone: (850) 644-0311; https://nationalmaglab.org/news-events/events/for-the-community/public-tours

Samuel P. Harn Museum of Art focuses on Asian, African, modern and contemporary art, as well as photography. FREE. 3259 Hull Rd; Gainesville, FL 32611; Phone: (352) 392-9826; https://harn.ufl.edu

Santa Fe College Teaching Zoo is the only college zookeeper training facility in the United States. It has its own AZA-accredited zoo on grounds. Guided tours are led by students in the program, or visitors can walk the grounds on their own. Santa Fe College; 3000 NW 83rd St; Gainesville, FL 32606; Phone: (352) 395-5633; https://www.sfcollege.edu/zoo/

Sweetwater Wetlands Park is a man-made wetland habitat shaped like the head of an alligator. Designed to improve water quality by filtering out pollution and nutrients, it's one of many throughout the state that helps improve water quality and creates a tranquil environment for visitors and inhabitants. Walk the nature trail to viewing decks to observe Sweetwater's diverse wildlife, including alligators, Florida cracker horses, bison, and more than 215 bird species. 325 SW Williston Rd; Gainesville, FL 32601; Phone: (352) 554-5871; https://www.sweetwaterwetlands.org

University of Florida Bat Houses offers visitors a bat-viewing experience. The bats emerge during a 15- to 20-minute period after sunset and before total darkness. The best viewing is spring through early summer on calm, warm evenings when temperatures are above 65 F. NOTE: Bats may swoop near observers however they will not attack or harm people if left alone. Best viewing is said to be over the western sky above the pine trees and around the street lights on

Museum Road on the UF campus.
https://www.floridamuseum.ufl.edu/bats/

Greenville, FL (Madison County)

Fans of legendary Ray Charles will want to pay homage to the town in which he was raised. Although he was born in Georgia in 1930, he soon moved with his mother to Greenville and lived there until around seven years of age when he left for St. Augustine where he lived at the Florida School for the Deaf and Blind.

Ray Charles Memorial is a statue of Ray Charles in Haffye Hays Park overlooking the lake. It was created as a gift by local father and son team of Bradley Cooley and Brad Cooley Jr. 140 SW Broad Ave; Greenville, FL 32331;
https://www.waymarking.com/waymarks/WM8459_Ray_Charles_Statue_Greenville_FL

Ray Charles Childhood Home was saved by one of his childhood friends who later became mayor. Visitors can call City Hall for a tour. 443 SW Ray Charles Ave; Greenville, FL 32331; Phone: (850) 948-2251;
https://mygreenvillefl.com/visitors-information/

High Springs, FL (Gilchrist County) (GMA)

One of the newest parks to join the state park system **Gilchrist Blue Springs State Park** offers several springs in one setting. The highlight is Gilchrist Blue, a large second-magnitude spring that produces an average of 44 million gallons of water per day, and is known for its water clarity. It discharges through a shallow spring that runs about one-quarter mile to the Santa Fe River. Popular for paddling, snorkeling, and swimming, the park closes when capacity is reached. 7450 NE 60th St; High Springs, FL 32643; Phone: (386) 454-1369;

https://www.floridastateparks.org/parks-and-trails/ruth-b-kirby-gilchrist-blue-springs-state-park

Ginnie Springs is privately owned but offers seven springs at a constant 72 degrees, tubing on the Santa Fe River, and three different dive sites for certified scuba divers. Equipment rental is available. 7300 Ginnie Springs Road, High Springs, FL 32643; Phone: (386) 454-7188; https://ginniespringsoutdoors.com/

Jasper, FL (Hamilton County)

Constructed as part of the Section of Fine Arts of the Works Progress Administration (WPA) the **Jasper Post Office** features two commissioned tempera frescoes. Completed by Pietro Lazzari in 1942 they are: *Harvest at Home* and *News from Afar*. 105 Martin Luther King Dr SE, Jasper, FL 32052; Phone: (386) 792-1304; http://wpamurals.org/florida.htm

Lake City, FL (Columbia County)

All Tech Raceway for fans who love dirt racing. Check the site for scheduled racing. 1024 SW Howell Rd; Lake City, FL 32024; Phone: (386) 754-7223; https://alltechraceway.com

Lee, FL (Madison County)

Madison Blue Spring State Park is an old-fashioned swimming hole and one of the state's first magnitude springs. But you can do more than swim. About 30 feet below the water's surface at Martz Sink is the opening to its extensive aquatic cave system. NOTE: Divers must have specialized training in cave diving. Check the website for water quality before you go. The spring is closed when rising water levels create brown-out water conditions. 300 NE SR 6; Lee, FL 32059; Phone: (850) 971-5003;

https://www.floridastateparks.org/parks-and-trails/madison-blue-spring-state-park

Live Oak, FL (Suwannee County)

International Falconry Academy has a range of programs from hawk (and owl) walks to multi-day falconry workshops. 15209 165th Rd; Live Oak, FL 32060; Phone: (386) 776-1960; https://www.birdsofprey.net/

Suwannee River State Park includes the remnants of a 19th-century steamship and two ghost towns that have been reclaimed by the wilderness. These can be found on the Earthworks Trail, and the Sandhill Trail. NOTE: The Stephen Foster Folk Culture Center State Park which honors Foster is in the town of White Springs listed below. 3631 201st Path; Live Oak, FL 32060; Phone: (386) 362-2746; https://www.floridastateparks.org/parks-and-trails/suwannee-river-state-park

Micanopy, FL (Alachua County) (GMA)

Founded in 1821, Micanopy is named for Chief Micanopy who was chief of the Seminole Nation during the Second Seminole War, 1835-1842.

Micanopy is Florida's self-proclaimed antiques capital and visitors can find shops along Cholokka Blvd as well as in **Antique City Mall**. Formerly known as Smiley's Antique Mall, today it's a 20,000 square foot, multi-dealer business with a wide array of items from primitives to mid-century modern furniture. 17020 SE CR 234; Micanopy, FL 32667; Phone: (352) 389-4688; https://antiquecitymall.com

Garden of Love Pet Memorial Park is the final resting place for dogs and cats, as well as a goat, rat, squirrel, hamster, duck, cockatiel, horse, and (rumored) a human. A variety of memorials mark the grave sites. The statue of an angel cradling a dog and cat while a horse stands by is considered one of the most beautiful in the park. 17027 US 441; Micanopy, FL 32667; Phone: (352) 377-7455; https://www.roadarch.com/petcem/fl2.html

Micanopy Historical Society hosts the town's museum in the warehouse formerly owned by J E Thrasher. The *Florida Under Five Flags* display illustrates the history of Florida as it was claimed by the Spanish, French, British, Confederacy, and finally, United States of America. NOTE: Open Wednesday through Sunday. 607 NE Cholokka Blvd; Micanopy, FL 32667; Phone: (352) 466-3200; http://micanopyhistoricalsociety.com/home.htm

Paynes Prairie Preserve State Park offers visitors free-roaming bison and horses plus nearly 300 species of birds. The visitor center has an exhibit on the role of the Paynes Prairie in the Seminole Wars. A 50-foot-high observation tower provides panoramic views. NOTE: This is a different park from Paynes Creek Historic State Park in Bowling Green. 100 Savannah Blvd; Micanopy, FL 32667; Phone: (352) 545-6000; https://www.floridastateparks.org/parks-and-trails/paynes-prairie-preserve-state-park

Newberry, FL (Alachua County) (GMA)

Ashton Biological Preserve is a working conservation facility that specializes in the care and conservation of tortoise species, including breeding the endangered radiated tortoise. Visitors are welcome, but reservations are required. 14260 W Newberry Rd; Newberry, FL 32669; Phone: (352) 538-9108; https://ashtonbiodiversity.com/

Dudley Farm Historic State Park is an actual historic

Florida farm that illustrates the evolution of farming through three generations of the Dudley family. Stroll the nature trail, enjoy a picnic, watch wildlife in the fields. The visitor center screens a 12-minute video plus there are interpretive exhibits. Download their self-guided cellphone tour. 18730 W Newberry Rd; Newberry, FL 32669; Phone: (352) 472-1142; https://www.floridastateparks.org/parks-and-trails/dudley-farm-historic-state-park

Perry, FL (Taylor County)

Forest Capital Museum State Park preserves an 1863 Cracker homestead interpreting the history of forestry in North Florida including early turpentine production. There's also wildlife exhibits and Terrie the Talking Tree, with her message about the importance of trees in our environment. 204 Forest Park Dr; Perry, FL 32348; Phone: (850) 584-3227; https://www.floridastateparks.org/parks-and-trails/forest-capital-museum-state-park

Perry Post Office hosts Florida artist George Snow Hill's *Cypress Logging* mural created as part of the Public Works of Art Project during the Great Depression. The panel honors the mostly Black laborers who contributed to the local lumber industry. In 1987 it was moved to its present location in the new post office. 1600 E Jefferson St; Perry, FL 32348; Phone: (850) 584-5627; https://livingnewdeal.org/projects/post-office-mural-perry-fl/

Rosewood, FL (Levy County) (GMA)

There is nothing left of the town that once stood just off SR 24 northeast of Cedar Key. It was a thriving community in the early 20th century until a White mob destroyed the Black town in the 1923 Rosewood Massacre. It began when a White woman in nearby Sumner claimed she had been assaulted by a

Black man. Several hundred White men combed the countryside and burned almost every building in Rosewood. No one was ever arrested. In 2004, the state designated the site of Rosewood as a Florida Heritage Landmark and erected a historical marker on State Road 24 that names the victims and describes the community's destruction.
https://en.wikipedia.org/wiki/Rosewood_massacre
https://dos.myflorida.com/library-archives/research/explore-our-resources/florida-history-culture-and-heritage/rosewood/

Starke, FL (Bradford County)

Camp Blanding Museum and Memorial Park is located in a WWII-era military barracks and is dedicated to the history of Camp Blanding with a collection of weapons (US and foreign) and a refurbished World War II barracks. The grounds showcase numerous WWI-era vehicles. 5629 SR 16 W; Starke, FL 32091; Phone: (904) 682-3196; http://www.30thinfantry.org/blanding.shtml

Suwannee, FL (Dixie County)

The Suwannee River is well known because of Stephen Foster's famous song, *Old Folks at Home* – or more popularly *Way Down Upon the Swanee River*. But fewer people know that Foster never visited Florida. He wrote the song in 1851 and reportedly chose the name because its two-syllable cadence fit into the music he had composed. It was written before the Civil War when the south was deep into slavery, and the words and images have been seen as offensive by today’s standards. Its lyrics were updated and adopted by the Center for American Music, Stephen Foster Memorial at the University of Pittsburgh. It is the amended lyrics that are officially used in the song that has been adopted as the Florida State Song. Although, all in all, perhaps an odd choice given that he never set foot in the state. The Stephen Foster Folk

Culture Center State Park which honors Foster is in the town of White Springs listed below. And his famous song spells the river as the Swanee but that is likely creative license. Learn more about the song at:
https://www.8notes.com/scores/Old_Folks_At_Home_(Swannee_River)_Foster_Stephen.asp;
https://www.pitt.edu/~amerimus/OldFolksatHome.html

White Springs, FL (Hamilton County)

Big Shoals State Park sometimes features whitewater rapids. When the water level on the Suwannee is between 59 and 61 feet above mean sea level, the Big Shoals rapids earn a Class III Whitewater classification. But visitors can also enjoy miles of wooded trails for hiking, biking, horseback riding, and wildlife viewing. NOTE: These rapids are not considered appropriate for beginners. 18738 SE 94th St; White Springs, FL 32096; Phone: (386) 397-4331;
https://www.floridastateparks.org/parks-and-trails/big-shoals-state-park

Stephen Foster Folk Culture State Park features exhibits about Foster's most famous songs, and his music can be heard from the park's 97-bell carillon throughout the day. There are also miles of trails, and demonstrations of quilting, black-smithing, stained glass making, and other crafts. The park also mounts a music festival and special events. The most famous is the Florida Folk Festival held Memorial Day Weekend. Over 300 performances and a special Folk Life area highlight the event. More at:
https://www.floridastateparks.org/FloridaFolkFestival
11016 Lillian Saunders Dr (US 41); White Springs, FL 32096; Phone: (386) 397-4331;
https://www.floridastateparks.org/parks-and-trails/stephen-foster-folk-culture-center-state-park

Williston, FL (Levy County) (GMA)

Cedar Lakes Woods and Gardens is filled with cascading waterfalls, garden displays, and koi ponds, all with a heart-warming backstory. In 1991 Dr. Raymond Webber discovered a century-old abandoned limestone quarry. With a small workforce, he made islands, pools, waterfalls, pavilions, and bridges to create a unique and spectacular botanical garden. 4990 NE 180 Ave; Williston, FL 32696; Phone: (352) 529-0055; https://cedarlakeswoodsandgarden.com/

Privately owned **Devil's Den Spring** is open to the public for snorkeling and scuba diving. Located in a karst cavern this subterranean natural pool (always 72 degrees) is lined with rock formations, and stalactites. It's said to resemble a Mexican cenote. NOTE: Reservations are currently required. Rental equipment is available. 5390 NE 180th Ave; Williston, FL 32696; Phone: (352) 528-3344; http://www.devilsden.com

The **Montbrook Fossil Dig** has recently made the news with the finding of a massive elephant graveyard described as perhaps the largest gomphothere (prehistoric elephant) ever discovered in Florida, going back about five and a half million years. Although the dig is not open to the public, the Division of Vertebrate Paleontology at the Florida Museum offers volunteers the opportunity to join a fossil collecting session. Learn more at: https://www.floridamuseum.ufl.edu/montbrook

Yankeetown, FL (Levy County) (GMA)

Founded in 1923, it was originally named for its founder A.F. Knotts, but the present name comes from a local mail carrier who supposedly would direct visitors to the settlement he called "that Yankee town". He didn't mean it as a compliment. Knotts wasn't even a Yankee – he was from Indiana and moved to the area for the hunting.

But the reason to visit, whether or not you come from the north, is the Withlacoochee River, regarded by many as one of the most beautiful coastal rivers in the state. **Withlacoochee Gulf Preserve** is 413 acres of mixed hardwood, pine, and cabbage palm forest, tidal marshes, and several salt ponds. Visitors can climb the 30-foot observation tower, stroll the boardwalk, or enjoy Gulf accessible canoe/kayak dock, and a 4500 square foot Education Center. 1001 Old Rock Rd; Yankeetown FL 34498; Phone: (352) 447-2511; https://wgpfl.org/

Region 3 Northeast Florida: Jacksonville, St. Augustine, and Amelia Island

Consistent with the early settlement of the area this part of Florida calls itself the First Coast.

> This region is home to some of Florida's most famous Scenic Highways.
>
> The 40-mile **A1A Ocean Islands Trail** connects beaches and barrier islands on Florida's Atlantic coast. It begins at Fernandina Beach on Amelia Island and ends at Jacksonville Beach to the south.
>
> **A1A Scenic & Historic Coastal Byway** runs 72 miles through lands of natural beauty, and history, often with rolling ocean views. The official byway starts at Ponte Vedra Beach, goes through historic St. Augustine, and ends at Gamble Rogers Memorial Park on Flagler Beach. It is a beautiful, although not time efficient, route to reach and explore some of the smaller towns along the coast. https://scenica1a.org

In the 1950s the city of Jacksonville and Duval County merged to create Metro Jacksonville, which instantly gave the city 840 square miles of territory, and made it the largest city in the continental US by land mass.

The **Jacksonville Metropolitan Area (JAX)** makes up most of the region with the counties of Duval, St. Johns, Clay, Nassau, and Baker County. Because the metropolitan area covers so much territory, the communities at the outskirts may not be near one another. NOTE: The Florida Regional Planning Council considers Flagler County to be part of the

Jacksonville area and this book follows that convention. However, Flagler County is also considered part of the Daytona area and its attractions are often convenient for visitors to the Daytona area.

FOCUS ON: East Florida Patriot Revolt

One of the provisions of the 1783 Treaty of Paris, which ended the Revolutionary War with the British, returned the Floridas to Spain. At the time Florida wasn't a state but an area of land often divided into East Florida and West Florida, together known as the Floridas. France and Spain went back and forth about ownership but during the War of 1812, Spain controlled the Florida peninsula which made the US government uncomfortable.

About this time a group that became known as the *Patriots* were eager for Florida to become American territory. The Patriot War in Spanish East Florida was an attempt by interested parties, and President James Madison to gain possession of that land from Spain, ensure British control didn't return, and open the area up to colonization.

In order to do that they needed to subjugate or eliminate fractious elements of the population – primarily the Seminoles, fugitive slaves, and the free Black militia in St. Augustine – who were either loyal to the Spanish or just likely to make trouble for colonization and slavery. This led to machinations by the Federal government, both in public and behind the scenes, to gain control.

March 17, 1812, the Patriots marched into Fernandina, removed the Spanish flag and raised the

Patriot flag. They made a speech, and then turned the land over to the United States. This became a pattern with the Patriot group stopping at each town on their way towards St. Augustine, taking the town in the Patriot's name and then immediately relinquishing the land to the Federal government. The Patriots went as far as capturing and setting up a headquarters at Fort Mose, outside of St. Augustine.

Eventually the United States lost interest in the enterprise, the Spanish made peace with the Patriots, and the movement collapsed. The Florida Territory was sold to the United States in 1821 and the town at the bend of the St. Johns River was named Jacksonville in honor of the territory's first provisional governor, Andrew Jackson.

That actually wasn't the town's first name. Jacksonville was originally Cowford, (sometimes Cow Ford) a place where cows could easily *ford* or cross the river.
https://www.researchgate.net/publication/265945762_The_Other_War_of_1812_The_Patriot_War_and_the_American_Invasion_of_Spanish_East_Florida_review

https://libcom.org/article/patriot-war-florida-manifest-destiny-slavery-covert-intervention-and-us-imperialism;
https://www.jaxhistory.org/patriot-war-1812/

Amelia Island, FL (Nassau County) (JAX)

This charming barrier island is a bit of old Florida that offers the pleasures of the ocean and the delights of Fernandina

Beach, the destination town on the island. Fernandina Beach is the only city in the US that has flown eight different national flags. In chronological order they were: French, Spanish, English, Spanish (again), Patriot, Green Cross of Florida, Mexican Rebel, Confederate, and finally, the United States. http://fbfl.us/190/Isle-of-Eight-Flags

Amelia Island is also famous for hosting the Concours d'Elegance. More information is available at: https://www.ameliaisland.com/concoursweek. Amelia Island includes the communities of Fernandina Beach, Amelia City, and American Beach.

American Beach has a fascinating history. In the years before the Civil Rights struggles, beaches in Florida were segregated. Black beaches were few, but one exception was the American Beach, created in 1935. The **American Beach Museum** explains how A. L. Lewis, President of the Afro-American Life Insurance Company and self-made millionaire, created the oceanfront resort of American Beach. In 2014 residents of the town founded the museum to honor Lewis' vision, the history of American Beach, and MaVynee Oshun Betsch, *The Beach Lady,* who brought the museum to fruition. NOTE: Limited hours. 1600 Julia St; American Beach, FL 32034; Phone: (904) 510-7036; https://americanbeachmuseum.org/

Amelia Island Light is the oldest existing lighthouse in the state of Florida. Located near the northern end of Amelia Island, it goes back to the Territorial Period of Florida history. The grounds are only open one day a month, but they offer tours two days a month. 215 O'Hagan Ln; Fernandina Beach, FL 32034; Phone: (904) 277-7300; http://www.fbfl.us/474/Amelia-Island-Lighthouse-Tour

Amelia Island Museum of History displays 4,000 years of island history with exhibits on the Timucuan Indians, Spanish missions, the Civil War, Florida railroads, and the turpentine industry. Area tours are included in the price of admission. 233 S Third St; Fernandina Beach, FL 32034; Phone: (904) 261-7378; https://ameliamuseum.org/

Fernandina Beach Pinball Museum is less a museum and more a chance to play pinball machines for hours (priced per hour). NOTE: Limited hours. 2106 Sadler Rd; Fernandina Beach, FL 32034; Phone: (904) 435-8424; https://pinball.trickett.org/

Fort Clinch State Park dates back to the Civil War and visitors can explore the fort's rooms, galleries, and grounds as well as enjoy their living history program. Like almost every Florida state park, there's hiking and biking on the park's many trails. Shark tooth hunters will want to visit the northern end of the island to try their luck finding these elusive teeth. 2601 Atlantic Ave; Fernandina Beach, FL 32034; Phone: (904) 277-7274; https://www.floridastateparks.org/fortclinch

Maritime Museum of Amelia Island displays maritime and pirate history through artifacts and treasures recovered from shipwrecks. This eclectic museum also holds US Navy memorabilia, weapons from multiple time periods, and a Soviet era KGB diving suit. 115 S Second St; Fernandina Beach, FL 32034; Phone: (904) 277-1948; https://maritimemuseumai.org/

Espanola, FL (Flagler County)

Sitting at the crossroads of CR 13, and CR 205, tiny Espanola is home to one of the few remaining sections of the **Old Dixie Highway**. The Dixie Highway was a patchwork of roads created between 1915 and 1929. There were several routes across the US that linked different parts of the country ending with cities in Florida. Eventually these roads became absorbed into the national and state highway systems. Some of these old roads maintain the name Old Dixie Highway as homage to its origins. However, Espanola has the **Old Brick Road**, literally paved with the old bricks, going about 9 miles to CR 204. NOTE: This is a rough and very narrow road. It is listed on the National Register of Historic Places. https://flaglercountyhistoricalsociety.com/espanola/

Flagler Beach, FL (Flagler County)

(See also Ormond Beach, FL)

Technically in another county and region, both Ormond Beach and Flagler Beach are actually located quite close together. In fact, two state parks cross county lines and are joined by a hiking trail.

Bulow Plantation Ruins Historic State Park contains the ruins of an antebellum plantation sugar mill. Built of coquina sedimentary rock (made up of crushed shells) it is a sight that draws photographers, and those interested in the state's complex history. The Bulow family grew sugar cane, cotton, rice and indigo, as did many across eastern Florida. The plantation was destroyed in 1836 during the Second Seminole War. Today the sugar mill, the spring house, and several wells are left. An interpretive center tells the plantation's history. NOTE: This park is adjacent to Bulow Creek State Park which is in Ormond Beach. 3501 Old Kings Rd; Flagler Beach, FL 32136; Phone: (386) 517-2084; https://www.floridastateparks.org/parks-and-trails/bulow-plantation-ruins-historic-state-park

Jacksonville, FL (Duval County) (JAX)

Jacksonville is the most populated city in Florida, but it is also the largest city by land size in the continental United States. How did this happen? In 1968 the city of Jacksonville and the county of Duval merged. Or as they like to say – consolidated. It made JAX a population powerhouse. It also means that the city sprawls over a huge area with some attractions located well outside of the heart of the city.

The consolidation also created a delightful mélange of different neighborhoods, each with their own atmosphere. San Marco is one of the local favorites for charm. But it's Springfield that hosts the much loved and quirky **PorchFest**. Music floats from the porches and the park to the delight of the audiences who move with the music from one historic home to another. Generally held in November, the event is FREE. http://www.jacksonvilleporchfest.org/

Jacksonville has another important distinction for locals and visitors. JAX hosts the largest urban park system in the United States with over 400 park and recreational sites. That isn't a typo – there's a lot of recreational opportunities in Jacksonville. https://www.visitjacksonville.com/things-to-do/outdoors/parks/

Big Talbot Island and Boneyard Beach is a local favorite, especially for photographers. The *bones* are the twisted dead trees and branches that were once live oak and cedar trees. Years of erosion stranded the ones that grew near the shore and created an other-worldly vista. SR A1A N; Jacksonville, FL 32226; Phone: (904) 251-2320; https://www.floridastateparks.org/parks-and-trails/big-talbot-island-state-park

Brumos Collection has more than three dozen rare, historically acclaimed race and collector cars including the iconic 1970 Gulf-liveried Porsche 917K driven by Steve McQueen in the legendary racing film *Le Mans*. The collection is a walk through automotive and racing history and lore. NOTE: Tickets must be purchased online in advance.

5159 San Pablo Road S; Jacksonville, FL 32224; Phone: (904) 373-0375; https://thebrumoscollection.com/

Catty Shack Ranch Wildlife Sanctuary provides a forever home for endangered big cats of all varieties. It also seeks to educate the public about their plight. 1860 Starratt Rd; Jacksonville, FL 32226; Phone: (904) 757-3603; https://cattyshack.org/

In the Riverside neighborhood, the **Cummer Museum of Art and Gardens** displays the art collection, house, and gardens of philanthropist Ninah Mae Holden Cummer. The galleries host permanent and changing exhibitions, as well as preserve one of the original rooms of the mansion. Outside, visitors can enjoy the lush Italian and English gardens. 829 Riverside Ave; Jacksonville, FL 32204; Phone: (904) 356-6857; https://www.cummermuseum.org/

Jacksonville Arboretum & Gardens highlights the natural beauty of north Florida. 1445 Millcoe Rd; Jacksonville, FL 32225; Phone: (904) 318-4342; https://www.jacksonvillearboretum.org/

Jacksonville Fire Museum details the history of the fire service from its beginnings in the 1850s to the present. Exhibits include photos from the Great Fire of 1901, a fully-restored 1902 American LaFrance horse-drawn fire engine, and a working 1926 American LaFrance fire engine. You'll find it adjacent to Metropolitan Park. Currently closed, the re-opening will be posted on their website. 1406 Gator Bowl Blvd; Jacksonville, FL 32202; Phone: (904) 630-2969; https://www.coj.net/departments/fire-and-rescue/fire-museum

Jacksonville Zoo and Gardens is home to more than 2,000 animals in habitats including African Forest, River Valley Aviary, Giraffe Overlook, and Land of the Tiger. It is one of only seven zoos in the United States with an animal wellness team. 370 Zoo Pkwy; Jacksonville, FL 32218; Phone: (904) 757-4463; https://www.jacksonvillezoo.org/

Outside the heart of the city in an area that was once a suburb, **Mandarin Museum and Schoolhouse** hosts exhibits on the history of the area, including the famous abolitionist Harriet Beecher Stowe who wintered in Mandarin from 1867 to 1884. The museum is currently closed, but the Mandarin Museum & Historical Society operates the **Walter Jones Historical Park**. There are several historic buildings on the site, and a paved path with informational signs leads to the river and a boardwalk. Take a stroll through old Florida. The historic buildings are generally open the first and third Saturdays, from 10 AM to 2 PM. FREE. 11964 Mandarin Rd; Jacksonville, FL 32223; Phone: (904) 268-0784; https://www.mandarinmuseum.net/

Museum of Contemporary Art (MOCA) is a downtown museum featuring eclectic permanent and temporary exhibits. Operated by University of North Florida. 333 N Laura St; Jacksonville, FL 32202; Phone: (904) 366-6911; https://mocajacksonville.unf.edu/

Museum of Science & History (MOSH) is downtown (Southbank) and specializes in science and local history with changing exhibits, as well as three floors of nature exhibits, a hands-on science area, and the Bryan Gooding Planetarium. 1025 Museum Cir; Jacksonville, FL 32207; Phone: (904) 396-6674; https://themosh.org/

Norman Studios was part of Jacksonville's movie-making history, but with an important difference. Started by the White silent film maker Richard Edward Norman (1891-1960) what stands out is that from 1919 to 1928 he wrote, produced, and distributed high-quality Black-oriented feature pictures with Black actors, eschewing the demeaning stereotypes of the day.

Its only surviving film, *The Flying Ace*, has been restored by the Library of Congress. The buildings have been purchased and renovation has begun on a museum. Check the website for information on its opening and special events. It is included in the National Register of Historic Places. 6337 Arlington Rd; Jacksonville, FL 32211; Phone: (904) 716-0706; http://normanstudios.org

An urban pleasure available 24/7 is **Riverwalk**. This mile long promenade along the St. Johns River offers beautiful city views and sunsets. It starts at 1001 Museum Circle adjacent to St. Johns River Park, also known as Friendship Park. https://www.coj.net/departments/parks-and-recreation/recreation-and-community-programming/parks/southbank-riverwalk

Sally Dark Rides hosts visitors and provides tours of their robot factory where they produce dark rides and animatronics. FREE. NOTE: Tours are currently suspended. Call or check the website for reopening. 745 W Forsyth St; Jacksonville, FL 32204; Phone: (904) 355-7100; https://www.sallydarkrides.com/tours

Timucuan National Preserve covers 46,000 acres of wetlands, waterways, and habitats. The preserve also protects important parts of Florida history – **Fort Caroline** and the **Kingsley Plantation**. https://www.nps.gov/timu/index.htm

Fort Caroline National Memorial honors the short-lived French presence in 16th century Florida. The interpretative exhibits explain first contact between Native Americans and Europeans as well as the horror that happened when the French and Spanish sparred for control. Walk down to an area that may have been the site of long-lost fort. FREE. 12713 Fort Caroline Rd, Jacksonville, FL 32225; Phone: (904) 641-7155; https://www.nps.gov/timu/learn/historyculture/foca.htm

Kingsley Plantation, located in another part of the preserve, was ironically once a slave plantation that came to be owned by a former slave. Visitors can learn the unusual history, explore the quarters of the enslaved people, as well as the barn, waterfront, plantation house, kitchen house, and interpretive garden. Ranger guided tours of the house are available on weekends during some parts of the year. Although there's not much to see inside, the stories of the owners of the plantation are fascinating and well worth the visit. FREE. 11676 Palmetto Ave; Jacksonville, FL 32226; Phone: (904) 641-7155;
https://www.nps.gov/timu/learn/historyculture/kp_visiting.htm
https://www.nps.gov/timu/planyourvisit/calendar.htm

Olustee, FL (Baker County) (JAX)

Although Florida didn't play a major role in the Civil War, the **Olustee Battlefield Historic State Park** was the site of Florida's largest Civil War battle. The battle on February 20, 1864 ended with the retreat of Union troops to Jacksonville until the war's end 14 months later. The visitor center has historical information and artifacts. Visitors walk the mile-long trail with interpretive signs describing the events of the battle. A reenactment is held every February. FREE (except during the reenactment). 5815 Battlefield Trail Rd; Olustee FL 32087; Phone: (386) 758-0400;
https://www.floridastateparks.org/parks-and-trails/olustee-battlefield-historic-state-park

Palatka, FL (Putnam County)

Ravine Gardens State Park is famous for its azaleas that bloom January through March. The park itself is unusual for its two steep ravines. In 1933, the ravines were transformed into a dramatic garden by the federal Works Progress Administration (WPA). Some of the original landscaping still exists as formal gardens, and a paved trail offers overlooks. Another trail takes strollers along the bottom of the ravine. 1600 Twigg St; Palatka, FL 32177; Phone: (386) 329-3721; https://www.floridastateparks.org/parks-and-trails/ravine-gardens-state-park

Palm Coast, FL (Flagler County)

Two stellar attractions can be found in this recently developed town (incorporated in 1999), and they are linked by something rarely found. Florida Agricultural Museum, and Princess Place Preserve are linked by an animal crossing. Both sites offer horse camping and the bridge over I-95 makes it possible for horses, animals, and riders to cross from one to the other.

Florida Agricultural Museum illuminates the history of Old Florida through a restored 1890s pioneer homestead, an early 20th century dry goods store, and five additional buildings. You'll also be able to learn about the history of Florida's unique Cracker cows, and Cracker horses. 7900 N Old Kings Rd; Palm Coast, FL 32137; Phone: (386) 446-7630; https://www.floridaagmuseum.org/

Princess Place Preserve offers history, hiking paths, fishing, kayaking, canoeing, and horse camping. Princess Place was actually a hunting lodge built by Henry Cutting in 1886 for his bride Angela. After Cutting died Angela went through another marriage and then divorce, finally marrying an exiled Russian prince in 1924. Fast forward almost 70 years to 1993 when Flagler County bought the land. Visitors are invited to take a scheduled tour of the building and learn its history. The preserve is also linked to Florida Agricultural Museum by an animal bridge across I-95. 2500 Princess Place Rd; Palm Coast, FL 32137; Phone: (386) 313-4020; https://www.flaglercounty.gov/Home/Components/FacilityDirectory/FacilityDirectory/2/339

Washington Oaks Gardens State Park preserves the one of the largest outcroppings of coquina rock on the Atlantic Ocean. Azaleas, camellias, and bird of paradise are only some of the plantings that comprise the formal gardens. Don't miss the spectacular Rose Garden. The park is split by the highway and offers an additional beach-side location. 6400 N Ocean Shore Blvd; Palm Coast, FL 32137; Phone: (386) 446-6780; https://www.floridastateparks.org/parks-and-trails/washington-oaks-gardens-state-park

St. Augustine, FL (St. Johns County) (JAX)

(See also Palm Coast, FL)

Founded in 1565, St. Augustine is the oldest continuously inhabited settlement established by Europeans in the continental United States. That's a lot of limiting words because there are other places in the southwest that are both older and continuously inhabited. The Taos and the Acoma Pueblos are Native American settlements established around the 12th century and thus predate the arrival of Europeans. Santa Fe, New Mexico is certainly another historic city, but it was founded 40 years later in 1607 (and is considered the oldest American capital).

It's worth remembering that the English colony at Jamestown, which is the much vaunted first English settlement in the New World, wasn't founded until May 14, 1607, over 40 years after the founding of St. Augustine. The Spanish had been busy, and earlier than the British.

St. Augustine has been ruled by Spanish and British in a tug of war that lasted until 1822 when Florida became a US Territory, achieving statehood in 1845.

Its history has made St. Augustine both a tourist attraction and a lovely place to stroll and explore. As befitting a city with a long history, it has numerous houses of worship. Some are open for tours, some just for prayers. Learn more about visiting these sacred places at: https://www.visitstaugustine.com/things-to-do/historic-churches

Castillo de San Marcos National Monument dates back to 1672 when Spanish Governor Francisco de la Guerra y de la Vega sought to protect the area after a 1668 raid by the English privateer Robert Searles. When Britain gained control of Florida almost a hundred years later in 1763, St. Augustine became the capital of British East Florida, and the fort was renamed Fort St. Mark. That lasted about 20 years until Florida was transferred back to Spain and the fort's original name restored. In 1819 a new owner appeared. Spain ceded Florida to the United States, the fort became a military base named Fort Marion. Under United States control the fort was used as a military prison to incarcerate members of Native American tribes including the Seminoles, and members of western tribes, including Geronimo's band of Chiricahua Apache, and the Cheyenne. In 1942 the original name, Castillo de San Marcos, was restored by an Act of Congress. It is the oldest masonry fortification in the continental United States and interprets more than 450 years of history. 11 S Castillo Dr; St. Augustine, FL 32084; Phone: (904) 829-6506; https://www.nps.gov/casa/index.htm

Classic Car Museum offers visitors a chance to peruse automotive classics. 4730 Dixie Hwy; St. Augustine, FL 32086; Phone: (904) 806-4610; https://www.ccmstaug.com/

Father O'Reilly House Museum is one of the oldest structures in St. Augustine, built during the first Spanish Period in 1691. Father Miguel O'Reilly bought the house in 1785 and left it to the Sisters of St. Joseph, who continue to preserve the museum today. Located on historic Aviles Street, the museum focuses on the history of the house, the Catholic tradition it represents, and the story of the Sisters of St. Joseph. FREE. 32 Aviles St; St. Augustine, FL 32084; Phone: (904) 826-0750; http://fatheroreilly.house

Fish Island Preserve, on Anastasia Island, opened to the public in 2021 with few amenities (although more are being planned). The 60 acres of maritime hammock and salt marsh offer birding, fishing, hiking, and appreciating the natural beauty of the area. An interesting side note is that in 2018, the developer, D.R. Horton sought to clear-cut and fill Fish Island to construct 170 new homes. The community thought otherwise and the housing plan was turned down. Plantation Island Dr S; St. Augustine, FL 32080; https://www.floridashistoriccoast.com/blog/explore-fish-island-preserve/

Flagler College was built as the Hotel Ponce de León for Henry Flagler in magnificent Spanish Renaissance architectural style. Today it is Flagler College and open to the public for guided tours. A highlight is the dining room with 79 Louis Comfort Tiffany stained glass windows, and hand-painted murals on the walls and ceiling. 74 King St; St. Augustine, FL, 32084; Phone: (904) 823-3378; https://legacy.flagler.edu/pages/tours

Established by the Spanish in 1738 **Fort Mose** was the first legally sanctioned free Black community. It both provided a refuge for escaping slaves, and enabled the Spanish to have additional fortifications. There were two requirements to join the refuge; residents had to convert to Catholicism, and they had to join the militia. Although nothing remains of the fort, there is a museum on the grounds and visitors can view the land where the settlement once stood. A militia demonstration is usually held the first Saturday of the month. FREE. 15 Fort

Mose Trail; St. Augustine, FL 32084; Phone: (904) 823-2232; https://www.floridastateparks.org/parks-and-trails/fort-mose-historic-state-park

Fort Matanzas National Monument preserves the fortified coquina watchtower, completed in 1742, which defended the southern approach to the Spanish military settlement of St. Augustine. The 300-acre island also contains dunes, marsh, maritime forest, and associated flora and fauna, including threatened and endangered species. FREE. NOTE: A free ferry takes visitors to the fort. 8635 A1A South; St Augustine, FL 32080; Phone: (904) 471-0116; https://www.nps.gov/foma

Governor's House Cultural Center and Museum served as the governor's official residence during the First Spanish Period, the British Period, and until 1812 in the Second Spanish Period. An exhibit in the grand lobby follows this history including a timeline to present-day. 48 King St; St. Augustine, FL 32084; Phone: (904) 825-5034; https://www.floridamuseum.ufl.edu/firstcolony/

Lightner Museum is located in the 1887 Spanish Renaissance Revival-style Hotel Alcazar and contains the eclectic collections of Otto Lightner (1887-1950). Lightner was known as *America's King of Hobbies* and delighted in collecting all manner of objects. Although known for his fine and decorative art from the 19th century, Lightner wasn't above amassing shrunken heads and humble buttons. A highlight is the exhibit of automated musical instruments. 75 King St; St. Augustine, FL 32084; Phone: (904) 824-2874; https://lightnermuseum.org/

Lincolnville Museum and Cultural Center uses exhibits and stories to chronicle 450 years of St. Augustine's Black history. The museum is housed in the historic Excelsior School Building, which served as the first public Black high school in

St Johns County. 102 M L King Ave; St. Augustine, FL 32084; Phone: (904) 824-1191; https://www.lincolnvillemuseum.org/

Oldest House Museum Complex is owned and operated by the St. Augustine Historical Society. The **González-Alvarez House** is the oldest surviving Spanish colonial dwelling in St. Augustine dating back to the early 1700s. Visitors are provided with a guided tour of the house, history museum, ornamental gardens, and an exhibit gallery. 14 St. Francis St; St. Augustine, FL, 32084; Phone: (904) 824-2872; https://saintaugustinehistoricalsociety.org/oldest-house-museum-complex/
https://www.nps.gov/nr/travel/american_latino_heritage/Gonzalez_Alvarez_House.html

Peña-Peck House was built circa 1750 for Royal Spanish Treasurer Juan Estevan de Peña, and occupied by the Peck family until 1931. It is among the oldest colonial buildings in St. Augustine. 143 St George St; St. Augustine, FL 32084; Phone: (904) 829-5064; https://penapeckhouse.com/history-and-tours/

Spanish Military Hospital offers guided tours that highlight medical practices during the Second Spanish Period (1784-1821). 3 Aviles St; St. Augustine, FL 32084; Phone: (904) 342-7730; https://www.smhmuseum.com/

St. Augustine Alligator Farm Zoological Park is one of Florida's oldest continuously running attractions, opening in 1893 as a roadside reptile showcase. Today it features exhibits, animal performances and educational demonstrations, and a zipline. 999 Anastasia Blvd; St. Augustine, FL 32080; Phone: (904) 824-3337; https://www.alligatorfarm.com/

St. Augustine Distillery invites visitors to tour their restored circa-1907 ice plant turned distillery and sample the products.

Self-guided tours are FREE. 112 Riberia St; St. Augustine, FL 32084; Phone: (904) 825-4962; https://www.staugustinedistillery.com/

St Augustine Lighthouse & Maritime Museum is an active, working lighthouse at the north end of Anastasia Island. View exhibits in the historic structures built between 1871 and 1874. Climb the tower and observe demonstrations including boat-building. NOTE: They recommend using 100 Red Cox Road for GPS navigation. 81 Lighthouse Ave; St. Augustine, FL 32080; Phone: (904) 829-0745; https://www.staugustinelighthouse.org/

St. Augustine Winery offers tours and tastings in Henry Flagler's East Coast Railway Building. FREE. 157 King St; St. Augustine, FL 32084; Phone: (888) 352-9463; https://www.sansebastianwinery.com/

Ximenez-Fatio House Museum highlights the independent women who owned the property (and operated it as an exclusive inn) as well as the visitors who wintered with them from the 1830s through the 1850s. Operated by National Society of the Colonial Dames of America – State of Florida. 20 Aviles St; St. Augustine, FL 32084; Phone: (904) 829-3575; https://www.ximenezfatiohouse.org/

Region 4 Central West Coast: Tampa, St. Petersburg, and Clearwater

Although the Florida Keys which spread south of Miami are more famous, the west coast of Florida has its own delightful set of tiny islands. It is also one of the best arts destinations in Florida. Sarasota and its nearby communities are often considered a different region, in terms of distance, but visitors can easily consider it for a day trip.
http://www.usa.com/tampa-st-petersburg-clearwater-fl-area-city-and-city-map.htm#fulllist

The **Tampa Bay Area (TBA)** encompasses several towns including St. Petersburg, and Clearwater. The counties included are Hernando, Hillsborough, Pasco, and Pinellas. Although they are all located near Tampa, the communities at the outskirts may not be near one another.

Apollo Beach, FL (Hillsborough County) (TBA)

Big Bend's discharge canal is a state and federally designated manatee sanctuary. **Tampa Electric's Manatee Viewing Center** provides critical protection from the cold for these beloved, gentle mammals. Inside the MVC are environmental education displays of the world of the manatee. Others show how Big Bend Power Station generates electricity for the community. Walk the habitat loop trail and climb the observation tower. Learn the story of how a power generating plant became a favored spot for manatees. FREE. 6990 Dickman Rd; Apollo Beach, FL 33572; Phone: (813) 228-4289; https://www.tampaelectric.com/company/mvc/

Brooksville, FL (Hernando County) (TBA)

Chinsegut Hill Historic Site includes an antebellum home located within a 114-acre preserve. There is no charge to visit the property, and several interpretive signs tell its history. There is an admission charge to tour the house and tickets can be purchased online (open Saturday and Sunday). 22495 Chinsegut Hill Rd, Brooksville, FL 34601; Phone: (352) 277-1227; https://www.tampabayhistorycenter.org/chinsegut/

May-Stringer House is the home of the Hernando Heritage Museum and highlights specific themes such as an Elegant Dining Room, Victorian Bedrooms, Military Room, an 1880s Doctor's Office, and a 1900s Communication Room. 601 Museum Ct; Brooksville, FL 34601; Phone: (352) 799-0129; https://www.hernandohistoricalmuseumassoc.com/may-stringer-house/

Chassahowitzka Wildlife Management area is home to Florida wildlife, and the **Njoy Distillery** sitting on 80 acres. Tours are free. Tastings will incur a fee (applied to your purchase). NOTE: You don't need to pay the reserve entrance fee if you are going to the distillery. Follow the NJOY signs for the entrance to Goff Ranch. Open Saturday and Sunday. 3243 Commercial Way (US 19); Brooksville, FL 34614; Phone: (352) 592-9622; https://njoyspirits.com/

The **1885 Train Depot** is part of the Hernando Historical Museum Association and focuses on the history of Hernando County. There's also 1925 LaFrance Fire Engine, and a reclaimed box car. NOTE: Hours are limited. 70 Russell St; Brooksville, FL 34601; Phone: (352) 799-4766; https://www.hernandohistoricalmuseumassoc.com/1885-brooksville-train-depot/

Clearwater, FL and Clearwater Beach, FL (Pinellas County) (TBA)

Another of the state's twinned cities, take Memorial Causeway back and forth, or the fee-based ferry to avoid traffic.

https://www.clearwaterferry.com/

Clearwater, FL

Clearwater Marine Aquarium is home to bottlenose dolphins, loggerhead sea turtles, Kemp's Ridley sea turtles, river otters, sting rays, fish, coral reefs, mangroves, and more. The aquarium also offers a 60-minute dolphin and wildlife boat tour, including a bird sanctuary. 249 Windward Passage; Clearwater, FL 33767; Phone: (727) 441-1790; https://www.cmaquarium.org/

Moccasin Lake Nature Park showcases plant and animal species native to the area with a preserve for rescued and rehabilitated birds. The 51-acre park is crossed with trails and boardwalks under a canopy of mature oaks. 2750 Park Trail Ln; Clearwater, FL 33759; Phone: (727) 793-2976; https://www.myclearwaterparks.com/facilities/facilities-amenities-locator/moccasin-lake-environmental-education-center

OCC Roadhouse and Museum is part entertainment/restaurant and part homage to Orange County Choppers' Paul Teutul Sr and his custom motorcycles (featured on the *American Chopper* series). Memorabilia, photos and posters, and even some of his creations are on display. 10575 49th St N; Clearwater, FL 33762; Phone: (727) 231-1510; https://www.occroadhouse.com/

Philadelphia Phillies Spring Training at Spectrum Field is a must for Philly fans. The Grapefruit League generally begins the end of February. 601 Old Coachman Rd; Clearwater, FL 33765; Phone: (727) 467-4457;
https://www.mlb.com/phillies/spring-training
https://www.mlb.com/phillies/spring-training/ballpark

Showtime Speedway Pinellas Park offers races on Saturday nights. According to the website: "We even invite *you*, our fans, to bring your cars onto the track for fan participation "oval drags" – a crowd favorite!" 4398 126th Ave N; Clearwater, FL 33762; Phone: (727) 561-9646; http://showtimespeedway.us/

Clearwater Beach, FL

Pier 60 Park, and Sunsets at Pier 6 is known for its daily sunset celebration two hours before until two hours after sunset, weather permitting. 10 Pier 60 Dr; Clearwater Beach, FL 33767; Phone: (727) 449-1036; https://www.sunsetsatpier60.com/

Crystal River, FL (Citrus County)

Coastal Heritage Museum/Crystal River Heritage Council features an array of exhibits, artifacts, furniture, and photographs of the early history of the west side of Citrus County. FREE. 532 Citrus Ave; Crystal River, FL 34428; Phone: (352) 341-6428; https://cccourthouse.org/

Crystal River Archaeological State Park, within Crystal River Preserve State Park, is a 61-acre complex with burial mounds, temple/platform mounds, a plaza area, and a substantial midden (mound of ancient domestic waste). 3400 N Museum Pt; Crystal River, FL 34428; Phone: (352) 795-3817; https://www.floridastateparks.org/parks-and-trails/crystal-river-archaeological-state-park

Crystal River National Wildlife Refuge is the only refuge created specifically for the protection of the beloved and endangered Florida manatee. Its Three Sisters Springs is considered crucial for wintering manatees and the boardwalk is very popular for manatee viewing. Interpretive talks take place daily in the winter months. 865 N Suncoast Blvd; Crystal River, FL 34429; Phone: (352) 563-2088; https://www.fws.gov/refuge/Crystal_River/

Dade City, FL (Pasco County) (TBA)

Giraffe Ranch describes itself as *hands-on real working game farm and wildlife preserve where animals have room to roam.* Several different types of explorational safaris are available. Advance registration is required. 38650 Mickler Rd; Dade City, FL 33523; Phone: (813) 482-3400; https://girafferanch.com/

Enjoy a drive-in movie at **Joy-Lan Drive-In**. There's one screen showing double features. NOTE: Check the website for further information. 16414 US-301; Dade City, FL 33523; Phone: (352) 567-5082; https://www.joylandrivein.com/

Pioneer Florida Museum and Village brings visitors a one-room schoolhouse, church, train depot, train engine, and a museum exhibition of tools, household items, antiques, and farm equipment. 15602 Pioneer Museum Rd; Dade City, FL 33523; Phone: (352) 567-02621; https://www.pioneerfloridamuseum.org/

Dunedin, FL (Pinellas County) (TBA)

Caladesi Island State Park offers its popular white sand beaches, as well as a three-mile nature trail through the island's interior, and a three-mile kayak trail through the mangroves and bay. NOTE: The park is only accessible by boat. Ferry service is available from Honeymoon Island State Park. https://www.floridastateparks.org/parks-and-trails/caladesi-island-state-park

Honeymoon Island is a much-loved island on the Gulf of

Mexico with miles of nature trails, four miles of beach, and a three-mile trail through one of the last remaining virgin slash pine forests. You can rent a bike or a kayak as well as beach chairs and umbrellas. The nature center offers exhibits on the park's history and natural resources. You can take a ferry from Honeymoon Island to Caladesi Island. NOTE: The southern portion of beach has a special Pet Beach. However, pets must stay on a six-foot hand-held leash at all times. One Causeway Blvd; Dunedin FL 34698; Phone: (727) 241-6106; https://www.floridastateparks.org/honeymoonisland

Self-billed as *the ultimate* Beatles Museum, **Penny Lane Beatles Museum** contains everything from signed guitars to strands of the Beatles' hair… and much in between. NOTE: Open Thursday through Sunday with limited hours. FREE. 730 Broadway; Stirling Commons (Second Floor); Dunedin, FL 34698; Phone: (727) 281-8130; https://www.pennylanebeatlesmuseum.com

Dunedin is the home of the Toronto Blue Jays for spring training, and for the Dunedin Blue Jays year-round. **Toronto Blue Jays Spring Training** takes place in TD Ballpark generally beginning at the end of February. 373 Douglas Ave; Dunedin, FL 34698; Phone: (727) 733-0429; https://www.mlb.com/bluejays/spring-training; https://www.mlb.com/bluejays/spring-training/ballpark

Gibsonton, FL (Hillsborough County) (TBA)

Originally famous as a sideshow wintering town (the showman's museum is about four miles away in Riverview), little is left of the people of the sideshows who once made Gibsonton home. It is also known as Gibtown.

Holiday, FL (Pasco County) (TBA)

If you love comedy, take the time to visit this town hosting the country's only Hall of Fame for comedy. **National Comedy Hall of Fame** began in 1991with comedy stars Morey Amsterdam, Jan Murray, Sid Caesar, Milton Berle, and Tony Belmont, and evolved into the National Comedy Hall of Fame. The complex includes the National Comedy Hall of Fame Museum, Hall of Fame Event Center, Hall of Fame Comedy School, and Hall of Fame Comedy Club. View its collection of memorabilia with original movie posters, albums, authentic puppets, studio photographs and more. Short films and rare footage accompany each comedian's exhibit, like Charlie Chaplin's slapstick, Jack Benny's violin dexterity, and Phyllis Diller's wit. There's even an in-house movie theater that screens short films and comedy sketches. NOTE: To preserve the collection, the climate is set at 68-72 degrees. 2435 US 19; Suite 102; Holiday, FL 34691; Phone: (727) 656-9867; https://nationalcomedyhalloffame.com

Homosassa, FL (Citrus County)

Homosassa Springs State Park is known for its Underwater Observatory allowing visitors to walk beneath the spring's surface and watch the fish and manatees. Its Wildlife Walk consists of elevated, and accessible boardwalks providing a view of the natural habitats. Tours and wildlife encounters are also offered. 4150 S Suncoast Blvd; Homosassa, FL 34446; Phone: (352) 628-5343; https://www.floridastateparks.org/parks-and-trails/ellie-schiller-homosassa-springs-wildlife-state-park

Homosassa is home to several semi-feral monkeys. Monkeys are not indigenous to Florida but **Monkey Island** is nonetheless the residence of spider monkeys. The island is owned by the Lowman family who purchased the Florida Cracker Riverside Resort, which included Monkey Island.

They are planning an upgrade during which time the monkeys will be temporarily relocated. 5297 S Cherokee Way; Homosassa, FL 34448; Phone: (352) 628-2474; https://www.historicmonkeyisland.com/

Yulee Sugar Mill Ruins Historic State Park preserves the remains of David Levy Yulee's 5,100-acre sugar plantation including the steam engine, boiler, and crushing machinery of the mill, as well as the large cast iron cooking kettles. Labor for the plantation was provided by enslaved people, and the plantation including Yulee's home was burned down and abandoned during the Civil War. FREE. CR 490; Homosassa, FL 34448; Phone: (352) 795-3817; https://www.floridastateparks.org/parks-and-trails/yulee-sugar-mill-ruins-historic-state-park

Inverness, FL (Citrus County)

Citrus County Speedway is the stop for the thrill of figure-eight races, demolition derby, and its famous *Bring on the Carnage*. NOTE: Payment is by CASH ONLY and there is currently NO ATM on site. 3600 S Florida Ave; Inverness, FL 34452; Phone: (352) 341-5764; http://www.citruscountyspeedwayandtrack.com/

Old Citrus County Courthouse displays artifacts from Citrus County's pre-history and its pioneer days, and offers time-limited, themed exhibits. FREE. One Courthouse Sq; Inverness, FL 34450; Phone: (352) 341-6428; https://www.cccourthouse.org/courthouse-museum.php

Largo, FL (Pinellas County) (TBA)

Located on the west coast, the town of Largo is not to be confused with Key Largo in the Florida Keys. The two attractions below share the Pinewoods Campus along with

Pinellas County Extension and Creative Pinellas (an arts initiative complete with exhibits in their gallery space).

Florida Botanical Gardens covers over 30 acres with cultivated gardens and 90 acres of natural landscapes. A new Children's Discovery Garden will soon be added. FREE. 12520 Ulmerton Rd; Largo, FL 33774; Phone: (727) 582-2100; http://www.flbg.org

Heritage Village combines museum exhibits about local history with live re-enactments and historic village buildings. FREE. 11909 125th St; Largo, FL 33774; Phone: (727) 582-2123; http://www.pinellascounty.org/heritage/

Lecanto, FL (Citrus County)

Mertailor's Mermaid Aquarium Encounter is a small family run attraction featuring mermaid shows. The back story is charming – they started as tailors, making mermaid tails, so what could be more natural than have mermaids too. 4100 W Gulf to Lake Hwy; Lecanto, FL 34461; Phone: (352) 513-3278; https://www.mermaidaquariumencounter.com/

Madeira Beach, FL (Pinellas County) (TBA)

John's Pass Village and Boardwalk is filled with shops and eateries on a 1,100-foot boardwalk along the Intracoastal. The Pass was created by a hurricane about 150 years ago. Pirate John Levique was reputed to have made the first passage. 12945 Village Blvd; Madeira Beach, FL 33708; Phone: (727) 394-0756; http://johnspassvillage.net/

Palm Harbor, FL (Pinellas County) (TBA)

One of the few cemeteries that honor K-9 officers can be found at **Curlew Hills Memory Gardens**. The donated burial plots in their pet cemetery are the final resting place for nearly 60 deceased service animals from the Pinellas County Sheriff's office and the Clearwater Police Department. Each grave has a granite marker. 1750 Curlew Rd; Palm Harbor, FL 34683; Phone: (727) 789-2000; http://curlewhillspetcemetery.com/k-9-heroes

Suncoast Primate Sanctuary Foundation provides a safe haven and home to over 130 residents including apes, birds, small primates, and reptiles. 4600 Alt Hwy 19; Palm Harbor, FL 34683; Phone: (727) 943-5897; http://www.spsfi.org/

Pinellas Park, FL (Pinellas County) (TBA)

Tampa Bay Automobile Museum encapsulates the history and engineering behind the design and manufacturing of some of the world's most innovative cars. 3301 Gateway Centre Blvd; Pinellas Park, FL 33782; Phone: (727) 579-8226; https://www.tbauto.org/

Showtime Speedway offers professional racing and more. NOTE: Races held Saturday evenings. 4550 Ulmerton Rd; Pinellas Park, FL 33762; Phone: (727) 561-9646; http://showtimespeedway.us/

Plant City, FL (Hillsborough) (TBA)

Named after railroad developer Henry B. Plant today the town is more famous as the self-proclaimed Winter Strawberry Capital of the World and hosts the annual Florida Strawberry Festival http://www.flstrawberryfestival.com/.

Bing Rooming House African American Museum is primarily known for being one of the few hotels for people of color during the period of segregation. The hotel operated from 1928 through 1975. It interprets and preserves the city's

Black history. NOTE: Hours are limited. 205 South Allen St; Plant City, FL 33563; Phone: (813) 757-6760; http://www.plantcitybinghouse.com/

Dinosaur World is a prehistoric theme park featuring 200 life size dinosaurs along with shows and exhibits. NOTE: There is an additional fee for the Fossil Dig and the Dino Gem Excavation. 5145 Harvey Tew Rd; Plant City, FL 33565; Phone: (813) 717-9865; https://dinosaurworld.com/

Glover School Campus & Museum is in the Bealsville community which was settled by freed slaves in 1865. Using the Southern Homestead Act of 1866, the 12 original families acquired land ranging from 40 to 160 acres. They eventually constructed a wood-frame school in 1933 and named it the Glover School after one of the pioneer families. The campus and museum are open for tours but the hours are limited. 5104 Horton Rd; Plant City, FL 33567; Phone: (813) 737-1352 https://bealsville.com/glover-school-campus/

Plant City Photo Archives & History Center collects and preserves the community's photographs and documents with over 250,000 historic photos, slides, and documents digitally stored on their servers. FREE. 106 S Evers St; Plant City Fl 33566; Phone: (813) 754-1578; https://www.plantcityphotoarchives.org/

Robert W. Willaford Railroad Museum in the historic train depot features a completely restored Seaboard Air Line, #5735 Caboose (built in 1963), and a 1942 Whitcomb Locomotive. FREE. The Train Viewing Platform, located adjacent the museum, is open seven days a week and is currently lit for evening viewings. 102 N Palmer St; Plant City, FL 33563; Phone (813) 719-6989; https://www.willafordrailroadmuseum.com/

Riverview, FL (Hillsborough County) (TBA)

International Independent Showmen's Museum honors the heritage of American carnivals with exhibits, memorabilia, and antique rides which span over a century of traveling shows in America. 6938 Riverview Dr; Riverview, FL 33578; Phone: (813) 671-3503; https://showmensmuseum.org/

Ruskin, FL (Hillsborough County) (TBA)

For over 50 years, **Ruskin Family Drive-In Theatre** has been welcoming people to watch movies from their cars. NOTE: Cash only and prices are per person. 5011 US Hwy 41 N; Ruskin, FL 33572; Phone: (813) 645-1455 (answering machine); http://www.ruskinfamilydrivein.com

Safety Harbor, FL (Pinellas County) (TBA)

The city reportedly derived its name from the time of the pirates – if a ship could make it to the small harbor, it would supposedly be safe from attack. The town also gained fame for its Espiritu Santo Springs, named in 1539 by the Spanish explorer Hernando de Soto while he was searching for the legendary Fountain of Youth. Although neither de Soto or his compatriot Juan Ponce de Leon ever succeeded in locating the elusive (and fictitious) waters.

Safety Harbor Museum of Regional History features 12,000 years of dioramas and displays that tell the story of Florida's first people and the arrival of Spanish explorers. Photographs and memorabilia illustrate Safety Harbor at the turn of the century. 329 S Bayshore Blvd; Safety Harbor, FL 34695; Phone: (727) 726-1668; http://www.cityofsafetyharbor.com/573/Museum-Cultural-Center

WhimzeyLand, or as it is also called, the *Bowling Ball House*, is home to artists Todd Ramquist and Kiaralinda. The couple have created a blizzard of color, form, art, and (of course) whimsy. Although not open for tours, the public can certainly drive and stroll by to see their over 20 years of work. If you are so inclined, make a reservation to stay in the guest house *Casa Loca*. 1206 3rd St; Safety Harbor, FL, 34695; http://www.kiaralinda.com/

Spring Hill, FL (Hernando County) (TBA)

The lure of Spring Hill is the enticement of Old Florida – the fun and quirky attractions that once delighted visitors. Or, as it might be known, before Disney, when Florida was home to a plethora smaller, homey attractions. One of the more famous and much-loved was the underwater theater at the Weeki Wachee Springs in the town that was then called Weeki Wachee.

Weeki Wachee Springs State Park is built around the deepest natural spring in the United States, releasing 117 million gallons of fresh water every day. When road trips lost their appeal in favor of destination travel, Weeki Wachee and its famous mermaids foundered. The performers sought to raise money and public interest to help save this iconic destination. In 2008 the state of Florida got involved and made Weeki Wachee Springs a state park. And they saved the mermaid shows along with it. The park also offers a riverboat ride, wildlife program, and swimming in the pristine waters at Buccaneer Bay, Florida's only spring-fed waterpark. Weeki Wachee also has the deepest known freshwater cave system in the United States. NOTE: Mermaid performances can be delayed or canceled due to weather-related issues. This includes, but not limited to, lightning in the area and temperatures below 50° at showtime. 6131 Commercial Way;

Spring Hill, FL 34606; Phone: (352) 592-5656; https://www.floridastateparks.org/WeekiWachee

St. Pete Beach and St. Petersburg, FL (Pinellas County) (TBA)

These two cities are another town/beach combination with the St. Pete Beach as a resort city set on a barrier island and the city of St. Petersburg on the mainland. Both are gateways to the tiny island keys that dot Tampa Bay area. This is also an art mecca. Lovers of glass art will definitely want to add St. Petersburg to their itinerary.

FOCUS ON: The Naming of St. Petersburg

In a state filled with towns named after Native Americans, Native Tribes, and famous people, how did this Florida town end up with the same name as a famous Russian city?

It started with the assassination of a Russian Czar, and a retired member of the Imperial Russian Guard. Pyotr Dementyev (spellings vary including Demens) was educated, and wealthy but felt the need to leave Russia possibly the result of his political beliefs. It gets a bit murky but at some point during the political chaos, Demens either left voluntarily or was exiled after the assassination of Czar Alexander II. He ended up in the United States around 1880 or 1881, finally settling in Longwood, FL. Americanizing his name to Peter Demens, he became a successful businessman eventually coming to own a small railroad.

Meanwhile, in 1875 John Constantine Williams of Detroit, Michigan moved to Tampa and bought 2,500 acres of waterfront land. He eventually transferred part of the land to Demens for the development of the railroad which would run to his tiny settlement from Sanford, FL. In 1888 Demens achieved his dream and the railroad became reality, at least for a short time.

But the name itself is rumored to have come from Demens winning a bet. Legend says that Demens won and named the town after Saint Petersburg, Russia. The newly minted town thrived, but sadly the railroad did not. Demens eventually settled on a ranch in Alta Loma, California, where he died in 1919.

Peter Demens is remembered with a monument and historical marker in Demens Landing Park, site of the first railroad pier in St. Petersburg. You can find it at Bayshore Dr SE & 2nd Ave SE; St. Petersburg, FL 33701

St. Pete Beach, FL

Home to Don CeSar resort since 1928, the structure resembles a castle blending Mediterranean and Moorish styles. Its hot pink architecture has also led to its nickname as the Legendary Pink Palace®

Gulf Beaches Historical Museum is located in Pass-A-Grille National Historic District. The museum is housed in what was the first church built on the St. Petersburg/Clearwater area barrier islands. The exhibits trace the history of the area's barrier islands through photographs, news clippings, and artifacts dating from the 1500s through modern times. 115 10th Ave; St. Pete Beach, FL 33706; Phone: (727) 552-1610; http://gulfbeachesmuseum.com/

St. Petersburg, FL

Mural Tours enable this art-focused city to strut its creativity. Learn about the murals and artists at: https://www.visitstpeteclearwater.com/list/ultimate-list-of-street-art-st-pete
Tours of over 30 murals found in the four-block area are also available. StPeteMuralTour.com and Florida CraftArt have partnered to create guided walking tours: https://floridacraftart.org/product/mural-tours/ or create your own with this interactive map: https://stpetemuraltour.com/map-of-st-pete-murals/ https://floridacraftart.org/product/mural-tours/

Dali Museum is home to the world's most comprehensive collection of works by the late Spanish surrealist Salvador Dali. The collection includes 94 original oils, more than 100 watercolors and drawings, plus 1,300 graphics, sculptures, holograms, objects of art, and photographs. One Dali Blvd; St. Petersburg, FL 3370; Phone: (727) 823-3767; https://thedali.org/

DMG School Project is a glass art mecca in the heart of the Warehouse Art District combining fruit bearing trees with rotating exhibitions showcasing nationally and internationally recognized glass artists. 2342 Emerson Ave S; St. Petersburg, FL 33712; Phone: (855) 436-4527; https://dmgschoolproject.org/gallery

Dr. Carter G. Woodson African American Museum presents the historic voice of this community. 2240 9th Ave S; St. Petersburg, FL 33712; Phone: (727) 323-1104; https://woodsonmuseum.org/

Florida CraftArt is part exhibition space, part artist studios located in an old department store. ArtLofts are open by appointment or by chance, and on ArtWalk, every second

Saturday from 5 to 9 PM. Fine jewelry, clay, glass, ornaments and more handcrafted by Florida's craft artists. FREE. 501 Central Ave; St. Petersburg, FL 33701; Phone: (727) 821-7391; https://floridacraftart.org/; https://floridacraftart.org/about-florida-craftart-gallery/

Florida Holocaust Museum documents the experiences of Holocaust survivors and liberators who eventually settled in Florida and other areas of the United States. The museum's core exhibition, *History, Heritage and Hope* presents the history of the Holocaust beginning with anti-Semitism and life before World War II, followed by the rise of Hitler and the Nazis and anti-Jewish legislation. The history of other victim groups, ghettos, and rescues are also included. 55 Fifth St S; St. Petersburg, FL 33701; Phone: (727) 820-0100; https://www.flholocaustmuseum.org/

Great Explorations Children's Museum stresses creativity and discovery. Launch a tennis ball to the top of the museum, create art masterpieces, join a workshop. Located next to Sunken Gardens. 1925 Fourth St N; St. Petersburg, FL 33704; Phone: (727) 821-8992; https://greatex.org/

Historic Outdoor Museum of Roser Park currently features twenty-eight markers describing the neighborhood's attributes and the history of the community. The route initially wound along Booker Creek from Fourth St S. to Martin Luther King, Jr. St S. Since then, it has been expanded to most of the other streets in the neighborhood. NOTE: Markers are currently in the process of being renovated and restored. Check the website for updates.
https://www.historicroserpark.org/outdoormuseum

Imagine Museum is another of the city's major glass art destinations. It showcases major works of contemporary American and International art with over 500 glass pieces from the early works of the American Studio Glass Movement and the first pioneer, Harvey Littleton, to those he influenced in the early 1960s, and on to the current works from artists around the world. 1901 Central Ave; St. Petersburg, FL 33713; Phone: (727) 300-1700; https://www.imaginemuseum.com/

James Museum of Western & Wildlife Art contains part of the personal collection of Western and wildlife art of Tom and Mary James. Themed galleries include Early West; Native Life; Native Artists; Frontier; Wildlife; and New West. 150 Central Ave; St. Petersburg, FL 33701; Phone: (727) 892-4200; https://thejamesmuseum.org/

Morean Arts Center encompasses several locations focused on glass, clay, and other media, including a FREE contemporary art gallery. Lovers of Dale Chihuly and his stylistically lush blown glass can visit **Chihuly Collection** then watch local glass artists in the **Morean Glass Studio and Hot Shop**. Admission is fee-based. **Morean Center for Clay** (MCC) is located in the 1926 Seaboard Freight Train Depot in the Warehouse Arts District. Admission to its rotating exhibits of ceramic art and pottery is FREE. **Morean Arts Center**; 719 Central Ave; St. Petersburg, FL 33701; Phone: (727) 822-7872; https://www.moreanartscenter.org/morean-galleries/
Chihuly Collection; 720 Central Ave; St. Petersburg, FL 33701; Phone: (727) 896-4527;
https://www.moreanartscenter.org/chihuly/
Glass Studio and Hot Shop (behind the Morean Arts Center); 714 First Ave N; St. Petersburg, FL 33701; Phone: (727) 827-4527 Ext 2220; https://www.moreanartscenter.org/hot-shop/
Clay Center; 420 22nd St S; St. Petersburg, FL 33712; Phone: (727) 821-7162; https://www.moreanartscenter.org/center-for-clay/

Museum of the American Arts and Craft Movement is reported to be the only museum in the world dedicated exclusively to the American Arts and Crafts movement. It encompasses all the aspects of the movement from furniture and photography to woodblocks and textiles. 355 Fourth St N; St. Petersburg, FL 33701; Phone: (727)-440-4859; https://www.museumaacm.org/

Museum of Fine Arts features 4,000 years of art including African art, European paintings, and American photography. 255 Beach Dr NE; St. Petersburg, FL 33701; Phone: (727) 896-2667; https://mfastpete.org/

Red Cloud Indian Arts introduces visitors to the unexpected beauty of the art of the First Nations and the Pueblos. They like to call themselves *A little bit of Santa Fe in Downtown St. Petersburg, Florida.* 214 Beach Dr. NE; St. Petersburg, FL 33701; Phone: (727) 821-5824; http://www.redcloudindianarts.com/

The city has also just unveiled its 9/11 memorial **Rise St. Pete Memorial** in the Warehouse Arts district. The centerpiece is a nine-foot-fall, 4,000-pound steel beam. 515 22nd St S, St. Petersburg, FL 33712; https://www.risestpete.org/; https://stpetecatalyst.com/rise-st-petersburgs-9-11-memorial-dedicated/

Sawgrass Lake Park allows you to walk through one of the largest maple swamps on the Gulf Coast of Florida. Take the elevated boardwalk to the observation tower for panoramic views of Sawgrass Lake. FREE. 7400 25th St N; St. Petersburg, FL 33702; Phone: (727) 217-7256; http://www.pinellascounty.org/park/16_Sawgrass.htm

St. Petersburg Museum of History on the pier covers the area's history from the world's first commercial airline to the world's largest collection of autographed baseballs. 335 Second Ave NE; St. Petersburg, FL 33701; Phone: (727) 894-

1052; https://spmoh.com/

St. Pete Pier lines Tampa Bay with 26 acres for strolling, biking, dining, shopping, and entertainment. Learn more about parking options here: https://stpetepier.org/getting-here-parking. Another highlight is the four-mile-long, cable-stayed Sunshine Skyway Bridge (I-275) spanning Lower Tampa Bay. 600 Second Ave NE, St. Petersburg, FL 33701; https://stpetepier.org/

Sunken Gardens started as a roadside attraction over 100 years ago. Today it is home to some of the oldest tropical plants in the region and offers meandering paths, cascading waterfalls, demonstration gardens, and more than 50,000 tropical plants, and flowers. 1825 Fourth St N; St. Petersburg, FL 33704; Phone: (727) 551-3102; http://www.stpete.org/attractions/sunken_gardens/index.php

Tampa Bay Watch Discovery Center is located at the city's signature St. Pete's Pier and delights visitors with its 1,800-gallon Estuary Habitat that replicates the living habitat of many of the species found in local waters. There are interactive displays, video presentations, a touch tank and docent-led tours. 700 Second Ave NE; St. Petersburg, FL 33701; Phone: (727) 291-4103; https://tbwdiscoverycenter.org/

Weedon Island Preserve invites visitors to explore nature with almost two miles of handicap-accessible boardwalks and pavement through tidal flats and mangrove forests, providing viewing opportunities over saltwater ponds, pine flatwoods, and a 45-foot observation tower. The Weedon Island Preserve Cultural and Natural History Center offers interpretive hikes, workshops, and exhibits. FREE. 1800 Weedon Dr NE; St. Petersburg, FL 33702; Phone: (727) 453-6500; http://www.weedonislandpreserve.org/

Zen Glass Studio specializes in glass blowing and flamework glass art. Special workshops are offered. 600 27th St S; St. Petersburg, FL 33712; Phone: (727) 323-3141; https://zenglass.com/

Tampa, FL (Hillsborough County) (TBA)

In 1885 cigar manufacturer Vicente Martinez-Ybor founded a city that bore his name. Martinez-Ybor built small houses (casitas) which the Spanish and Italian workers could buy at cost, and the city thrived. But Tampa city leaders became concerned about an area that felt to them a bit too much like an ungoverned frontier town and annexed the city in 1887, folding it into Tampa. Today it's a National Historic Landmark District and a popular and lively area.

To help visitors navigate the city, the TECO Line Streetcar is a heritage streetcar transit line that connects parts of the city. http://www.tecolinestreetcar.org

SS American Victory is one of only four fully-operational WWII ships in the country. 705 Channelside Dr; Tampa, FL 33602; Phone: (813) 228-8766; http://www.americanvictory.org/

Busch Gardens Tampa Bay is the popular 335-acre African animal theme park. 10165 McKinley Dr; Tampa, FL 33612; Phone: (813) 884-4FUN; https://buschgardens.com/tampa/

Cracker Country Living History Museum at Florida State Fairgrounds invites visitors to see how early Florida settlers lived through interpreters, skilled artisans, heritage livestock, and heirloom plants. NOTE: Open to the public only for select events. 4800 US 301 N; Tampa, FL 33610; Phone: (813) 627-4225; http://www.crackercountry.org/

East Bay Raceway Park is a 1/3-mile dirt/clay track. 6311 Burts Rd, Tampa, FL 33619; Phone: (813) 677-7223; https://www.facebook.com/eastbayracewaypark/

Florida Aquarium shelters over 8,000 aquatic animals and plants and offers opportunities to meet their animal ambassadors and talk with the biologists who care for them. 701 Channelside Dr; Tampa, FL 33602; Phone: (813) 273-4000; https://www.flaquarium.org/

Florida Museum of Photographic Art creates exhibits of historic and contemporary works by nationally and internationally known photographic artists. 1630 E Seventh Ave; Ybor, Tampa, FL 33605; Phone: (813) 221-2222; https://www.fmopa.org/; https://www.facebook.com/FloridaMuseumOfPhotographicArts/

Glazer Children's Museum has created exhibits and interactive experiences including building in Engineers' Workshop and learning the origins of our food in the Farm, even grocery shopping and banking. 110 W Gasparilla Plaza; Tampa, FL 33602; Phone: (813)443-3861; https://glazermuseum.org/

Henry B. Plant Museum in the Tampa Bay Hotel, depicts the opulence of the gilded age of the 1890s complete with actual furnishings. Built by Henry Bradley Plant, it was the palace of his empire of railroads, steamships, and hotels. 401 W Kennedy Blvd; Tampa, FL 33606; Phone: (813) 254-1891; http://www.plantmuseum.com/

Hindu Temple of Tampa is a place of worship and practice of Sanatana dharma brought to their new home. Temple tours are free (with donations gratefully accepted). NOTE: Modest clothing and reservations are required. 5509 Lynn Rd; Tampa,

FL 33624; Phone: (813) 962-6890; https://htfl.org/temple-tour/

J.C. Newman Cigar Company is America's oldest family-owned cigar company, and it has opened its doors to share the story with the pubic in its three-floor museum. Although the museum is free, there is a charge to take the tour. 2701 N 16th St; Tampa, FL 33605; Phone: (813) 248-2124; https://www.jcnewman.com/visit-us/

Museum of Science & Industry (MOSI) enables visitors to explore everything from dinosaurs to the moon. A Jurassic-themed exhibit invites guests to explore the world of paleontology, or visitors can choose to see NASA's vision for living on worlds beyond Earth, and much in between. 4801 E Fowler Ave; Tampa, FL 33617; Phone: (813) 987-6000; https://www.mosi.org

Sulphur Springs Museum and Heritage Center is a local history museum in Mann-Wagnon Memorial Park. Permanent exhibits outline the history of Sulphur Springs and some of its best-known landmarks. A four-panel exhibit tells the story of Mann-Wagnon Park, and the natural history museum that once stood here. There's also a three-panel exhibit on the history of the Black neighborhood of Sulphur Springs, during the segregation era. FREE with donations encouraged. 1101 E River Cove St; Tampa, FL 33604; Phone: (813) 935-9402; https://www.sulphurspringsmuseum.org/

Al Lopez was Tampa's first Major League player, manager, and Hall of Fame inductee. **Tampa Baseball Museum at the Al Lopez House** is located in the family home and celebrates local baseball culture – from Little League to Major League, and everything in between. 2003 N 19th St; Tampa, FL 33605; Phone: (813) 247-1434; https://www.tampabaseballmuseum.org/

For horse racing head to **Tampa Bay Downs** which offers live racing generally from December through April. 11225 Race Track Rd; Tampa, FL 33626; Phone: (813) 855-4401; https://www.tampabaydowns.com/

Tampa Bay History Center covers three floors exploring the stories and personalities from Florida's past. Exhibitions include the infamous pirate Jack Rackham, Teddy Roosevelt, Florida's first peoples, Cuban cigar rollers, and pioneering cattle ranchers. 801 Water St; Tampa, FL 33602; Phone: (813) 228-0097; https://www.tampabayhistorycenter.org/

Tampa Firefighters Museum, housed in the 1911 fire station, tells the stories that make up the history of the Tampa Fire Department. FREE. 720 Zack St; Tampa, FL 33602; Phone: (813) 964-6862; http://www.tampafiremuseum.com

Tampa Theatre, designed to mimic a spectacular outdoor setting, opened in 1926. Not only can you enjoy a special event or a movie, but their monthly Balcony to Backstage tours invite the public to learn more about its history and architecture, and treats guests to a demonstration of the Mighty Wurlitzer Theatre Organ. This is a nonprofit organization. NOTE: Tampa Theatre is wheelchair accessible and offers devices for assisted listening and audio narration. 711 N Franklin St; Tampa, FL 33602; Phone: (813) 274-8286; https://tampatheatre.org/tour/balcony-backstage-tour/

Tampa Museum of Art exhibits modern and contemporary art, as well as Greek, Roman, and Etruscan antiquities. 120 W Gasparilla Plaza; Tampa, FL 33602; Phone: (813) 274-8130; https://tampamuseum.org/

Tampa Police Museum remembers and honors officers killed in the line of duty and traces the history of the police force. Located on the ground floor of the Tampa Police Department headquarters. 411 N Franklin St; Tampa, FL 33602; Phone: (813) 276-3258; http://tampapolicememorial.org/museum/

University of South Florida Contemporary Art Museum (USFCAM) organizes and presents exhibitions of contemporary art from Florida, the United States, and around the world, including Africa, Europe, and Latin America. FREE. 3821 USF Holly Dr; Tampa, FL 33620; Phone: (813) 974-4133; http://cam.usf.edu/CAM/cam_about.html

University of South Florida Botanical Gardens consists of seven acres of developed gardens plus a natural greenbelt. FREE. 12210 USF Pine Dr; Tampa, FL 33612; Phone: (813) 974-2329; https://www.usf.edu/arts-sciences/botanical-gardens/

Wat Mongkolratanaram is a Buddhist Thai temple with an unusual and very popular twist – it hosts a food market specializing in Thai dishes held every Sunday. Temple grounds are open daily between 9 AM and 6 PM. Regular services are held on Sunday at 1 PM in Pali language. Most Sundays a representative will be in the main Temple between 11:30 AM and 12:45 PM to answer questions on the Temple and Temple activities. NOTE: Please remove your shoes before entering the Temple and follow the Temple rules of etiquette. 5306 Palm River Rd; Tampa, FL 33619; Phone: (813) 621-1669; https://wattampainenglish.com/

Ybor City Museum interprets the area's unique Cuban history. Once an independent town (Tampa annexed Ybor City in 1887), it was home to the immigrants who worked in the cigar industry. Today the area is a National Historic Landmark District in Tampa. Visitors can explore the main exhibit space, housed in the historic Ferlita Bakery building, as well as a Mediterranean-style garden and a recreated cigar worker's house. Walking tours of the Ybor City Historic District are also available. 1818 E Ninth Ave; Tampa, FL 33605; Phone: (813) 247-6323; https://www.ybormuseum.org/; https://www.floridastateparks.org/parks-and-trails/ybor-city-museum-state-park

ZooTampa at Lowry Park is home to a wide variety of exotic animals, some rare and threatened with extinction. Visitors can hear stories of wildlife conservation, walk through four free-flight aviaries, watch animal shows, and observe species from all over the world and understand the threats they face. 1101 W Sligh Ave; Tampa, FL 33604; Phone: (813) 935-8552; https://zootampa.org/

Tarpon Springs, FL (Pinellas) (TBA)

Named for the fish found in abundance in nearby waters, the town is also the self-proclaimed *sponge capital of the world*, and reasons to visit include its Greek heritage, and miles of waterfront.

Leepa-Rattner Museum of Art includes modern and contemporary paintings, photography, sculpture, prints. The works of figurative expressionist Abraham Rattner (1893-1978), printmaker, sculptor, and painter Esther Gentle (1889-1991), and abstract expressionist Allen Leepa (1919-2009) are considered highlights. Located on the Tarpon Springs campus of St. Petersburg College. 600 E Klosterman Rd; Tarpon Springs, FL 34689; Phone: (727) 712-5762; https://leeparattner.org/

Replay Museum is ground zero for those loving vintage arcade and pinball games. The collection of over 120 machines is ready to play. 119 E Tarpon Ave; Tarpon Springs, FL 34689; Phone: (727) 940-3928; https://www.replaymuseum.org/

Safford House Museum was home of one of the city's original developers and an example of late 19th century Florida vernacular architecture. It is filled with period furnishings and original family possessions. 23 Parkin Ct; Tarpon Springs, FL 34689; Phone: (727) 942-5605; https://tarponarts.org/event-location/safford-house-museum/

Saint Nicholas Greek Orthodox Cathedral domed main church building, designed by the Eugene Brothers of Chicago, was modeled in part after the Hagia Sophia in what is now Istanbul, melding Byzantine and Gothic Revival styles. The 23 stained glass windows surrounding the dome depict episodes in the life of Jesus and the saints. The interior features icons, many by Greek iconographer George Saklaridis. 36 N Pinellas Ave, Tarpon Springs, FL 34689; Phone: (727) 937-3540; https://stnicholastarpon.org/

Spongeorama's Sponge Factory is certainly a gift shop aimed at tourists, but that doesn't mean it can't be a bit of fun. After all, you are in the Sponge Capital of the World. Find out just what a sponge is and where they come. There's even a movie. FREE. 510 Dodecanese Blvd; Tarpon Springs, FL 34689; Phone: (727) 943-2164; https://spongeorama.com/

Tarpon Springs Area Historical Society, Inc. operates a depot museum emphasizing the important role the railroad played in the growth of the town. The front rooms of the building have been restored to when it was a working railroad station. FREE. NOTE: Hours are limited so check the website. 160 East Tarpon Ave; Tarpon Springs, FL 34689; Phone: 727-943-4624; http://tarponspringsareahistoricalsociety.org

Tierra Verde, FL (Pinellas) (TBA)

Take Pinellas Bayway South to explore the tiny keys (islands) dotting the Tampa Bay area. Many are reachable only by boat.

Fort De Soto Park includes five interconnected islands across 1,136 acres. The fort itself was a military outpost constructed during the Spanish American War, which had a big impact on Florida because of its proximity to Cuba. The Quartermaster Storehouse Museum is on Mullet Key. Visitors can walk through Battery Laidley, home to the last four surviving carriage-mounted 12-inch seacoast mortars in the continental United States. The historical trail leads park visitors from Battery Laidley to the locations of former post buildings. The Barrier-Free Nature Trail is a self-guided interpretive trail providing access to nature for all visitors to Fort De Soto Park. NOTE: Ferry service to Egmont and Shell Key is available from the park. 3500 Pinellas Bayway S; Tierra Verde, FL 33715; Phone: (727) 582-2100;
https://www.pinellascounty.org/park/Quartermaster_museum.htm;
https://www.pinellascounty.org/park/05_ft_desoto.htm

Egmont Key State Park is accessible only by boat and serves primarily as a wildlife refuge sprinkled with ruins of Fort Dade, a Spanish–American War era fort. A lighthouse is also on the island. Commercial guide boats provide daily tours of Egmont Key and there is a ferry from Fort de Soto State Park. The Egmont Key Guardhouse has been restored for future use as a museum and education center. NOTE: There is no water and no restroom facilities on the island.
https://www.fws.gov/refuge/Egmont_Key/;
https://www.floridastateparks.org/parks-and-trails/egmont-key-state-park/

Shell Key Preserve is an 1,828-acre preserve with access limited to water vessels, including private boats, public shuttles, and ferries. NOTE: This is undeveloped land and there are no services. Ferry service is available from Fort De Soto Boat Ramp. Phone: (727) 453-6900;

https://www.pinellascounty.org/park/managedlands/skp.htm
https://www.hubbardsmarina.com/shell-key-ferry/
http://shellkey.org/

Weeki Wachee, FL (Hernando) (TBA)

(See Spring Hill, FL)

The city of Weeki Wachee was founded in 1966 to promote the local mermaid attraction. With fewer than 15 residents, the city was dissolved in June 2020. The name of the town has changed, but the mermaids and their shows live on in the town of Spring Hill.

Ybor City, FL (Hillsborough County)

(See Tampa, FL)

Region 5 Central Florida: Ocala to Orlando

The theme parks of central Florida are certainly a destination for visitors, and the economic powerhouse city of Orlando is another great place to explore. But the many towns that make up this region offer their own special charms. Those who seek the beauty and activities of the outdoors will also find places to enjoy.

The 45-mile long **Green Mountain Scenic Byway** (think hills more than actual mountains) links several towns. https://greenmountainbyway.org/things-to-do/

The area also hosts an old railroad route transformed into the 22-mile **West Orange Trail**. https://www.traillink.com/trail/west-orange-trail/

Ocala National Forest encompasses 387,000 acres and spans parts of Marion, Lake, Putnam, and Seminole counties. Filled with natural pools, canoe runs, hiking trails, and the remains of 19th-century homesteads, it is the second largest nationally protected forest in Florida. https://www.fs.usda.gov/attmain/ocala/specialplaces

The **Ocala Metropolitan Area** covers all of Marion County. Although Ocala is in a different county and region from Gainesville (in Region Two) these cities are less than one hour apart.

Orlando anchors the **Greater Orlando Metropolitan Area (GOMA)** and includes Kissimmee, and Sanford as well as the towns in the counties of Lake, Orange, Osceola, and Seminole.

Altoona, FL (Lake County) (GOMA)

Alexander Springs Recreation Area (part of the Ocala National Forest) is considered to be one of the most beautiful and user-friendly areas, with a gently sloped clear spring pool (at the constant 72°F). The Timucuan Trail is a one-mile interpretive loop with a boardwalk through a jungle of palms along the spring run. NOTE: It is the only place in the Ocala National Forest where scuba diving is permitted. 49525 CR 445; Altoona, FL 32702; Phone: (352) 669-3522; https://www.fs.usda.gov/recarea/florida/recarea/?recid=83546

Apopka, FL (Orange County) (GOMA)

Proud of their heritage of agriculture, and foliage, the city holds its Apopka Art and Foliage Festival in April. https://www.apopkaartandfoliagefestival.org/

Avian Reconditioning Center rehabilitates raptors (birds of prey) and is open to the public on Saturdays, weather permitting. Closed the month of August. 323 W Lester Rd; Apopka, FL 32712; Phone: (407) 461-1056; https://arc4raptors.org/

Lake Apopka Wildlife Drive is a one-way 11-mile road that follows the lake's edge. It's part of the larger Lake Apopka Loop Trail. FREE. NOTE: The drive is open Friday through Sunday, and holidays. Entrance to the drive ends at 3 PM and all cars must leave by 5 PM. 2850 Lust Rd; Apopka, FL 32703; Phone: (386) 329-4404; https://www.sjrwmd.com/lands/recreation/lake-apopka

Wekiwa Springs State Park is a popular day trip from Orlando with its springs feeding the Wekiwa River and lush tropical hammocks. Visitors can swim, hike, bike, and horseback ride on the trails, or rent a canoe or kayak. NOTE: Wekiwa Springs will close when it reaches capacity (150 cars)

and no vehicles, cyclists, or pedestrians will be allowed to enter until space becomes available. 1800 Wekiwa Cir; Apopka, FL 32712; Phone: (407) 553-4383; https://www.floridastateparks.org/parks-and-trails/wekiwa-springs-state-park

Bushnell, FL (Sumter County)

Dade Battlefield Historic State Park focuses on US history, hiking, and wildlife photography. Every January they create a re-enactment of the 1835 battle said to be the largest Seminole Wars reenactment offered anywhere. 7200 Battlefield Pkwy; Bushnell, FL 33513; Phone: (352) 793-4781; https://www.floridastateparks.org/parks-and-trails/dade-battlefield-historic-state-park

Celebration, FL (Osceola County) (GOMA)

Located near Walt Disney World Resort, the town was part of the New Urbanism movement, and originally developed by the Walt Disney Company with a deliberate small-town feel.

FOCUS ON: The Naming of Osceola and Seminole Counties

There's almost always a story behind a county's name, but Osceola County may have one that is more than a bit perplexing. The county derives its name from Billy Powell, son of British trader William Powell who married a Creek woman named Polly Copinger. Powell adopted the name Osceola at a tribal ceremony around 1820 and became one of the best-known Seminole leaders. He was famous (or perhaps infamous) for conducting several raids against the Army as part of the Seminole wars. During the 1830s he led members of his tribe to resist the US Army's efforts to forcibly deport them to a reservation west of the Mississippi River. Captured under a false flag of truce, Osceola died a prisoner of the US Army at Fort Moultrie, South Carolina in January 1838. Because of his renown, Osceola attracted visitors in prison, including the famous artist George Catlin who painted perhaps the most well-known portrait of the Seminole leader.

And here is where the story gets mystifying. The body of Osceola is buried at the fort, but his head is likely not there. Rumors abound that Dr. Frederick Weedon, a contract surgeon to the US Army, was alone with the warrior's body and cut off Osceola's head before the body was buried. The story goes that Weedon eventually sold his head to Dr. Valentine Mott of New York City but that it was destroyed when Mott's museum burned down in 1866. Fast forward to 1887. After years of attempting to destroy the Seminoles, Florida created Osceola County in 1887. His likeness also is prominently placed on the county flag. https://www.nps.gov/people/osceola.htm

Similarly Seminole County, created on April 25, 1913, was carved out of Orange County and named after the Seminole people who had historically lived in that area… before they were forced to relocate to Indian Territory or flee into the Everglades.

Christmas, FL (Orange County) (GOMA)

The town derived its name from the date it was established – December 25, 1837. Christmas, the town, becomes quite popular in December with folks who want their cards postmarked Christmas, Florida.

Fort Christmas Historical Park shelters several restored and replicated buildings including the fort, traditional Florida Cracker and pioneer homes, a schoolhouse and lunchroom, and a sugar cane mill, as well as historical farming equipment. 1300 N Ft Christmas Rd (CR 420); Christmas, FL 32709; Phone: (407) 254-9312; http://www.nbbd.com/godo/FortChristmas

Jungle Adventures invites visitors to take a guided tour, enjoy a show, explore the Native American village, take a cruise, and stroll the park. 26205 E Colonial Dr; Christmas, FL 32709; Phone: (407) 568-2885; https://www.jungleadventures.com/index.html

Clermont, FL (Lake County) (GOMA)

Built in 1956 to allow visitors to observe the miles of surrounding orange groves, **Citrus Tower** was one of the most famous landmarks of the Orlando area. It rises 226 feet – about 22 stories. The glass-enclosed observation deck still provides a panoramic view of the Florida's ridge section and the hundreds of spring-fed lakes across an eight-county area. 141 US 27 S; Clermont, FL 34711; Phone: (352) 394-4061; https://citrustower.com/

Lakeridge Winery & Vineyards specializes in native grape varieties (Noble, Carlos, and Welder Muscadine) as well as Chardonnay, Pinot Grigio, Petite Sirah, and Cabernet Sauvignon. Visitors can enjoy free wine tours and tastings as well as special events. 19239 US 27 N; Clermont, FL 34715; Phone: (800) 768-9463; https://www.lakeridgewinery.com/

Presidents Hall of Fame started as a wax museum called the House of Presidents, but today includes animatronics, White House replicas, and Americana miniatures. 123 US 27 N; Clermont, FL 34711; Phone: (352) 394-2836.

Showcase of Citrus is a family owned and operated 2,500-acre estate cultivating over 50 varieties of citrus with a pick-your-own experience. Also available is a truck tour through native woods, groves, and swamps. 5010 US 27; Clermont, FL 34714; Phone: (352) 394-4377; https://showcaseofcitrus.com/

Dunnellon, FL (Marion County)

(See also Ocala, FL and Ocklawaha, FL)

A statue of the **Blues Brothers** catches Jake and Elwood Blues in a moment of dance. There's no particular association between the fictional musical duo and the city, but it is pretty cool as a selfie spot. West Pennsylvania Avenue and Cedar Street.

Grandview Clydesdale brings visitors through their farm with a two-hour tour that starts with the breeding and birth of the tiny Clydesdales, then follows them through training for the world championships. 10020 SW 125th Court Rd; Dunnellon, FL 34432; Phone: (260) 388-4279; https://grandviewclydesdales.tours/

Rainbow Springs State Park is another of the state's beautiful places. Today it is filled with ornamental gardens, built waterfalls, and sloping hills but the land was once the site of a phosphate mining operation, and then a privately owned tourist attraction called Rainbow Springs. The 72-degree spring pool is known for the clarity of the water. Kayak and canoe rentals are available. Tubing is also available. NOTE: This a very popular park and reaches capacity early in the day. 19158 SW 81st Place Rd; Dunnellon, FL 34432; Phone: (352) 465-8555; https://www.floridastateparks.org/parks-and-trails/rainbow-springs-state-park

Eatonville, FL (Orange County) (GOMA)

From the 1880s to the 1930s hundreds of communities founded by and for Black Americans were created throughout the south. Few have survived, but Eatonville is an exception. The Black settlers in the historic White community of Maitland wanted to establish their own town. That was the dream of Joseph E. Clarks. Eventually, Lewis Lawrence (a northern philanthropist), and Josiah Eaton (a local landowner), helped Clarks and others acquire the 112 acres that became the original city limits. The 20-acre historic district includes buildings constructed between 1882 and 1946. Read more at: http://www.townofeatonville.org/about/

FOCUS ON: Zora Neale Hurston

Eatonville's most famous resident was Zora Neale Hurston (1891–1960), a Black American writer and anthropologist. Hurston moved with her family to Eatonville when she was still a toddler and her father became one of the town's first mayors.

Hurston's mother died in 1904, and her father remarried a year later. It is likely Hurston and her stepmother did not get along since shortly after the marriage Hurston was sent to a boarding school and subsequently roamed from relative to relative. In 1917, Hurston enrolled at Morgan College, where she completed her high school studies. She then attended Howard University and earned an associate's degree. She later used Eatonville as the setting for many of her stories.

Despite an active and diverse career, she died with few resources and was initially buried in an unmarked grave in the Garden of Heavenly Rest in Fort Pierce.

In the early 1970s, author Alice Walker found what she believed to be the grave and provided a gravestone. Walker also resurrected Huston's fame with her article, *In Search of Zora Neale Hurston*, in the March issue of Ms. Magazine. There was so much renewed interest that additional work was published posthumously. The career of Zora Neale Hurston spanned over 30 years and included four novels, two books of folklore, as well as essays, short stories and even a play. Read more about her at: https://www.zoranealehurston.com and https://chdr.cah.ucf.edu/hurstonarchive/

See also Fort Pierce, FL for the Zora Neale Hurston Trail

Constructed between 1888 and 1889, the **Moseley House** is the second oldest remaining structure in Eatonville. It has been restored and is furnished with period pieces. 11 Taylor St; Eatonville, FL 32751; Phone: (407) 622-9382; https://www.themoseleyhouse.org/

The **Zora Neale Hurston National Museum of Fine Arts** features paintings, sculpture, films, and photography on permanent exhibit and temporary loans. 344 E Kennedy Blvd; Eatonville, FL 32751; Phone: (407) 647-3307; http://www.zoranealehurstonmuseum.com/

Eustis, FL (Lake County) (GOMA)

This town goes back to about 1825 with a historic waterfront and several buildings listed on the National Register of Historic Places. The town is also famous for its George Fest held yearly on the birthday of George Washington, although there is no known association between America's first President and the town. https://eustisgeorgefest.org/

Eustis Historical Museum highlights the story of the town through its two museums. The **Clifford House** features period antiques and displays of local history. The *Indiana Jones Room* is dedicated to Dr. Edgar J. Banks, a professor and archaeologist who spent time in Eustis and who many believe was the inspiration for the intrepid fictional Indiana Jones. The **Citrus Museum** features exhibits related the citrus industry, and displays include labels, posters, utensils, tools, equipment, and other memorabilia. NOTE: Hours are limited. 536 N Bay St; Eustis, FL 32726; Phone: (352) 483-0046; http://www.eustishistoricalmuseum.org/

Gotha, FL (Orange County) (GOMA)

Nehrling Gardens was the passion of Dr. Henry Nehrling, one of Florida's pioneer horticulturists and naturalists. His Palm Cottage Gardens became one of Florida's first USDA horticultural experimental stations where Dr. Nehrling tested thousands of plants and produced more than 300 plants of ornamental horticulture, including caladiums, palms, bamboos, magnolias, amaryllis, Indian Hawthorne, and crinum lilies. NOTE: The gardens are open to visitors with limited days and hours. 2267 Hempel Ave; Gotha, FL 34734; Phone: (407) 445-9977; https://nehrlinggardens.org/

Howey-In-The-Hills, FL (Lake County) (GOMA)

Howey-In-The-Hills was founded by William John Howey and incorporated as "Howey" on May 8, 1925. A few years later, in a move to highlight the area's rolling hills the name was changed to... Howey-in-the-Hills.

Howey Mansion was the home of the town's founder and is in the process of being restored. Designed in Mediterranean Revival style, the architect was Katherine Cotheal Budd

(1860–1951) who has her own interesting history. She was the first woman to be granted membership in the New York chapter of the American Institute of Architects. The Howey home is one of two existing examples of her work. The other is the Duncan House, or Harry C. Duncan House, a private home in Tavares, FL which is not open to the public. Advanced online registration is required for the guided tours. NOTE: The Howey Mansion is not ADA accessible.
1001 Citrus Ave; Howey-In-The-Hills, FL 34737; Phone: (407) 906-4918; https://www.thehoweymansion.com/historic-tours.html

Kissimmee, FL (Osceola County) (GOMA)

Disney Wilderness Preserve shelters over 1,000 species of plants and animals and is considered an essential part of the Everglades ecosystem. Its 3,500 acres of restored wetlands captures rain, and replenishes the groundwater. There's a heartening history. The land was once an 8,500-acre cattle ranch at the head of the Greater Everglades watershed. As with most of the land in Florida, it was slated for extensive development. Working with the Nature Conservancy, the State of Florida, and a number of other groups, the Walt Disney Co. purchased the property and transferred it to the Conservancy to create a nature preserve dedicated to wetlands restoration. Today visitors can hike, bird-watch, and enjoy old Florida's natural beauty. NOTE: It is advised bring drinking water, hats, sun protection and bug repellent and to use appropriate footwear. FREE. 2700 Scrub Jay Trail; Kissimmee, FL 34759; Phone: (407) 935-0002; https://www.nature.org/en-us/get-involved/how-to-help/places-we-protect/the-disney-wilderness-preserve/

Old Town Entertainment District is Kissimmee's fun zone self-described as a *recreation of a classic Florida town.* The 18 acres offer shops and restaurants plus free weekly events, live music, car shows, and amusement rides. For fans of magic, The Great Magic Hall offers fun shows throughout the day featuring magic on several intimate stages. Entrance and parking are FREE but many attractions charge for tickets. 5770 W Irlo Bronson Memorial Hwy; Kissimmee, FL 34746; Phone: (407) 396-4888; https://myoldtownusa.com/

Machine Gun America is quick to tell visitors that it is NOT a shooting range. Machine Gun America is a Shooting Attraction. No personal firearms are allowed. Instead, visitors are provided a selection of firearms, eye and ear protection, standard range target as well as one-on-one instruction and observation by one of their NRA Certified Range Safety Instructors. They also offer Tank America at a different location. 5825 W Irlo Bronson Memorial Hwy; Kissimmee, FL 34746; Phone: (407) 278-1800; https://machinegunamericaorlando.com

Dedicated in 1943, downtown Kissimmee's **Monument of States** is a 40-foot-tall pyramid constructed of stones, fossils, and rocky materials gathered from all 50 states and more than 20 countries. 300 E Monument Ave; Kissimmee, FL 34741

Carefully relocated from different parts of Osceola County, **Pioneer Village at Shingle Creek** demonstrates how life was once lived. The village includes a general store and post office, schoolhouse, church, train depot, homesteads from Osceola settlers, a Seminole settlement, a cow camp and working structures such as a blacksmith shop, citrus packing plant, cane grinder, and barn. Guided tours are available. 2491 Babb Rd; Kissimmee, FL 34746; Phone: (407) 396-8644; https://osceolahistory.org/pioneer-village/

Wat Florida Dhammaram monastery observes religious functions of the Buddhist calendar and provides daily chanting and meditation practice. All are welcome. 2421 Old Vineland

Rd; Kissimmee, FL 34746; Phone: (407) 397-9552; http://www.watfloridadhammaram.com/

Maitland, FL (Orange County) (GOMA)

Art & History Museums of Maitland encompasses several museums on two separate campuses. The largest is the **Maitland Art Center** founded in 1937 by artist and architect J. André Smith (1880-1959) who designed it in a style called Mayan Revival. It is one of the rare examples in the southeast. The Maitland Historical Society brought the **Telephone Museum**, and the **Waterhouse Residence Museum** as examples of Florida living in the Victorian period. There's also the **Carpentry Shop Museum** with its hands-on antique tools. Maitland Art Center, Maitland Historical Museum, and the Telephone Museum are on the main campus on W Packwood Ave – adjacent one another at 221 and 231. The Waterhouse Residence Museum, and Carpentry Shop Museum are at 820 Lake Lily Dr. The grounds are free to visit but there is a fee to enter the museums. Phone: (407) 539-2181; https://artandhistory.org/

Audubon Center for Birds of Prey rehabilitates injured birds at a restored lakefront 1920s bungalow. View bald eagles, ospreys, kites, owls, and falcons. Learn about the unique adaptations of raptors. 1101 Audubon Way; Maitland, FL 32751; Phone: (407) 644-0190; https://cbop.audubon.org/

Holocaust Memorial Resource and Education Center of Florida communicates the history and lessons of the Holocaust using artifacts, videos, text, photographs, and artwork. There are also recorded testimonies of Holocaust survivors who settled in Central Florida. Their Displaced Person exhibit traces the journey of Oswald "Valdik" Holzer, a Czech Jewish doctor. Behind The Bookcase is a virtual reality experience of the secret annex where Anne Frank and her family hid from the Nazis. FREE. 851 N Maitland Ave; Maitland, FL 32751; Phone: (407) 628-0555; https://www.holocaustedu.org/

Mount Dora, FL (Lake County) (GOMA)

Known for its antique shops (which are generally open only on weekends) the town also hosts one of the few objects-as-art museums in the country. Mount Dora is one of the access points to the Dora Canal. The canal is considered one of the more beautiful stretches in central Florida. Tours ply the waterway between Mount Dora and Tavares. The best access is in Mount Dora with Premier Boat Tours of Mount Dora (https://www.doracanaltour.com/) and Rusty Anchor Mount Dora Boat Tours (https://www.rustyanchormountdora.com/).

Modernism Museum introduces visitors to functional objects as art and new expressive possibilities in the field. 145 E Fourth Ave; Mt Dora, FL 32757; Phone: (352) 385-0034; https://www.modernismmuseum.org

Mount Dora Center for the Arts highlights local and regional artists in their gallery. FREE. 136 E Fifth Ave; Mt Dora, FL 32757; Phone: (352) 383-0880; https://mountdoraart.com/

Mount Dora History Museum is located in the first fire station and city jail dating back to 1923. The exhibits highlight activities in Mount Dora from the 1880s to the 1930s. NOTE: Hours are limited. 450 Royellou Ln; Mt Dora, FL 32757; Phone: (352) 383-0006; http://www.mountdorahistorymuseum.com/

Despite being only 35-feet tall **Mount Dora Lighthouse** is a real and registered inland aid to navigation, the only one in Florida. The tiny lighthouse guides boaters navigating Lake

Dora after dusk. Grantham Point (next to Mount Dora Marina).
https://www.whattodoinmtdora.com/attractions/iconic-mount-dora-lighthouse/

Both indoor and outdoor spaces fill **Renninger's Twin Markets** with everything from produce and clothing, to high end antiques and collectibles. The flea market and farmers stand are open Saturday and Sunday. The indoor antique center is open Friday through Sunday. 20651 US 441; Mount Dora, FL 32757; Phone: (352) 383-3141; https://renningers.net/mt-dora/explore-the-market-3

Oakland, FL (Orange County) (GOMA)

Despite similar names, Oakland, Florida is about three hours away from Oakland Park, Florida which is part of the Greater Miami Metro area.

Located on 150-acres surrounding Lake Apopka, **Oakland Nature Preserve** has an important past. By the early 1920s sewage discharge into the lake, and then fertilizer runoff and pesticides from the nearby farms had created an environmental disaster for the fish. The folks who started the preserve were instrumental in saving the lake and creating a healthy environment for both the fish and the land. FREE. 747 Machete Trail; Oakland, FL 34760; Phone: (407) 905-0054; https://oaklandnaturepreserve.wildapricot.org/

Ocala, FL (Marion County)

(See also Dunnellon, FL and Ocklawaha, FL)

Officially named **Horse Capital of the World**, Ocala is one of only four major thoroughbred centers in the world. Marion County is truly horse country with 600 thoroughbred horse farms that have produced 45 national champions, six

Kentucky Derby winners, 20 Breeders' Cup champions and six Horses of the Year. Numerous horse farms in the area offer tours by appointment. Learn more at: https://www.ocalamarion.com/things-to-do/equestrian/local-horse-farms/

The city is also the gateway to **Ocala National Forest**, one of the major recreation areas in the state filled with 600 lakes, rivers and springs, including three first-magnitude springs. https://www.fs.usda.gov/ocala

FOCUS ON: Marjorie Harris Carr Cross Florida Greenway

Ocala is a major part of the Marjorie Harris Carr Cross Florida Greenway. It was originally going to be the Cross Florida Barge Canal linking the Atlantic Intracoastal Waterway with the Gulf Intracoastal Waterway, facilitating commerce across central Florida. Starting in 1935, about 5,000 acres had been cleared and four bridge piers constructed when the money ran out. In 1942 it was started again and over the years bits and pieces of funding was provided.

But there was plenty of controversy over the environmental impact. Whole swaths of land were devastated, communities were destroyed. When the canal was finally de-authorized in 1990, approximately $74 million had been spent.

The land was turned over to the state of Florida and became the Greenway, a 110-mile linear park with more than 300 miles of trails of all types — paddling, hiking, mountain biking, equestrian, and paved multi-use. The Greenway is also the site of first wildlife land bridge in Florida, with a crossing over a major

interstate for both humans and wildlife. The **Land Bridge Trail** over Interstate 75 is one of the most popular trails in the park.
https://www.floridastateparks.org/parks-and-trails/landbridge-trailhead

It was named in honor of Marjorie Harris Carr, a nationally recognized environmentalist of Alachua County, who led the effort to stop the construction. Learn more about the Greenway, and the places you want to visit at:
https://www.floridastateparks.org/parks-and-trails/marjorie-harris-carr-cross-florida-greenway/experiences-amenities-0

Learn more about the history of the Cross Florida Barge Canal in this excerpt from *Ditch of Dreams: The Cross Florida Barge Canal and the Struggle for Florida's Future* by Steven Noll at:
https://www.ocalastyle.com/floridas-folly/

Appleton Museum of Art provides art and artifacts representative of European, American, Asian, African, Contemporary, and pre-Columbian styles. The museum also collects works of Florida artists and showcases the history and progression of Central Florida culture. 4333 E Silver Springs Blvd; Ocala, FL 34470; Phone: (352) 291-4455; http://www.appletonmuseum.org/

Dating back to 1952, **Bubba Raceway Park** is the oldest continuously operating race track in the state of Florida. The track is 3/8-mile, D shaped with a clay surface. Check the website for the racing schedule. 9050 NW Gainesville Rd; Ocala, FL 34482; Phone: (352) 622-9400; https://bubbaracewaypark.com

Brick City Center for the Arts features changing exhibits. The first Friday of the month is an opening reception for the new exhibit and a chance to meet the artist. 23 SW Broadway St; Ocala, FL 34471; Phone: (352) 369-1500; https://www.ocalamarion.com/directory/brick-city-center-for-the-arts/

Don Garlits Museum of Drag Racing chronicles the history of drag racing with almost 300 vehicles in two buildings. 13700 SW 16th Ave; Ocala, FL 34473; Phone: (352) 245-8661; https://www.garlits.com/

Fort King was a United States military fort near what later became the city of Ocala. The fort was built in 1827 as a buffer between new settlers and the Seminole. It later became a base for the United States Army during the forced removal of the Seminole and the Seminole Wars. The site was abandoned and materials used as salvage, but it was recently reconstructed to be as historically accurate as possible. 3925 E Fort King St; Ocala, FL 34470; Phone: (352) 368-5533; https://ftking.org/

Gypsy Gold Horse Farm introduces the public to the regal but relatively unknown Gypsy Vanner horses first imported into the US in 1996 by Dennis and Cindy Thompson. The tours provide an overview and introduction to the breed and its history. On the walking tour you'll meet the stallions, mares, foals and various other animals living on the farm. Read the fascinating history about how this rare horse came to live in Florida at: https://gypsygold.com/gypsy-vanner-history; 12501 Eighth Ave; Ocala, FL 34473; Phone: (352) 307-3777; https://gypsygold.com/book-a-tour/

If you're itching to drive your 4 x 4, dirt bike, or side x side, head to **Hardrock Offroad Park** with 70 acres of trails and tracks. If watching is more your style, **Marion County Speedway** is located on the grounds. 6849 NW Gainesville Rd; Ocala, FL 34475; Phone: (352) 732-6697; https://hardrockoffroadpark.net/

Juniper Springs is known for the hundreds of springs shaded by palms and oaks. A water wheel and old mill building which was constructed in the 1930s by members of the Civilian Conservation Corps now contain interpretive and historical exhibits. A barrier-free, self-guided trail parallels the spring outflows and provides information on the semi-tropical vegetation plus views of the waterways. 26701 E Hwy 40; Silver Springs, FL 34488; Phone: (352) 625-3147; https://www.fs.usda.gov/recmain/florida/recreation

Marion County Museum of History and Archaeology, in the McPherson County Government Complex, displays 13,000 years of human history in Marion County. 307 SE 26th Ter; Ocala, FL 34471; Phone: (352) 236-5245; http://marioncountyarchaeology.com/mcmha/mcmha.htm

Marion County Speedway is a 1/4-mile dirt flat track for Sprint cars, motorcycles and more. 7197 NW Gainesville Rd; Ocala, FL 34475; Phone: (352) 812-3922; https://marioncountyspeedway.com/

Ocala Drive-In is proudly still open for business. 4850 S Pine Ave; Ocala, FL 34480; Phone: (352) 629-1325; https://ocaladrivein.info/

Ocala Fire Museum invites visitors to a self-guided tour through the Fire Department's history. FREE. The Ocala Fire Museum is in Ocala Fire Rescue's Administration site. 3001 NE 21st St; Ocala, FL 34470; Phone: (352) 629-8306; https://www.ocalafl.org/government/city-departments-a-h/ocala-fire-rescue/fire-museum

Ocala Model Railroaders have created a museum in their clubhouse with items from the Atlantic Coast Line, Seaboard Air Line, Union Pacific, Southern and many other railroads on display. NOTE: Limited hours. FREE. 1247 NE Third St; Ocala, FL 34470; Phone: (352) 401-0747 http://www.ocalamodelrailroaders.com/

Petting Zoo Ocala invites families to enjoy petting, feeding, and viewing farm animals along with monkeys, camels, and other non-native creatures. They note that most of their animals were rescued or unwanted. 11150 W Hwy 40; Ocala, FL 34482; Phone: (352) 300-6688; https://www.pettingzooocala.com/

Silver Springs State Park offers the **Silver River Museum** known for its signature exhibit *Dugout Canoes: Paddling the Americas*. These ancient dugouts range in age from 500 to 5,000 years old. The original excavation uncovered the world's largest find of ancient watercraft. Explore their Cabinet of Curiosities and learn about truly giant shrimp – Big Claw River Shrimp whose body can reach 12 feet in size. The **Cracker Village** replicates a 19th century pioneer settlement. The buildings are open on the twice monthly tours. 1445 NE 58th Ave; Ocala, FL 34470; Phone: (352) 236-5401; https://silverrivermuseum.com/ Finally, the park still has their much-loved **glass bottom boat tours** of the spring, as well as kayaking the five-mile Silver River. 1425 NE 58th Ave; Ocala FL 34470; Phone: (352) 236-7148; https://www.floridastateparks.org/silversprings

Tuscawilla Art Park is more than a community park, it features outsized outdoor sculptures from painted bridges to a metal dragon. 213 NE Fifth St; Ocala, FL 34470; Phone: (352) 368-5517; https://www.ocalamarion.com/directory/tuscawilla-art-park/

Webber Center Gallery at College of Central Florida hosts time-limited exhibits as well as curates its own shows. FREE. 3001 SW College Rd; Ocala, FL 34474; Phone: (352) 873-5809; https://www.cf.edu/student-life/arts-and-culture/webber-gallery/

Ocklawaha, FL (Marion County)

(See also Dunnellon, FL and Ocala, FL)

The **Ma Barker House** – named after that Ma Barker – is famous for being the location of the longest recorded gun battle in FBI history. Built in 1930, the Bradford-Ma Barker house is a two-story Florida Cracker style home that was the hideout for the Barker gang. The house was owned by the Bradfords who built it as a retreat. Given an offer too good to refuse, they agreed to rent it to what has been described as a *sweet little old lady.* Next thing they knew, the house was riddled with bullets. The FBI had come for the Barker-Karpis gang. Fill out the form on the website to schedule a tour. https://mabarkerhouse.org/book-tour/; 13279 SE 115th Ave; Ocklawaha, FL 32179; Phone: (352) 671-8560; https://mabarkerhouse.org/

Orlando, FL (Orange County) (GOMA)

Home to numerous theme parks, resorts, restaurants, and nightlife, detailing them would require a book of its own. Rather than listing all the places that are already famous, visitors should check out the city's excellent website: https://www.visitorlando.com/en/things-to-do.

Below you'll find some lesser-known attractions, but don't neglect the nearby cities and towns for more things to do. They are indicated as being **GOMA (Greater Orlando Metropolitan Area).**

Chocolate Kingdom - Factory Adventure Tour is an interactive exploration of how chocolate goes from bean to bar. 9901 Hawaiian Ct; Orlando, FL 32819; Phone: (407) 705-3475; https://www.chocolatekingdom.com

Chocolate Museum & Café is another chocolate-themed destination. The hour-long guided tour takes visitors through the origins of chocolate and its history, continues through the artistic portion with 25 solid chocolate sculptures of some of the world's most recognizable landmarks, and ends with (of course) tastings. 11701 International Dr; Suite 400; Orlando, FL 32821; Phone: (407) 778-4871; https://wocorlando.com/

Gatorland is much like it sounds -- a 110-acre theme park and wildlife preserve focused on Florida's 'gators. Started in 1949, it's one of the state's earliest theme parks that is still in existence. In addition to everything 'gator (and crocodile) there's an aviary, petting zoo, animal shows, zip line, and off-road adventures. 14501 S Orange Blossom Trail; Orlando, FL 32837; Phone: (407) 855-5496; https://www.gatorland.com/

Guang Ming Temple is the largest Buddhist temple in Central Florida. The public is invited to weekly services on Sunday mornings or to visit the shrine as a place of meditation. There is also a public tea house. Please check the website or call for current information. 6555 Hoffner Ave; Orlando, FL 32822; Phone: (407) 281-8482; https://www.orlandobuddhism.org

Owned by the city of Orlando, **Greenwood Cemetery** is the only Orlando cemetery located within the city limits. Visitors can take a tour to learn the history of Orlando through the unique stories of its deceased residents. FREE. 1603 Greenwood St; Orlando, FL 32801; Phone: (407) 246-2616; https://www.orlando.gov/Our-Government/Departments-Offices/Executive-Offices/City-Clerk/Greenwood-Cemetery

ICON Park is filled with restaurants, bars, shopping, and amusement park rides. 375 International Dr; Orlando, FL 32819; Phone: (407) 601-7907; https://iconparkorlando.com/

Nearly 50 acres of landscaped grounds and lakes make up **Harry P. Leu Gardens**. The Leu House Museum is a restored 19th century home that was owned by four families before it was opened to the public. The gardens are a photographer favorite. 1920 N Forest Ave; Orlando, FL 32803; Phone: (407) 246-2620; https://www.leugardens.org/

Mennello Museum of American Art can be found in the Howard Phillips' house in Loch Haven Park and highlights the permanent collection of paintings by Earl Cunningham. On the grounds visitors will find large-scale sculpture exhibitions by nationally renowned American artists. 900 E Princeton St; Orlando, FL 32803; Phone: (407) 246-4278; https://www.mennellomuseum.org/

Orange County Regional History Center, in the historical Orange County Courthouse, covers five floors with local and regional history starting from 12,000 years ago. 65 E Central Blvd; Orlando, FL 32801; Phone: (407) 836-8500; http://thehistorycenter.org

Orlando Fire Museum highlights local fire department history in the 1926 firehouse. A highlight is the restored 1926 American LaFrance fire engine. NOTE: Open Friday and Saturday only. FREE. 814 E Rollins St; Orlando, FL 32803; Phone: (407) 246-3468; https://www.orlandofiremuseum.org/

Orlando Museum of Art includes artworks in all media focused on American art, art of the Ancient Americas, and African art. Recent acquisitions are enhancing its modern and contemporary collections. 2416 N Mills Ave; Orlando, FL 32803; Phone: (407) 896-4231; https://omart.org/

Orlando Science Center uses exhibits, as well as live and screened programming. 777 E Princeton St; Orlando, FL 32803; Phone: (407) 514-2000; https://www.osc.org/

Randall Knife Museum displays Randall Knives, old and new, along with the work of other knife artisans. Think pocket knives, military knives, axes, swords, machetes, and over 7,000 items. NOTE: Visitors must stop by the business showroom first. 4857 S Orange Blossom Trail; Orlando, FL 32839; Phone: (407) 855-8075; https://www.randallknives.com/faqs/museum-hours/

Shooters World bills itself as *the largest indoor gun range in the United States*. Their firearms instructors and range safety officers will help new visitors every step of the way. This is their largest location with 58 shooting lanes. NOTE: There are two other locations – in Tampa, and The Villages – with 39 shooting lanes. 4850 Lawing La; Orlando, FL 32811; Phone: (407) 500-4867; https://www.shootersworld.com/orlando/

WonderWorks in Orlando is one of two Florida locations for this small chain of science-based attractions. The other one is in Panama City Beach. The upside-down facility is explained as the result of an attempt to harness the power of tornadoes that went literally in an unexpected direction. 9067 International Dr; Orlando, FL 32819; Phone: (407) 351-8800; https://www.wonderworksonline.com/orlando/

In 1921 Dr. William M. Wells, a prominent Black physician in Orlando, built a hotel for Black Americans who were barred from Florida's segregated hotels. **Wells'Built Museum of African American History and Culture** houses memorabilia of Orlando's Black community and contains displays on the civil rights movement in Orlando. Exhibits include a 1930s period hotel guestroom with authentic furniture, beading and decorations, and the Chitlin' Circuit performance hall that was formerly located next to the hotel. NOTE: Currently operating with limited hours. 511 W South St; Orlando, FL 32805; Phone: (407) 245-7535; http://www.wellsbuilt.org/

Oviedo, FL (Seminole County) (GOMA)

Lukas Nursery Butterfly Encounter takes place with hundreds of flying butterflies among the flowering plants that feed them. There's even a room set aside for visitors to interact with these flying pieces of visual art. 1909 Slavia Rd; Oviedo, FL 32765; Phone: (407) 365-6163; https://lukasnursery.com/butterfly-encounter/

Pinball Lounge welcomes lovers of pinball games to play the day away. They even have leagues, although that's more for locals. NOTE: Special prices on Friday. 376 E Broadway St; Oviedo, FL 32765; Phone: (407) 495-2875; http://www.thepinballlounge.com

Sanford, FL (Seminole County) (GOMA)

For drivers coming down from the north, Sanford is famous as the final stop of Amtrak's Auto Train. It runs between Lorton, VA (Washington, DC) and Sanford, FL (Orlando) and takes just over 17 hours. But this small charming town also boasts a historic center with local shops and restaurants. One favorite is **Hollerbach's Willow Tree Cafe**. This large friendly German restaurant offers true on-tap German beers. Check their website for dates and times that diners can enjoy folksy music (and fun toasts). Of course, every October is a weekend of Oktoberfest. 205 E First St; Sanford, FL 32713; Phone: (407) 321-2204; https://www.hollerbachs.com/

St. Cloud, FL (Osceola County) (GOMA)

In the early years of the 20th century, developers reached out to Civil War veterans to populate an area of St. Cloud. The colony was the brainchild of the National Tribune newspaper which formed a holding company in 1909 to sell 25-by-50 lots to Union veterans. By 1911, the city of St Cloud was officially established. Today, both Union and Confederate graves co-exist in the same cemetery, although at opposite ends, watched over by separate memorials.

Amazing Animals Inc provides a sanctuary for animals needing a home as well as a breeding program for some endangered, threatened, and at-risk animals from around the world. The public is invited to take a private tour of the facility and meet a variety of their Ambassador Animals. 4235 Rambler Ave; St. Cloud, FL 34772; Phone: (407) 719-6269; https://www.amazinganimalsinc.org/

Explore the world of snakes at the **Reptile World Serpentarium** with more than 75 species as well as lizards, crocodiles, alligators, and turtles. The Serpentarium is also a working venom factory and visitors are invited to watch a live venom milking show. 5705 E Irlo Bronson Memorial Hwy; St Cloud, FL 34771; Phone: (407) 892-6905; https://www.reptileworldserpentarium.net/

St. Cloud Heritage Museum showcase St. Cloud's early beginnings as *Soldier City*. Located in the Veterans Memorial Library the museum is operated by the Woman's Club of St. Cloud, and the City of St. Cloud. FREE. NOTE: Hours are limited. 1012 Massachusetts Ave; St. Cloud, FL 34769; Phone: (407) 957-7587; http://www.stcloudheritagemuseum.com/

Tavares, FL (Lake County) (GOMA)

Calling itself *America's Seaplane City (R)* Tavares invites visitors to watch these air-water vehicles take off and land. Tavares Seaplane Base & Marina (FA1) is a seaplane airport and part of the Downtown Waterfront Entertainment District at Ruby St and Main St along with Wooton Park on Lake Dora. NOTE: Alcohol is permitted within the entertainment district in approved plastic cups.

The **Dora Canal** is just over a mile and links Lake Dora and Lake Eustis and is one of the more beautiful and pristine stretches in central Florida. Boat tours take visitors along the waterway between Mount Dora and Tavares but the best access to the tours is from Mount Dora.

Discovery Gardens shows off different gardens of Central Florida – over 20 major themes highlight more than 700 different plants. FREE. 1951 Woodlea Rd; Tavares, FL 32778; Phone: (352) 343-4101; http://sfyl.ifas.ufl.edu/lake/lawn-and-garden---florida-friendly-landscaping/discovery-gardens/

Lake County Historical Museum is on the first floor of the historic courthouse. FREE. 317 W Main St; Tavares, FL 32778; Phone: (352) 343-9890; https://lakecountyhistoricalmuseum.org/

Lake County Museum of Art exhibits historic and contemporary artwork from local, regional, and national sources. FREE. 213 W Ruby St; Tavares, FL 32778; Phone: (352) 483-2900; https://lakeartmuseum.com/

Umatilla, FL (Lake County) (GOMA)

What to do when big, beautiful trees have died? Bring in chain saw artists and create big, beautiful sculptures. Chad Gainey and Mark Rice have created full-throttle art at two locations in Umatilla. Most of the work is at **Cadwell Park** on Cassady St.

Webster, FL (Sumter County)

For intriguing opportunities to interact with rescued animal residents head to **Chase Animal Rescue and Sanctuary, Inc**. Among the unusual offerings are painting amidst lemurs who jump from tree to tree, and yoga among these same curious primates. Of course, there's also standard guided tours through their preserve. 6127 SE 122nd Blvd; Webster, FL 33597; Phone: (352) 988-8014; https://www.chasesanctuary.org/

Florida Bass Conservation Center is a major freshwater fish production hatchery. It provides largemouth bass, crappie, catfish, bream, triploid grass carp, striped bass, and sunshine bass. Stop by the visitor center to learn more. 3583 CR 788; Webster, FL 33597; Phone: (352) 583-4518; https://myfwc.com/fishing/freshwater/stocking/fbcc/

Richloam General Store is a bit of old Florida, having been both a store, and post office for the once-upon-a-time town of Richloam. It carries products the store would have carried in the 1920s. 38219 Richloam Clay Sink Rd; Webster, FL 33597; Phone: (800) 915-8027; http://www.richloamstore.com

Wildwood, FL (Sumter County)

GatorWorld Parks of Florida has rescued and relocated over 400 alligators and invites visitors to see them in the drive-through park. Then, feed the 'gators from the specially constructed platform. There are photo ops. NOTE: Temporarily closed. Future is unknown. 492 FL 44; Wildwood, FL 34785; Phone: (352) 462-9500; https://www.gatorworldparks.com/

Winter Garden, FL (Orange County) (GOMA)

Winter Garden was settled in 1908 and the town's Historic Downtown is listed on the National Registry of Historic

Places. Winter Garden is on the West Orange Trail, part of the 250-mile Coast to Coast (C2C) Connector Trail. When completed the biking, walking, hiking trail will link communities between St. Petersburg and Titusville across Central Florida.

As its name implies farmers settled the area because the mild climate enabled them to grow crops all year long. Tourism followed in the 1920s when the largemouth bass in Lake Apopka drew fishermen. It is a separate town from Winter Park, and the two are about 20 miles apart.

Central Florida Railroad Museum can be found in the former Tavares and Gulf depot built in 1913. Focused on Central Florida's railroading history a highlight is considered to be its large collection of dining car china. It is operated by the Central Florida Railway Historical Society. Children are invited to enjoy their Thomas layout. FREE. 101 S Boyd St; Winter Garden, FL 34787; Phone: (407) 656-0559; https://www.cfrhs.org/

Crooked Can Brewing Company Brewery offers fee-based brewery tours. Tours can be booked on their website. Located in Plant Street Market, the local indoor artisan marketplace. 426 W Plant St; Winter Garden, FL 34787; Phone: (407) 395-9520; https://crookedcan.com/

Heritage Museum contains over 5,000 artifacts documenting the town's rich history. One N Main St; Winter Garden, FL 34787; Phone: (407) 656-5544; http://www.wghf.org/

SOBO Art Gallery offers monthly exhibitions with opening receptions on the first Thursday of the month. FREE. 127 S Boyd St; Winter Garden, FL 34787; Phone: (407) 347-7996; https://wgart.org/

Winter Garden Heritage Museum focuses on the history of West Orange County through its associated museums of **Central Florida Railroad Museum** and the **Heritage Museum**. The foundation also offers both walking and biking tours of Historic Downtown Winter Garden. Phone: (407) 656-3244; http://www.wghf.org

Winter Park, FL (Orange County) (GOMA)

Florida charm and culture is on display in this delightful town. Founded in 1881 as a winter destination for northerners it was planned for walkability and beauty. A separate town from Winter Garden, the two are about 20 miles apart.

Albin Polasek Museum & Sculpture Gardens preserves the works of Czech sculptor Albin Polasek. Although not well-known in this country, his sculptures are massively impressive and dot the grounds of the garden. Inside, there is more of his work plus representational art and exhibits of regional and international artists. The museum offers guided tours of the historical Polasek residence and chapel, and the outdoor sculpture garden. Visitors are invited to picnic on the landscaped grounds bordering on Lake Osceola. 633 Osceola Ave; Winter Park, FL 32789; Phone: (407) 647-6294; http://polasek.org

Casa Feliz Historic Home Museum is a Spanish farmhouse turned museum, sitting in the heart of Winter Park. Tours during their Open House highlight the architecture and legacy of James Gamble Rogers II, a famous local architect. NOTE: Open House hours are limited. 656 N Park Ave; Winter Park, FL 32789; Phone: (407) 628-8200; https://casafeliz.us

Charles Hosmer Morse Museum of American Art is the formal name but it is more a trove of Tiffany and glass art. The galleries are filled with his lush and colorful lamps (many of which were designed and fabricated by Clara Driscoll and the women who worked with her) as well as his stunning three-dimensional stained-glass murals and panels. The highlight is the recreation of the chapel interior that Tiffany designed for the 1893 World's Columbian Exposition in Chicago. 445 N Park Ave; Winter Park, FL 32789; Phone: (407) 645-5311; https://www.morsemuseum.org

Hannibal Square Heritage Center is located in a historical Black neighborhood and hosts *Photographs and Oral Histories of West Winter Park*, a permanent exhibition of more than 100 framed, archival pieces that capture the lives of Winter Park's Black population since the Emancipation Proclamation. Special exhibits and events are also held. 642 W New England Ave; Winter Park, FL 32789; Phone: (407) 539-2680; http//www.hannibalsquareheritagecenter.org/

Rollins College offers one of the most beautiful campuses in the state with its Spanish Mediterranean architecture bordering Lake Virginia. **Cornell Fine Arts Museum** has a permanent collection of paintings from the 14th through the 21st centuries, plus works on paper (prints, drawings, and photographs), sculpture, decorative objects, and archaeological artifacts. If you grew up (or watched your children grow up) with Mr. Rogers' Neighborhood you'll want to visit the college and learn more about its most loved alumnus – **Fred Rogers**. There's even a self-guided walking tour. **Bach Festival Society**, also located on the campus, offers musical programs open to the public. 1000 Holt Ave; Winter Park, FL 32789; Phone: (407) 646-2526; https://www.rollins.edu/cornell-fine-arts-museum/; https://www.rollins.edu/mister-rogers; https://www.bachfestivalflorida.org

Winter Park History Museum curates a diversity of temporary exhibits ranging from lavish luxury hotels of the late 1800s built to attract wealthy northerners, to growing up in Winter Park. FREE. 200 W New England Ave; Winter Park, FL 32789; Phone: (407) 647-2330; https://www.wphistory.org

Yalaha, FL (Lake County) (GOMA)

Certified organic and family-owned and operated **Blue Bayou Farms** is open for their U-Pick blueberry season, generally beginning late April or early May. NOTE: Call ahead to verify the opening of the season, and wear closed-toe shoes. Part of the farm includes **Yalaha Bootlegging Co. at Blue Bayou Farms** offering tastings of their moonshine, blueberry brandy, and a blueberry flavored rum. 8222 CR 48; Yalaha, FL 34797; Phone: (352) 324-4069;
https://www.yalahabootleggingco.com/

Region 6 East Central: Daytona and More

The town and cities of the middle of the east coast of Florida offer a tempting series of destinations. Ormond Beach, Holly Hill, Daytona Beach, Port Orange, Ponce Inlet, and New Smyrna Beach make up a compact and easy-to-explore area bordering on the Atlantic Ocean. Go inland a bit and you can visit with psychics in Cassadaga, and explore the Volusia county capital of DeLand. A bit further south and you're in the Space Coast with the must-visit Kennedy Space Center.

Deltona–Daytona Beach–Ormond Beach is a metropolitan statistical area which consists of Volusia County. Sometimes Flagler County is added, but for visitor ease, only Volusia County is considered the Daytona metro area. Everything in Volusia would make a good day trip. Flagler county has also been considered part of the Jacksonville metropolitan area and is therefore included in Region Three. **Palm Bay-Melbourne-Titusville** in Brevard County make up another metro area.

One of the highlights of the region is the **Indian River Lagoon National Scenic Byway** which meanders through three national wildlife refuges, a national seashore, as well as state and local parks, and sanctuaries.
http://www.indianriverlagoonbyway.com/

Barberville, FL (Volusia County)

Barberville Pioneer Settlement invites visitors to discover their 18 historical structures across the 30-acre site. Some of the buildings and artifacts have been saved from destruction, others are reproductions which offer unusual collections. Barberville also hosts festivals, and special events featuring living history demonstrations of the pioneer way of life in

Florida. 1776 Lightfoot La; Barberville, FL 32105; Phone: (386) 749-2959; https://www.pioneersettlement.org/

Barberville Yard Art Emporium entices visitors with unique furniture and decor items inside and out. NOTE: Technically located in the town of Pierson the Yard Art Emporium is less than a half-mile from Barberville Pioneer Settlement. 140 West SR 40; Pierson, FL 32180; Phone: (386) 749-3562; http://www.barbervilleroadside.com/

Cape Canaveral and Port Canaveral, FL (Brevard County)

Port Canaveral, FL

Located in the city of Cape Canaveral, Port Canaveral is the departure point for the cruise lines.

The Cove at Port Canaveral Exploration Tower is seven floors of exhibits, interactive games, and observation decks overlooking the port. NOTE: Currently undergoing maintenance. Check the website for updates. 670 Dave Nisbet Dr; Port Canaveral, FL 32920; Phone: (321) 394-3408; http://www.explorationtower.com/

Cape Canaveral, FL

Canaveral Lock Visitor Viewing Area enables visitors to watch the largest navigation lock in Florida as vessels go from the Banana River to Port Canaveral Harbor and then to the Atlantic Ocean. Fun Fact: The lock was built larger than originally planned to allow passage of the Saturn rocket's first stage which was used to put Apollo rockets into space. Mullet Rd; Cape Canaveral, FL 32920; Phone: (321) 783-5421; https://www.saj.usace.army.mil/CanaveralLock/

Cape Canaveral Air Force Station is part of the US Space

Forces' 45th Space Wing and offers visitors several places to explore space travel history and its achievements with numerous missiles, rockets, and related space equipment, as well as Launch Complex 26 and Launch Complex 5/6. Because many of the sites are within the Air Force Station, visitors to **Air Force Space and Missile Museum** must schedule an escorted tour. https://afspacemuseum.org/visit-us/ However, the **Sands Space History Center** is located outside the south gate and is open to the public without a tour or reservation. The History Center contains historical information and displays for each Launch Complex (LC) at Cape Canaveral Air Force Station. FREE. If you time your visit for a launch, walk down the road a bit to the **Rocket Launch View Point** to witness space history. 100 Spaceport Way; Cape Canaveral, FL 32920; Phone: (321) 853-1919; http://afspacemuseum.org/historycenter

Parker Brothers Concepts designs and creates custom vehicles. Their **Hollywood Auto Museum** includes favorites like the Batmobile, the Ecto-1 from Ghostbusters, and Optimus Prime from Transformers. Self-guided and guided tours are available. NOTE: They closed for COVID and an opening date is not yet available. 730 Mullet Rd; Cape Canaveral, FL 32920; Phone: (321) 868-2174; https://www.parkerbrothersconcepts.com/showroom/

The recently opened **Wizard of Oz Museum** goes well beyond the movie version of L. Frank Baum's Wizard of Oz and dives into the history of the book and the series of books Baum wrote. The lovingly collected 2000 pieces of related objects is organized by decade starting in 1850. Immersive experiences of both the land of Oz and other 3D projections are under development. 7099 N Atlantic Ave; Cape Canaveral, FL 32920; Phone: (888) 949-6369; https://www.wizardofozflorida.com

Cassadaga, FL (Volusia County)

Established in the 1890s, the **Southern Cassadaga Spiritualist Camp Meeting Association** has been designated a Historic District and placed on the National Register of Historic Places. It is home to healers and spiritualists and offers events that are open to the public. There's also fee-based tours and readings. Check their calendar for a complete listing. https://www.cassadaga.org/calendar.html. 1112 Stevens St; Cassadaga, FL 32744; Phone: (386) 228-2880; https://www.cassadaga.org/

Cocoa, FL and Cocoa Beach, FL (Brevard County)

Cocoa, FL is a separate town from famous Cocoa Beach; one is on the mainland, and the other is on the ocean, about 13 miles away.

Cocoa, FL

Brevard Museum of History & Natural Science combines a museum with a nature preserve. Inside, there's a timeline of the history of Florida and rotating exhibits. The centerpiece of the museum, *The People of Windover* features implements used by inhabitants 8,000 years ago. The Windover site is famous for the well-preserved remains of 168 individuals buried in the peat at the bottom of the pond. The museum features an interactive archaeology lab space, a recreated excavation, a video, and a lifelike sculpture of Windover Woman which was created using forensic reconstruction techniques. The Windover site is considered one of the most important archeological sites ever excavated. FREE. NOTE: Limited hours. 2201 Michigan Ave; Cocoa, FL 32926; Phone: (321) 632-1830; https://www.brevard-museum.com

Cocoa Beach, FL

Already famous for its surfing Cocoa Beach has another take on this popular sport. Growing larger each year, **Surfing Santas** are folks who love surfing and dressing up as Santa, elves, or whatever Christmas-y outfit (or beard) appeals to them. The day of Christmas Eve – December 24 – they take to the waves from 8 AM to Noon. Three Minutemen Causeway Beach. https://surfingsantas.org/

Florida Surf Museum (formerly the Cocoa Beach Surf Museum) explores the history and evolution of surfing. 4275 N Atlantic Ave; Cocoa Beach, FL 32931; Phone: (321) 720-8033; http://www.floridasurfmuseum.org

Westgate Cocoa Beach Pier stretches over the Atlantic Ocean and is home to restaurants, bars, gift shops, and live musical entertainment. 401 Meade Ave; Cocoa Beach, FL 32931; Phone: (321) 783-7549; https://www.cocoabeachpier.com/

Daytona Beach, FL (Volusia County)

Daytona's slogan is *The World's Most Famous Beach*, coined in the 1920s when the town gained popularity and attention for its ocean-side racing. Although its hard-packed sand has been the scene of racing since the beginning of the 20th century, the first beach race was actually held in Ormond Beach, giving that historic town the nickname of *Birthplace of Speed.*

Over the years cars racing up and down the beach caused problems and in 1959 racing moved to the Daytona International Speedway. Cars can still drive and park on the beach at Daytona, but the speed is limited to 10 MPH. The beach is always free for pedestrians, but vehicles will pay an entry fee at the permitted locations.

Daytona is also famous for its barrier-breaking Black history.

Jackie Robinson played in the first integrated baseball game, and Mary McLeod Bethune opened one of the early schools for Black girls in Daytona.

Although the beach is one of the major attractions, **Riverfront Shops of Daytona** is more of a local secret. Perfect for strolling, it has local shops, galleries, and restaurants. The new **Riverfront Esplanade** that runs along the Halifax River adds another reason to visit. Some of the highlights include Galerie Elan, Sweet Marley's, the Halifax Historical Museum, Tic Toc, Angell & Phelps Chocolate Factory, and diverse restaurants. There's even Cinematique, a non-profit art cinema screening movies you're unlikely to find elsewhere. There's always something happening from Wine Walks to First Friday celebrations. https://riverfrontshopsofdaytona.com/

Cici and Hyatt Brown Museum of Art, which shares a campus with **Museum of Arts and Sciences (MOAS)**, displays the largest collection of Florida art in the world with a rotating collection of 2,600 Florida-themed oil and watercolor paintings. You will be surprised and delighted with the depth and variety of the art. 352 S Nova Rd; Daytona Beach, FL 32114; Phone: (386) 255-0285; https://www.moas.org/explore/cici-and-hyatt-brown-museum-of-art/index

Daytona International Speedway is a must-visit for any NASCAR lover. And even non-racing folks will find it fascinating. In addition to catching big races and taking track tours, visitors can explore racing history at the **Motorsports Hall of Fame of America**. 1801 W International Speedway Blvd; Daytona Beach, FL 32114; Phone: (800) 748-7467; https://www.daytonainternationalspeedway.com/

Hanksters Hot Rods of Daytona is 25,000 square foot former skating rink turned into a 1960s-themed classic cars salesroom. Browsers are welcomed. FREE. 1790 S Nova Rd; Daytona Beach, FL 32119; Phone: (386) 944-9219; https://hanksters.com/museum

Halifax Historical Museum invites visitors to learn the local history from 5,000 BC to the present day. Located in a 1910 building on the National Register of Historic Places it is also a reminder that Daytona is a town with much fascinating history. 252 S Beach St; Daytona Beach, FL 32114; Phone: (386) 255-6976; https://halifaxhistorical.org/

Jackie Robinson Ballpark opened on June 4, 1914 and is still used in professional baseball by the local Daytona Tortugas. It is also famous as the place where Jackie Robinson broke the color barrier in professional baseball. Robinson was recruited by Dodgers president Branch Rickey but ballparks in Sanford and Jacksonville wouldn't allow Robinson to play and games were canceled when Robinson couldn't take the field. In contrast, Daytona welcomed him. On March 17, 1946, Jackie Robinson integrated modern professional baseball playing in the Daytona stadium in a spring training game for the Montreal Royals (the Brooklyn Dodgers' Triple-A farm team). The next year, Robinson would integrate major league baseball when he was called up by the Dodgers. Visitors can see a statue of Robinson and there's a free open-air museum dedicated to Robinson, the history of the park, and other famous ground-breaking Black athletes. 105 E Orange Ave (City Island); Daytona Beach, FL 32114; Phone: (386) 257-3172; https://www.milb.com/daytona/ballpark/jackierobinsonballpark

Lilian Place was the Victorian home of the Thompsons, one of the founding families of Daytona. The heritage center offers special events, including opportunities for paranormal exploration, but this 1884 home is open for fascinating afternoon guided tours. Check the website or call to verify the schedule. 1000 S Peninsula Dr; Daytona Beach, FL 32118; Phone: (386) 256-4810; https://www.lilianplacehc.org/

Living Legends of Auto Racing is a tiny space in an almost defunct shopping center but it is crammed with treasures. A few cars are the centerpiece, but there are memorabilia a plenty, and a fascinating video about an almost unknown legend of racing, Wendell Oliver Scott (1921 – 1990). One of the first Black drivers in NASCAR, Scott was also the first Black American to win a race in the Grand National Series. He was inducted into the NASCAR Hall of Fame Class in 2015. FREE. NOTE: Hours are limited and a phone call is suggested to verify. Sunshine Plaza; 2400 S Ridgewood Ave #36; South Daytona, FL 32119; Phone: (386) 763-4483; https://www.facebook.com/livinglegendsofautoracing/

Mary McLeod Bethune was born in 1875, child of formerly enslaved parents who became one of the county's most important Black educators, as well as civil and women's rights leaders of the 20th century. Bethune opened the Daytona Beach Literary and Industrial School for Training Negro Girls which became a college, eventually merging with the nearby all-male Cookman Institute to form Bethune-Cookman College in 1929. It issued its first degrees in 1943. Bethune's 1920s home is now the **Mary McLeod Bethune Home** on the grounds of the college she founded. It is maintained exactly as it was when she lived there until her death on May 18, 1955. Her gravesite is nearby. The house is temporarily closed. NOTE: This is separate site from the Mary McLeod Bethune Council House National Historic Site in Washington, DC. 640 Dr. Mary McLeod Bethune Blvd; Bethune-Cookman University; Daytona Beach, FL 32114; Phone: (386) 481-2121; https://www.cookman.edu/mmbhome/index.html

Museum of Arts & Science (MOAS) is one of the largest

museums in central Florida. Included within MOAS is Root Family Museum with one of the largest Coca-Cola memorabilia collections in the world as well as other themed collections included Teddy Bears, and two restored vintage trains. There's also a digital planetarium and a children's area. The campus also includes the stunning Tuscawilla Preserve with its 90 acres of virgin Old Florida. Located on the same campus is the **Cici and Hyatt Brown Museum of Art**. **Gamble Place** is part of MOAS but located in nearby Port Orange. 352 S Nova Rd, Daytona Beach, FL 32114; Phone: (386) 255-0285; https://www.moas.org/

Riverfront Esplanade is downtown Daytona's revitalized waterfront promenade with paved trails overlooking the Halifax River. There are gardens, children's areas, special events, and planted gardens. Their Riverfront Market takes place on the last Sunday of each month. 249 N Beach St; Daytona Beach, FL 32114; Phone: (386) 882-2731; https://www.riverfrontesplanade.com/

On the grounds of Daytona State College, **Southeast Museum of Photography** highlights the work of students in the photography program as well as curates thoughtful and thought-provoking temporary themed exhibits. It is one of the few museums totally devoted to photography. FREE. 1200 W International Speedway Blvd; Daytona Beach, FL 32114; Phone: (386) 506-447; https://www.smponline.org/

Tuscawilla Preserve is part of MOAS and a visit is included in admission. Described as a lush 90-acre virgin Florida coastal hydric hammock and a habitat, this is truly Old Natural Florida. Stroll through nature on boardwalks. 352 S Nova Rd; Daytona Beach, FL 32114; Phone: (386) 255-0285; https://www.moas.org/explore/tuscawilla-preserve/index

Veterans Museum and Educational Center has found

permanent home in the historic Cornelia Young Library building. Their excellent collection includes items from all the wars beginning with the Revolutionary War. The facts about these conflicts are simply and factually stated. There are also stories of people adding a human element, including the priest who created communion cups of unfired 50-caliber bullets. FREE with donations appreciated. NOTE: Limited hours. 302 Vermont Ave; Daytona Beach, FL 32118; Phone: (386) 679-4812.

DeBary, FL (Volusia County)

DeBary Hall Historic Site covers 10 acres and includes the hunting lodge, stables, and other structures. The site offers exhibits, multimedia programs, guided tours, and hikes. The visitors center presents the history of the St. Johns River and Frederick DeBary's role in its development. 210 Sunrise Blvd; DeBary, FL 32713; Phone: (386) 668-3840; https://www.volusia.org/services/community-services/parks-recreation-and-culture/parks-and-trails/park-facilities-and-locations/historical-parks/debary-hall-historic-site/

DeLand, FL (Volusia County)

Part of historic Florida's rich past, the area was settled as part of the Homestead Acts that provided 160 acres of surveyed government land to anyone who would build a house and cultivate the land. After five years on the land, the original filer was entitled to the property, free and clear. After the Civil War, homesteaders headed to the area, cultivated citrus trees, and started a lumber industry as the pine woods were felled for orchards.

FOCUS ON: Founding of DeLand

In addition to the Homestead Acts, there was another

way to acquire land. Newcomers to the area now known as DeLand could purchase acreage. **Henry DeLand** was visiting from upstate New York when he became entranced by the beauty of the area, and its possibilities. He bought land in what was then called Persimmon Hollow and proceeded to create a town, donating land for a school, a church, and the main street. DeLand's goal was to make the city the *Athens of Florida.* When the county seat moved to the city of DeLand, he built the courthouse.

But DeLand was as much a visionary as a developer. He guaranteed the land. Anyone who had planted citrus trees but experienced the devastation of a crop freeze would be reimbursed for the cost of the land. That guarantee was put to the test in the freeze of 1894-95. A man of honor, he made good on his promise to reimburse his farmer-settlers for their losses.

One of those who became interested in the town was **John B. Stetson**, of cowboy hat fame, who built a mansion and made it his winter home. Stetson then went on to modernize DeLand with the state's first electrical plant and ice plant, and made it the first place in Florida to have streets illuminated by the incandescent light bulbs. He also endowed an academy in DeLand which today has become Stetson University.
Read more about Henry DeLand at:
https://www.perintonhistoricalsociety.org/history/people-of-perinton/perinton-historical-society-henry-addition-deland

This delightful town is also the origin of the visitor initiative **Wings of the West** (for the area of West Volusia). It began when artist Erica Group needed to take clothing photographs for a local boutique, eventually discovering that the place with the most perfect light was in the nearby alley. The backdrop was less than attractive, but Ms. Group knew how to fix that, deciding to draw a set of angel wings to inspire and add an extra dimension to the photographs. Visitors soon discovered the wings on Persimmon Lane, and turned it into a major selfie destination.

Soon, other towns and attractions wanted wings. West Volusia Tourism asked Ms. Group to paint a series of them around the area and now there's a Wings of the West trail with Group's wings across the county. https://erica.group/deland-wings/

African American Museum of the Arts is an art museum, art gallery, and performance space. FREE. 325 S Clara Ave; DeLand, FL 32720; Phone: (386) 736-4004; https://www.africanmuseumdeland.org/

Athens Theatre was built in 1921 and is considered one of central Florida's best examples of Italian Renaissance architecture. Renovated and updated, it presents live theater, concerts, and special programs. 124 N Florida Ave; DeLand, FL 32720; Phone: (386) 736-1500; https://athensdeland.com

Gillespie Museum on the Stetson University campus houses a small delightful museum with gem and mineral exhibits focused on earth science and natural history topics. FREE. 234 E Michigan Ave; DeLand, FL 32724; Phone: (386) 822-7330; https://www.stetson.edu/other/gillespie-museum/

Henry A. DeLand House Museum showcases period photographs, artifacts, and memorabilia that trace the history and development of DeLand and the surrounding area. A guided tour introduces visitors to the fascinating history of the town he founded, the challenges faced, and the role played by his friend John Stetson. 137 W Michigan Ave; DeLand, FL 32720; Phone: (386) 740-6813; https://www.delandhouse.com/

Homer and Dolly Hand Art Center highlight the work of Oscar Bluemner, a collection of over 1,000 pieces of his art and personal effects. Time-limited exhibits are also provided. 139 E Michigan Ave; Stetson University; Deland FL, 32723; Phone: (386) 822-7270; https://www.handartcenter.org/

Museum of Art - DeLand encompasses both the main gallery on Stetson campus and the Downtown Gallery. The original Museum is home to several galleries. 600 N Woodland Blvd; DeLand, FL 32720. The Downtown Gallery and Museum Store is located in downtown DeLand. 100 N Woodland Blvd; Deland, FL 32720; Phone: (386) 734-4371; https://moartdeland.org/

Old DeLand Colored Hospital and Black Museum details the history of the original Colored Hospital as well as Black heritage in the city. From 1926 to 1948, when Black citizens of DeLand required surgery, equipment was wheeled from the White hospital to the Black facility, other surgeries were conducted in the basement of the White hospital during the night. The exhibits, in the Elizabeth Roe Burgess Pavilion, focus on family, faith, education, and work. The gallery also honors the efforts of early medical professionals like midwives, doctors, and dentists. NOTE: Hours are limited. FREE. Enter through the Memorial Hospital building. 230 N Stone St; DeLand, FL 32720; Phone: (386) 490-6204; https://www.delandhouse.com/deland_memorial_hospital_museum.html

Old DeLand Memorial Hospital dates back to the 1920s and contains a local history museum including 1920s operating room, apothecary exhibit, and a gallery of military memorabilia, as well as tools, equipment, and appliances from the early days of the area's ice and electric business. 230 N Stone St; DeLand, FL 32720; Phone: (386) 490-6204; https://www.delandhouse.com/deland_memorial_hospital_museum.html

Reptile Discovery Center certainly offers their outdoor nature trail, but the center is also home to Medtoxin Venom Laboratories which collects venom from a wide variety of snakes. Visitors are invited to witness the process. 2710 Big John Dr; Deland, FL 32724; Phone: (386) 740-9143; https://reptilediscoverycenter.com

Stetson House is one of the few Florida Gilded Age mansions. Two of the others are Whitehall in Palm Beach, and Vizcaya in Miami. Stetson House bears the unusual nickname of *The House That Hats Built* after the business that made Stetson both a household name and fabulously wealthy. Tours are offered February through September with special Christmas tours. 1031 Camphor La; DeLand, Fl 32720; Phone: (386) 873-0167; https://www.stetsonmansion.com/

De Leon Springs, FL (Volusia County)

De Leon Spring State Park is another of the state's popular parks offering hiking, boating, swimming, snorkeling and even scuba diving (with an instructor) in the natural springs. NOTE: The park will shut down when capacity is reached. There is a swimmer chair lift and handrails into the water. 601 Ponce De Leon Blvd; De Leon Springs, FL 32130; Phone: (386) 985-4212; https://www.floridastateparks.org/parks-and-trails/de-leon-springs-state-park

Volusia Speedway Park calls itself the world's fastest half-mile. 1500 Hwy 40, De Leon Springs, FL 32130; Phone: (386) 985-4402; https://volusiaspeedwaypark.com/

Deltona/Enterprise, FL (Volusia County)

Green Springs Park has one of Florida's few green sulfur springs, and it is magical. The tiny springs make visitors feel that they have stumbled upon someplace other-worldly. Located on 31 acres, there are short hiking trails, and a small playground with picnic area. FREE. 994 Enterprise Osteen Rd; Deltona, FL 32725; Phone: (386) 736-5953; https://www.volusia.org/services/community-services/parks-recreation-and-culture/parks-and-trails/park-facilities-and-locations/ecological-nature-parks/green-spring-park.stml

Holly Hill, FL (Volusia County)

Although it is its own town, Holly Hill is adjacent to Daytona Beach – literally about two miles away.

If you like rum or simply want to learn more about the magic that turns sugar cane into spirits, **Copper Bottom Craft Distillery** welcomes you with a tour and tasting. The tour explains the process, as well as how they re-use oak barrels to provide distinctive notes to their aged rum. Sample the different rums and experience how barrels influence the flavors. FREE. 998 N Beach St; Holly Hill, FL 32117; Phone: (386) 267-5104; https://www.copperbottomspirits.com

Merci Train Boxcar has an important and uplifting history. In 1947, after World War II had concluded and Europe was in desperate need of supplies, the people of the USA donated food to the people of France and Italy. It was called the American Friendship Train and it made stops across the country to collect the donations. It is said that Washington journalist Drew Pearson proposed the train idea in his daily column. Soon other newspapers took up the cause and America embraced it. Over 700 cars of food, clothing, and fuel made its way across the Atlantic. Much appreciated, the French decided to reciprocate two years later with the Merci

Train (Merci is French for *Thank You*), a group of 49 French train cars arrived in New York Harbor on February 2, 1949. There was one car for each state, and one shared by the District of Columbia and Hawaii (which was then a territory). The cars were filled with wine, perfumes, art, bicycles, and more. Many of the gifts and cars remain on display at local museums throughout the USA and several of the cars are also displayed. Other countries also expressed their gratitude, but the Merci Train remains the most famous. Veteran's Memorial Park (next to City Hall); 1065 Ridgewood Ave; Holly Hill, FL 32117;
https://www.hometownnewsvolusia.com/news/boxcar-is-a-monument-to-appreciation/article_0b6ca826-4123-11ea-b0bd-e388c8dfcdd2.html

Melbourne, FL and Melbourne Beach, FL (Brevard County)

The city has an unusual history. It was first named Crane Creek and was founded in 1867 by three freed Black men who were the first settlers in the area. Captain Peter Wright settled in with his wife Leah, although he eventually left to become one of the area's earliest letter carriers. He was joined by Wright Brothers (that was his name – first name Wright, second name Brothers), and his wife Mary Silas Brothers. Balaam Allen was the third member and he was instrumental in establishing the church that became the Allen Chapel AME Church.

It's worth noting that the founding of Melbourne is sometimes attributed to Cornthwaite John Hector. However, by the time he arrived in the area, Crane Creek had already been established. Hector did however become the first postmaster and was there when the city was renamed Melbourne. The reason for the name change is unknown.

Despite being in different counties and regions, Melbourne and Vero Beach are only about 35 miles apart.

Melbourne, FL

Melbourne and Melbourne Beach are two separate towns, but they are located only a few miles apart and are often marketed together as Melbourne and The Beaches.

Brevard Zoo is a 75-acre nonprofit facility home to more than 900 animals representing more than 195 species. It started as a community project and now features animal feedings, behind-the-scenes tours, and Treetop Trek. They also offer guided kayak tours. 8225 N Wickham Rd; Melbourne, FL 32940; Phone: (321) 254-9453; https://brevardzoo.org

Melbourne is proud of its **Eau Gallie Arts District** providing strollers with their Outdoor Art Museum with over 30 murals and sculptures, as well as shops, restaurants, fine art galleries, live entertainment, and crafters. Take a guided mural tour or download the audio walking tour using your smart phone. https://www.egadlife.com/

Green Gables was the Queen Anne style riverside home of William and Nora Wells dating back to 1896. Tours of Green Gables are currently available on Saturdays from 10 AM to 2 PM. 1501 S Harbor City Blvd; Melbourne, FL 32901; Phone: (321) 794-8901; https://greengables.org

Joy & Gordon Patterson Botanical Garden at Florida Institute of Technology maintains the natural hammock that threaded through the original property. Melbourne's Little Red Schoolhouse built in 1883 has been relocated to the garden. FREE. 150 W University Blvd; Melbourne, FL 32901; Phone: (321) 674-8000; https://www.fit.edu/garden/

Liberty Bell Memorial Museum honors the famous bell with a replica in the Rotunda of American History. Visitors can also study a timeline of American history as well as historic documents, and other patriotic memorabilia. Other exhibits depict the history of Florida. FREE. 1601 Oak St; Melbourne, FL 32901; Phone: (321) 727-1776; http://honoramerica.org/liberty-bell-memorial-museum-2/

Renningers Flea & Farmers Market in Melbourne is one of their two Florida locations (the other is in Mount Dora). The market is the largest on the Space Coast, with both open and enclosed shops. 4835 W Eau Gallie Blvd; Melbourne, FL 32934; Phone: (321) 242-9124 https://renningers.net/melbourne/

Rossetter House Museum & Gardens provides tours of the interior of the Rossetter House Museum including the history of the area and the people who made that history. It includes the Roesch House, the Rossetter House, Rossetter gardens, the garage, and the Houston family cemetery. Visitors will also learn the story of Carrie Rossetter, the first woman to hold the position of oil agent in one of the largest companies in America. 1320 Highland Ave; Melbourne, FL 32935; Phone: (321) 254-9855; https://rossetterhousemuseum.org

Melbourne Beach, FL

Located just across the Indian River, the town of Melbourne Beach has its own attractions.

Archie Carr National Wildlife Refuge, part of the United States National Wildlife Refuge System, is located along a twenty-mile section of coastline from Melbourne Beach to Wabasso Beach, along State Road A1A. It was named in honor of the late Dr. Archie Carr, Jr. for his contribution to sea turtle conservation and the attention he brought to the world's declining turtle populations. The best time to view sea turtles nesting is in June and July when guided, night-time sea turtle watch programs are offered. The best time to see hatchlings emerge from their nest is during August and early September. The visitor center is on the Barrier Island Sanctuary and it provides exhibits, movies, programs, and trails. There is also an accessible ocean view boardwalk. FREE (although certain areas within Sebastian Inlet State Park may charge a fee). 8385 S Hwy A1A; Melbourne Beach, FL 32951; Phone: (321) 723-3556; https://www.fws.gov/refuge/Archie_Carr/

Sebastian Inlet State Park includes two attractions – **Fishing Museum,** and **McLarty Treasure Museum**. The fishing museum chronicles the history of the area's fishing industry. The treasure museum highlights the 1715 Spanish treasure fleet and screens *The Queen's Jewels and the 1715 Fleet,* the story of the ill-fated fleet lost when struck by a hurricane off the Florida coast. NOTE: The north and south catwalks under the A1A bridge are temporarily closed. Check the website for opening. 9700 South A1A; Melbourne Beach, FL 32951; Phone: (321) 984-4852; https://www.floridastateparks.org/parks-and-trails/sebastian-inlet-state-park

Mims, FL (Brevard County)

The **Harry T. and Harriette V. Moore Cultural Center and Museum** honors the legacy of Harry and Harriette Moore. Educators by profession, they taught in segregated public schools, but were also the first true activists of the modern Civil Rights era in Florida. They helped register over 100,000 Black voters, brought attention to the lynching of Black teenager Willie James Howard in 1944, and to the miscarriage of justice in the Groveland Rape case in 1949. Then the Moores became victims of the intolerance and hate they fought. In 1951 on Christmas night a bomb exploded under their bedroom. Mr. Moore was killed instantly, Mrs. Moore died nine days later. The Moore Museum is a replica of their home and it stands on the site of the original home. The interior has also been recreated. The museum explores their history through interactive exhibits, and historic collections. Both guided and self-guided tours are available. FREE. 2180 Freedom Ave; Mims, FL 32754; Phone: (321) 264-659; https://www.harryharriettemoore.org/activities

White Sands Buddhist Monastery welcomes visitors from dawn to dusk. The grounds feature the three largest granite statues of the Buddha in the state of Florida. Meditation services are held every Sunday. There's a gift shop and information on tours. 4640 Knost Dr; Mims, FL 32754; Phone: (321) 383-0723; https://www.tvct.org/

New Smyrna Beach, FL (Volusia County)

This is one of Florida's inviting small towns with local shops, galleries, and restaurants along tree-lined streets. But in addition to the charm, there's some darker history that is fairly emblematic of Florida's development. The town was originally part of the British plan to colonize northeast Florida. It was settled by Minorcan, Greek, Italian, and Corsican indentured immigrants between 1768 and 1777 who were brought over by Dr. Andrew Turnbull under a land grant. The settlement struggled from the beginning and many of the settlers were misused and mistreated. They eventually gained their freedom and most resettled up the coast in St. Augustine.

Little of that history remains. The town today is a major tourist destination with two main areas. Flagler Avenue is oceanside and is a quintessential beach town. Its historic buildings are filled with eateries, and gift shops. Across the bridge Canal Street is the other major area. It has more of an art vibe. Its historic buildings are filled with shops, restaurants, and art galleries. The First Saturday is their monthly art walk.

Arts on Douglas, associated with Atlantic Center for the Arts, curates over a dozen exhibits a year. FREE. 123 Douglas St; New Smyrna Beach, FL 32168; Phone: (386) 428-1133; https://artsondouglas.net/

Atlantic Center for the Arts showcases eclectic art in two locations. The main center is on 11 lush acres and includes the Pabst Visitors Center and Gallery. The other is Arts on Douglas (see above). 1414 Art Center Ave; New Smyrna Beach, FL 32168; Phone: (386) 427-6975; https://atlanticcenterforthearts.org/

Canaveral National Seashore is a pristine barrier island with historical sites, Native American mounds, and sanctuary for thousands of species of plants and animals. Historic sites include Seminole Rest (with the story of the Timucua Indian tribe), and Eldora (a pioneer village). NOTE: The website notes that there are mosquitoes on the trail most of the year. Bringing water and mosquito repellent is suggested. 7611 S Atlantic Ave; New Smyrna Beach, FL 32169; Phone: (321) 267-1110; https://www.nps.gov/cana/index.htm

HUB on Canal combines two historical buildings into one fine art destination. There's also classes, workshops, and special events. A photography gallery is next door. FREE. 132 Canal St; New Smyrna Beach, FL 32168; Phone: (386) 957-3924; https://thehuboncanal.org

Jane's Art Center is small but with a provocative range of art. Browsers can also peek into the art studio where pottery classes and workshops are held. FREE. Around the corner from the HUB on Canal. 199 Downing St; New Smyrna Beach, FL, 32168; Phone: (386) 402-8673; https://www.janesartcenter.com

Marine Discovery Center offers what they like to call *hands-on, feet-wet* learning opportunities through classes, camps, lectures, as well as boat and kayak eco-tours with certified naturalists and teachers. Indoors there are interactive exhibits, aquaria, and live marine creatures. Outdoors enjoy a butterfly garden, wildflower garden, nature playground, observation mound, restored salt marsh, and nature trail. 520 Barracuda Blvd; New Smyrna Beach, FL 32169; Phone: (386) 428-4828; https://www.marinediscoverycenter.org/

Mary S. Harrell Black Heritage Museum preserves and displays photos, oral histories, and memorabilia about the history of race relations in small town Florida over the course of the twentieth century. It is located in the old Sacred Heart/St. Rita church building, constructed in 1899. FREE. Donations welcomed. The museum is ADA compliant. Hours may be limited. 314 N Duss St; New Smyrna Beach, FL 32168; Phone: (386) 478-1934; https://www.blackheritage.org/

New Smyrna Museum of History introduces visitors to the unusual history of the town. 120 Sams Ave; New Smyrna Beach, FL 32168; Phone: (386) 478-0052; https://www.nsbhistory.org/

New Smyrna Speedway has two tracks – a 1/2-mile asphalt oval, and an infield track. 3939 FL-44; New Smyrna Beach, FL 32168; Phone: (386) 427-4129; http://www.newsmyrnaspeedway.org/

New Smyrna Sugar Mill Ruins preserves the remains of the sugar mill that was once part of the Cruger-dePeyster Plantation but was destroyed during the Seminole wars. FREE. 600 Mission Dr; New Smyrna Beach, FL 32168; Phone: (386) 736-5953; https://www.volusia.org/services/community-services/parks-recreation-and-culture/parks-and-trails/park-facilities-and-locations/historical-parks/sugar-mill-ruins.stml

Sugar Works Distillery is a favorite for their varied rums, whiskey, and moonshine (also known as corn whiskey). Tours and tastings are FREE. 214 N Orange St; New Smyrna Beach, FL 32168; Phone: (386) 463-0120; https://sugarworksdistillery.com

Orange City, FL (Volusia County)

Blue Spring State Park is one of the most popular state parks, and visitors are advised to arrive early during peak season and on weekends. The reason for its popularity is the first-magnitude spring which discharges 104 cubic feet of water per second flowing into the St. Johns River. The reliable and cooling flow beckons tubers (who can rent a tube at the gift shop). Below the tubing area, kayakers are welcome to navigate the water into the river. Want to just swim? There's even an area for that at the top by the boil. The steady temperature of the water attracts manatees during the winter months. NOTE: Water related activities are prohibited during manatee season (mid November through March). 2100 W French Ave; Orange City, FL 32763; Phone: (386) 775-3663; https://www.floridastateparks.org/parks-and-trails/blue-spring-state-park

Ormond Beach, FL (Volusia County)

Visitors can explore the **Ormond Scenic Loop & Trail** on both the barrier island and along the mainland. http://www.ormondscenicloopandtrail.com/

Although Flagler Beach is officially in another county and part of Northeast Florida, it's quite close to Ormond Beach and a visit to both of these towns can easily be accomplished.

FOCUS ON: Racing on the Beach

Proudly known as the *Birthplace of Speed* Ormond Beach was the site of the first beachside car race in the nation which took place in 1903. Cars had recently become popular among the wealthy who wanted to a place to play with their new toys. Roads were little more than trails for horses and were rutted and often muddy.

But the sands of Ormond were hard packed, wide, and stretched for miles. In 1902, J F Hathaway, a retired businessman, sent photos of the beach to leading automobile journals and newspapers along with a story extolling the hard-packed sand of Ormond Beach as the ideal race course. These sparked the interest of William J. Morgan, a correspondent for Automobile Magazine, as well as John Anderson and Joseph Price, managers of the Hotel Ormond. The idea of a race that would also promote their hotel was hatched.

On March 26, 1903, the first timed trials were held. The newly formed Florida East Coast Automobile Association built a clubhouse at the Silver Beach approach, which became the starting point for runs headed northward. Racing eventually moved more towards Daytona Beach which then dubbed itself *The World's Most Famous Beach.*

When the Florida real estate bubble of the 1920s collapsed and the stock market crashed in 1929, the city's finances stumbled. But racing continued and speeds increased until beach racing was no longer safe – the beach wasn't wide enough or flat enough for the speeds reached by the ever-more sophisticated engines. In 1935 Sir Malcolm Campbell set the last land speed record clocked at over 276 miles per hour... on the sand. He then moved to the salt flats of Utah, and broke the 300 miles per hour boundary.

Although beach sand wasn't the best surface, racing continued until World War II put a temporary halt. When it restarted in 1947 Bill France took the lead, forming the National Association for Stock Car Auto Racing, or NASCAR on February 21, 1948. He developed a plan to construct a permanent speedway in Daytona that would become Daytona International Speedway. The first Daytona 500 took off in 1959.

Racing had officially moved from sand and beach to asphalt in a brand-new arena. Motorcycle racing also resumed after the war and the races were held beachside until 1961 when they too moved to the speedway.

Markers are located throughout the area to help visitors explore the places where speed happened. https://www.hmdb.org/m.asp?m=134177

A small beachfront park, **Birthplace of Speed Park** tells the abbreviated story of racing through markers, and contains a small replica of the original garage, which sadly burned down in 1976. FREE. 21 Ocean Shore Blvd (A1A and SR40); Ormond Beach, FL 32176; https://www.ormondbeach.org/87/Birthplace-of-Speed

Bulow Creek State Park covers over 5,000 acres but is best known for its southern live oak forest and the Fairchild Oak. The famous tree is one of the largest live oaks in the south and is reported to be over 400 years old. The park is adjacent to Bulow Plantation Ruins Historic State Park (located just down the road and technically in Flagler Beach) and one of the hiking trails leads to Bulow Creek Plantation Ruins State Park. FREE. 3351 Old Dixie Hwy; Ormond Beach, FL 32174; Phone: (386) 676-4050; https://www.floridastateparks.org/parks-and-trails/bulow-creek-state-park

Casements was the winter home of John D. Rockefeller and is open for tours and special exhibits. Riverside Park is across from the Casements' entrance. Both admission and tours are FREE. 25 Riverside Dr; Ormond Beach, FL 32176; Phone: (386) 676-3216; http://www.thecasements.net/index.html

Rather than offering race car repair, **Ormond Garage** offers pub food and craft beers. But it is a beloved landmark with an interesting history. The original garage, located beachside, was the first *gasoline alley* for the race cars who tore up the sand on the wide, hard-packed beach. It burned down in 1976. There is a historical marker on that site as well as a scaled down replica of the garage. So, why is this Ormond Garage special? The management of the original Ormond Garage did not want repairs done there, so a second garage was built in 1919 by Robert E. Lowe as a repair and engine shop. That building has morphed in the popular eatery with car racing memorabilia. 48 W Granada Blvd; Ormond Beach, FL 32174; Phone: (386) 492-7981; https://www.ormondgarage.beer/

Ormond Memorial Art Museum & Gardens was founded as a tribute to veterans with beautifully landscaped grounds offering tranquility to everyone. Inside are changing exhibits as well as pieces from their permanent collection. 78 East Granada Blvd; Ormond Beach, FL 32176; Phone: (386) 676-3347; https://www.ormondartmuseum.org/

Tomoka State Park is a sparsely used park along the Tomoka River. Excellent for picnics as well as canoeing and kayaking.

2099 N Beach St; Ormond Beach, FL 32174; Phone: (386) 676-4050; https://www.floridastateparks.org/Tomoka

Pierson, FL

(See Barberville, FL)

Ponce Inlet, FL (Volusia County)

Marine Science Center and Bird Rehabilitation Center offers small aquaria, including an artificial reef. There is an overlook for the turtle hospital tanks. This is a family destination, geared to educating children about marine science. Due to an outbreak of avian flu the bird exhibits and walk are currently closed. Special activities (tank feeding, touch tanks) are held throughout the day. Call for updated information. 100 Lighthouse Dr; Ponce Inlet, FL 32127; Phone: (386) 304-5545; http://www.marinesciencecenter.com/

Ponce de Leon Inlet Light reaches 175 feet and is the tallest lighthouse in the state. The complex includes several exhibit buildings in addition to the tower itself, and the keepers' quarters. Much of the site is wheelchair accessible. https://www.ponceinlet.org/visit/accessibility 4931 S Peninsula Dr, Ponce Inlet, FL 32127; Phone: (386) 210-3660; https://www.ponceinlet.org/

Port Orange, FL (Volusia County)

Dunlawton Sugar Mill Gardens started as a 19th-century sugar cane plantation but was destroyed by the Seminoles during the Seminole Wars. The ruins are there, along with the remnants of the dinosaurs of Bongoland which had once been an attraction on the site. Trails go through and around the beautiful informal gardens. FREE. 950 Old Sugar Mill Rd; Port Orange, FL 32129;

https://www.dunlawtonsugarmillgardens.org/index.html

Gamble Place derives its name from James N. Gamble of Procter & Gamble fame. The 175-acre property features a historic home, cottage, and Citrus Packing House. The architecture is Florida Cracker. The Citrus Packing House is the only one currently in existence in its original location in Florida. NOTE: Self-guided tours are currently unavailable. Check the website for further information. 1819 Taylor Rd; Port Orange, FL 32128; Phone: (386) 304-0778; https://www.moas.org/explore/gamble-place/index

Rockledge, FL (Brevard)

Part of the EEL (Environmentally Endangered Lands) program, the **Helen & Allan Cruickshank Sanctuary** offers winding trails among its 140 acres. But it's a special place for Florida's endangered scrub jays who have made the sanctuary a favorite for birders who want to enjoy watching these colorful birds, and have the chance of a personal encounter. The birds have been known to land on visitors. FREE. NOTE: There are no facilities. 360 Barnes Blvd; Rockledge FL 32955; Phone: (321) 449-4720; https://www.brevardfl.gov/EELProgram/Sanctuaries/HelenAndAllanCruickshankSanctuary

Titusville, FL (Brevard County)

American Police Hall of Fame & Museum provides visitors with a large collection of antique law enforcement vehicles, decommissioned fire arms, and tools used by law enforcement officers. Kids can dress the part of their favorite law enforcement officer. There's also an indoor shooting range. 6350 Horizon Dr; Titusville, FL 32780; Phone: (321) 264-0911; https://www.aphf.org/

American Space Museum and Space Walk of Fame offers an eclectic array from spacecraft parts to astronaut suits and even working launch consoles, as well as Soviet cosmonaut mementos. Down the street visitors can stroll the Space Walk of Fame Riverwalk. 308 Pine St; Titusville, FL 32796; Phone: (321) 264-0434; https://spacewalkoffame.org/

Kennedy Space Center Visitor Complex is easily the number one attraction in the area. Think of it as Space Science meets Disney. It features exhibits and displays, historic spacecraft and memorabilia, two IMAX theaters, and a range of tours of the spaceport. Although much of the complex appeals to older children and adults, the most recent addition is a play area for children two to twelve. Don't miss the Space Shuttle Atlantis exhibit. SR 405 (Merritt Island); Titusville, FL 32899; Phone: (855) 433-4210; https://www.kennedyspacecenter.com/

Another reason to visit the area is **Merritt Island National Wildlife Refuge**. This 140,000-acre wildlife refuge offers an observation deck to view manatees, and the seven-mile (one way) Black Point Wildlife Drive which hugs the marsh. In addition, there's a variety of long and short trails. Visitors can also canoe and kayak in the protected waters of the creeks. The refuge is a starting point for bioluminescence tours offered by private companies. Facilities are in the visitor center open Tuesday through Saturday from 8 AM to 4 PM. SR 406; Titusville, FL 32781; Phone: (321) 861-0669; https://www.fws.gov/refuge/Merritt_Island/

Valiant Air Command, Inc. and the Warbird Museum contains almost 50 vintage aircraft and a 30,000-square-foot hangar with a restoration area. Space Coast Regional Airport; 6600 Tico Rd; Titusville, FL 32780; Phone: (321) 268-1941; https://www.warbirdairmuseum.com/

Windover Archeological Site is a major site with a striking history. It contained the remains of over 160 individuals (including children) dating back over 7,000 years with both their remains and artifacts in a remarkable state of preservation due to the acidic soil. The only accessible part of this site today is a historical marker. The Brevard Museum in Coco, FL has an exhibit on the Windover site. Learn more about Windover and its people here: http://nbbd.com/godo/history/windover/

Region 7 South West: Sarasota, Naples, Sanibel, and Fort Meyers

North Port–Sarasota–Bradenton metropolitan statistical area includes Manatee County and Sarasota County (**SBMA**). The principal city of Manatee County (Bradenton) and Sarasota County (Sarasota) are only about 13 miles apart.

Collier County includes the cities of **Naples**, and **Marco Island**. Adjacent Lee County to the north comprises the **Cape Coral - Fort Myers** metro area. These two popular areas are only about an hour apart.

The region hosts **Ten Thousand Islands National Wildlife Refuge**. Located between Marco Island and Everglades City, Florida, the refuge is best accessed by boat. It protects 35,000 acres of mangrove habitats and a diversity of native wildlife, and several endangered species including the beloved Florida manatee, peregrine falcon, wood stork, as well as the green, Atlantic loggerhead, and Kemp's ridley sea turtles.
https://www.fws.gov/refuge/Ten_Thousand_Islands/visit/plan_your_visit.html

Anna Maria, FL (Manatee County) (SBMA)

Anna Maria Island Historical Society Museum is housed in a building that has gone from icehouse to sea turtle hatchery, and now a museum describing the story of the first settlers on the island and the legacy they left behind. It also covers the island's fishing, and baseball history. FREE. 402 Pine Ave; Anna Maria, FL 34216; Phone: (941) 778-0492; https://www.amihs.org/

Mote's Marine Science Education & Outreach Center showcases the local marine environment and the research conducted by Mote Marine Laboratory scientists. It provides an underwater view of everything happening below the pier and an interactive touch pool. FREE. Anna Maria City Pier; 100 N Bay Blvd; Anna Maria, FL 34216; https://mote.org/locations/details/marine-science-education-outreach-center-on-anna-maria-city-pier

Boca Grande, FL (Lee County)

The village of Boca Grande is entirely located in Lee County; however, the village is on Gasparilla Island, which spans Charlotte and Lee counties.

Historic Gasparilla Island Light is a 105-foot steel skeleton with a cylindrical tower. It is open for climbing. 220 Gulf Blvd; Boca Grande, FL 33921; Phone: (941) 964-0060; https://www.barrierislandparkssociety.org/gasparilla-island-lighthouse/

Port Boca Grande Lighthouse Museum was home to a succession of five families of light keepers. Today, each room of the museum displays a place in local Charlotte Harbor history spanning 12,000 BC to current day. This circa-1890 lighthouse is in Gasparilla Island State Park. 880 Belcher Rd; Boca Grande, FL 33921; Phone: (941) 964-0060 https://www.bips.org/port-boca-grande-lighthouse

Bonita Springs, FL (Lee County)

Center for the Arts Bonita Springs features galleries, exhibitions, and art studios as well as a nature preserve. 26100 Old 41 Rd; Bonita Springs, FL 34135; Phone: (239) 495-8989; http://www.artcenterbonita.org/

Everglades Wonder Gardens started in the mid-1930s as one of Florida's roadside attractions. Today it is home to rescued tropical birds and reptiles with a flamingo pond, alligator pool, and aviary, as well as turtle and tortoise exhibits. The Natural History Museum features artifacts collected beginning in 1936. 27180 Old 41 Rd; Bonita Springs, FL 34135; Phone: (239) 992-2591; https://wondergardens.org/

Bradenton, FL (Manatee County) (SBMA)

Buried in shallow water, Regina (also known as the *Sugar Wreck* or *Molasses Barge)* is Florida's tenth Underwater Archaeological Preserve and is popular with snorkelers and divers due to its proximity to Bradenton beach. https://www.museumsinthesea.com/_docs/Regina_brochure.pdf

Bishop Museum of Science and Nature highlights Florida history from the prehistoric to the present. Exhibits explain manatee anatomy and offer above- and below-water viewing. Visitors can attend presentations about manatee habitat, nutrition, and physiology. 201 10th St W; Bradenton, FL 34205; Phone: (941) 746-4131; https://bishopscience.org/

De Soto National Memorial reminds visitors of the real story of the 1539 landing of Conquistador Hernando de Soto. His army of soldiers and hired mercenaries came with craftsmen, and clergy all seeking gold. In a fury when he found no treasure, de Soto attacked the native population, who fiercely resisted. The visitor center includes displays of historic armor, weapons, and related period items. An orientation film depicts the de Soto expedition, and a half-mile nature trail takes visitors through four distinct natural ecosystems. FREE. 75th St NW; Bradenton, FL 34209; Phone: (941) 792-0458; https://www.nps.gov/deso/index.htm

Family Heritage House Museum at State College of Florida features displays on African heritage, American experiences in slavery, fights for freedom, the Harlem Renaissance, Civil Rights struggle, and more. 5840 26th St; W Building 3; Bradenton, FL 34207; Phone: (941) 752-5319; https://www.familyheritagehousemuseum.com/

Jiggs Landing Preserve has a freshwater reservoir fed by the Braden River, and live music several afternoons a week. 6106 63rd St E; Bradenton, FL 34203; Phone: (941) 727-4181; https://www.facebook.com/jiggslandingoutpost

Manatee Village Historical Park highlights the restored, historical buildings from Manatee County's pioneer past. Explore the courthouse, one-room schoolhouse, farmhouse, general store, boat shop, steam engine, and even a Florida cowboy bunkhouse. FREE. 1404 Manatee Ave E; Bradenton, FL 34208; Phone: (941) 749-7165; https://www.manateevillage.org/

Palma Sola Botanical Park showcases its collections of rare palms, fruits, and flowering trees. Enjoy the lakes, and a butterfly garden. FREE. 9800 17th Ave NW; Bradenton, FL 34209; Phone: (941) 761-2866; http://palmasolabp.org/

Village of the Arts is a live-work community made up of historic cottages turned into restaurants, shops, bakeries, art galleries, and studios. On the first Friday night and Saturday afternoon of every month there's live music, food, and art. 1017 12th Ave W; Bradenton, FL 34205; https://www.villageofthearts.com/

Cape Coral, FL (Lee County)

Once a year, generally in April, Cape Coral's Seahawk Park is filled with unusual boats. These people-powered crafts are

made of corrugated cardboard and covered with lots of waterproof materials (paint, and liquid nails are popular choices) to keep them afloat at the Cape Coral Cardboard Boat Regatta. More information at:
https://capecoralregatta.com/index.html

Composed of three historical buildings, as well as gardens, **Cape Coral Museum of History** offers guided tours of the museum and gardens. 544 Cultural Park Blvd; Cape Coral, FL 33990; Phone: (239) 772-7037;
https://www.capecoralhistoricalmuseum.org/

At 365 acres, **Four Mile Cove Ecological Preserve** is the one of the largest preserved green spaces in Cape Coral. It features a walking trail, and a boardwalk through the mangroves along the Caloosahatchee River. The visitors center has information on programs, local wildlife, trail guides, and the facilities. For fisher folks there is a platform over the river. East end of SE 23 Ter; Cape Coral, FL 33990; Phone: (239) 549-4606;
https://www.capecoral.net/department/parks_and_recreationhome/four_mile_cove_eco_preserve.php

Wicked Dolphin Rum Distillery takes visitors through the steps of sourcing ingredients, cooking, fermenting, and distilling their signature rums. Currently there is no charge for tours. 131 SW Third Pl; Cape Coral, FL 33991; Phone: (239) 242-5244; https://wickeddolphin.com/

Captiva Island, FL (Lee County)

(See Sanibel, FL)

Cayo Costa, FL (Lee County)

Accessible only by boat or kayak **Cayo Costa State Park** was the former fishing ground of the Calusa Indians and features nine miles of undeveloped shoreline as well as several walking and bicycling trails through the island's interior. A ferry service runs to the island from mainland locations. Cayo Costa State Park is currently closed due to damage from Hurricane Ian. Check the website for updates. Cayo Costa FL 33922; Phone: (941) 964-0375; https://www.floridastateparks.org/CayoCosta

Chokoloskee, FL (Collier County)

Started as a general store **Ted Smallwood's General Store** has morphed into a museum. Smallwood opened in 1906, but when the store closed in 1982 almost all the goods were still intact. Eight years later Lynn Smallwood McMillin, Ted's granddaughter, reopened it as a time capsule of Florida pioneer history. 360 Mamie St; Chokoloskee, FL 34138; Phone: (239) 695-2989; http://www.smallwoodstore.com

Clewiston, FL (Hendry County)

Located on the Big Cypress Indian Reservation, **Ah-Tah-Thi-Ki** is a museum of Seminole culture and history. They proudly note that they are a Federally Recognized Indian Tribe, and that the Seminole are the only Native American tribe who never signed a peace treaty with the Federal Government. Ah-Tah-Thi-Ki means a place to learn and remember, and it includes 180,000 unique artifacts and archival items. 34725 W Boundary Rd; Clewiston, FL 33440; Phone: (877) 902-1113; https://www.ahtahthiki.com/

The **Billie Swamp Safari** is a Seminole-related enterprise on 2,200 acres offering airboat, and swamp buggy tours, as well as critter shows, Everglade exhibits, and an otter habitat. Check the website for updates on hours. 30000 Gator Tail Trail; Clewiston, FL 33440; Phone: (863) 983-6101; https://billieswamp.com/

Clewiston Museum documents the history of the Clewiston area. 109 Central Ave; Clewiston, FL 33440; Phone: (863) 983-2870; http://www.clewistonmuseum.org/

Hendry County Motorsports Park is a ¼ mile banked clay oval. 9985 US 27; Clewiston, FL 33440; Phone: (863) 983-3478; https://hendryracing.com/

Copeland, FL (Collier County)

Fakahatchee Strand State Park is known for its unique micro-climate that supports the rare Ghost orchid as well as other plants and animals not be found anywhere else in the continental United States. Sadly, poachers have seriously reduced the Ghost orchid population. Read more at: https://orchidswamp.org/the-park/orchids/ The park's Big Cypress Bend Boardwalk winds through a pristine section of the Fakahatchee Strand swamp and ends at an alligator pond and observation deck. Janes Memorial Scenic Drive is the main access point for the majority of hiking and biking trails in the park. The East Main tram passes through the central slough, said to be one of the most beautiful places in the park. Currently The East River Paddle Trail is open by appointment. The Big Cypress Bend Boardwalk is closed. Check the website for updates. 137 Coastline Dr; Copeland FL 34137; Phone: (239) 695-4593; https://www.floridastateparks.org/parks-and-trails/fakahatchee-strand-preserve-state-park

Cortez, FL (Manatee County) (SBMA)

Cortez is considered one of the last remaining fishing villages on Florida's southwest Gulf coast boasting a working waterfront. A walking tour map is available at: https://www.floridamaritimemuseum.org/_files/ugd/890b23_8a01c39114bb49deb3e6ece7816f5884.pdf

Each year the town hosts a Commercial Fishing Festival the third weekend of February. https://fishcortez.org/

Florida Maritime Museum lays out Florida's maritime history through historical photographs, boat models, tools, instruments, and other artifacts. The museum also features a large collection of shells from the Gulf of Mexico. Other historical structures are located on the site including the 1890 Burton store, a wood cistern, and the Pillsbury boat shop. The museum is housed in a 1912 schoolhouse on the 95-acre Cortez Nature Preserve. FREE. 4415 119th St W; Cortez, FL 34215; Phone: (941) 708-6120; https://www.floridamaritimemuseum.org/visit

Ellenton, FL (Manatee County) (SBMA)

Gamble Plantation Historic State Park preserves the antebellum home of Major Robert Gamble, the only surviving plantation house in south Florida. It is believed that Confederate Secretary of State Judah P. Benjamin took refuge there after the fall of the Confederacy until safe passage to England could be arranged. In 1925, the house and 16 acres were saved by the United Daughters of the Confederacy and donated to the state. Today, the mansion is furnished in the style of a successful mid-19th century plantation. Guided tours are available. 3708 NE US-301; Ellenton, FL 34222; Phone: (941) 723-4536; https://www.floridastateparks.org/parks-and-trails/judah-p-benjamin-confederate-memorial-gamble-plantation-historic-state-park

Englewood, FL (Sarasota County) (SBMA)

Lemon Bay Park and Environmental Center encompasses 210 acres with just under two miles of shoreline along the preserve. Within the park are nature trails with interpretive signage, a butterfly garden, and a canoe/kayak launch. 570 Bay Park Blvd; Englewood, FL 34223; Phone: (941) 861-5000; https://www.visitsarasota.com/parks/lemon-bay-park-and-environmental-center

Estero, FL (Lee County)

Estero is a village on the mainland in Lee County. There's also an island with the same name located about 20 miles away (and about 40 minutes). Despite the same name, they are different entities.

Koreshan State Park offers a window into the lives of an eccentric pioneer group known for its unusual beliefs. The Koreshan Unity was founded by Cyrus R. Teed in 1893. He built a settlement based on a commitment to celibacy, and communal living... and a belief that the universe existed on the inside of the Earth. The campus is composed of 11 restored and nationally registered historical buildings erected by the Koreshans between the late-19th and early-20th centuries. 3800 Corkscrew Rd; Estero FL 33928; Phone: (239) 992-0311; https://www.floridastateparks.org/parks-and-trails/koreshan-state-park

Mound Key Archaeological State Park has no facilities, but it does offer a trail over the shell mounds created by the Calusa Indians -- the tallest being 33 feet high. Interpretive displays help visitors discover the history of the island. NOTE: There is no land access to this park. Visitors typically launch from Koreshan State Park. FREE. 3800 Corkscrew Rd; Estero FL 33928; Phone: (239) 992-0311; https://www.floridastateparks.org/parks-and-trails/mound-key-archaeological-state-park

Everglades City, FL (Collier County)

Everglades National Park has one of its three entrances in Everglades City (the other entrances are in Miami, and Homestead). This is also one of the gateways for exploring **Ten Thousand Islands**, a maze of mangrove islands and waterways accessible only by boat in this region. The visitor center for this entrance is the Gulf Coast center, currently operating in a temporary building. Boat tours and equipment rentals are provided by concessionaires. Call or check the website for a list of service providers. 815 Oyster Bar La; Everglades City, FL 34139; Phone: (239) 695-3311; Alternative (temporary) phone at Reed Visitor Center at Big Cypress National Preserve: (239) 695-4758; https://www.nps.gov/ever/planyourvisit/gcdirections.htm; https://www.nps.gov/ever/planyourvisit/gulf-coast-ranger-guided-tours.htm

A historical 1920s building that once housed a laundry has been repurposed as the **Museum of the Everglades**. Permanent and rotating exhibits look at over 2,000 years of history and the people determined to live there. FREE. 105 West Broadway Ave; Everglades City, FL 34139; Phone: (239) 252-5026; https://colliermuseums.com/locations/museum-of-the-everglades

Fort Myers, FL (Lee County)

The Fort Myers area is home to the towns of Fort Myers, Fort Myers Beach, and North Fort Myers. There are also several popular islands including Pine Island and tiny Matlacha in addition to better known Sanibel and Captiva. The island of Estero is the location of the town of Fort Myers Beach. Both Fort Myers, and North Fort Myers are located on the mainland.

Fort Myers, FL

Arts for ACT Gallery is owned by Abuse Counseling and Treatment, Inc., and benefits their domestic violence, sexual assault, and human trafficking efforts. 2265 First St; Fort Myers, FL; Phone: (239) 337-5050; http://www.artsforactgallery.com

Bob Rauschenberg Gallery derives its name from the long relationship between the gallery and world-renowned contemporary artist Robert Rauschenberg. It is not affiliated with the Robert Rauschenberg Foundation, but the artist gave permission for the use of his name. Located on the grounds of Florida Southwestern State College, the gallery creates time-limited exhibitions. It is closed between shows. College Pkwy Bldg L; Fort Myers, FL 33919; Phone: (239) 489-9313; http://www.rauschenberggallery.com/

Spring training for the **Boston Red Sox** is part of Florida's Grapefruit League season. It takes place at JetBlue Park. 11500 Fenway South Dr; Fort Myers, FL 33913; Phone: (239) 226-4700; https://www.mlb.com/redsox/spring-training

Burroughs Home and Gardens, built in 1901, was the scene of much high society living. Learn about the Burroughs family, as well as the array of famous Americans who visited, including Thomas Edison, Henry Ford, Harvey Firestone, and aviator Charles Lindbergh. Costumed guides share the history and lives. NOTE: Advance reservations are required. 2505 First St; Fort Myers, FL 33901; Phone: (239) 337-9505; https://burroughshome.com/

Edison Ford Museum reflects the close friendship of Thomas Edison and Henry Ford. In 1916 Ford bought land in downtown Fort Myers next to Edison. Visitors enjoy 20 acres of historic buildings, historic gardens, the Edison Botanic Research Lab, and the Edison Ford Museum. The restored buildings include the Edison Main House, Guest House, Caretaker's House, and the Ford House. Garden-lovers will enjoy the 1929 historical landscape including the award-winning Moonlight Garden. Visitors who are more tech and history oriented will want to visit the Edison Ford Museum filled with hundreds of inventions, artifacts and special exhibits. 2350 McGregor Blvd; Fort Myers, FL 33901; Phone: (239) 334-7419; https://www.edisonfordwinterestates.org/

Florida Gulf Coast University Art Galleries mounts curated exhibitions from professional and noteworthy artists. Painting, sculpture, photography, as well as performance and video art are all represented. Lovers of art glass will want to see the Littleton Studios Collection which is the work of pioneer artist Harvey Littleton, one of the founders of the studio glass movement. 10501 FGCU Blvd S; Fort Myers, FL 33965; Phone: (239) 590-1894; https://www.fgcu.edu/artgalleries

Florida Native Butterfly Society is dedicated to saving the state's native butterfly population. They hand raise every butterfly and provide tours. 1815 Fowler St; Fort Myers, FL 33903; Phone: (239) 690-2359; http://www.thebutterflyestates.com/home.html

Focused on STEM (Science, Technology, Engineering, and Math), **IMAG History & Science Center** provides interactive exhibits, an aquarium, history displays, 3D theater, and a 3D Virtual Reality experience. 2000 Cranford Ave; Fort Myers, FL 33916; Phone: (239) 243-0043; https://theimag.org

Looking Glass Gallery explores the melding of traditional art and new media, encouraging guests to interact with the pieces. Work of local artists is available for sale. 5240 Bank St; Suite #8; Fort Myers, FL 33907; Phone: (239) 214-3595; https://www.lookingglassfortmyers.com/

Minnesota Twins Spring Training takes place at Hammond Stadium at the CenturyLink Sports Complex. There's also the Ft. Myers Miracle, a professional minor league baseball team and class A affiliate of the Minnesota Twins. 14400 Six Mile Cypress Pkwy; Fort Myers, FL 33912; Phone: (239) 768-4210; https://www.mlb.com/twins/spring-training/ballpark

Railroad Museum of South Florida Interpretive Center is housed in a railroad depot-style building in Lakes Regional Park. Outdoor exhibits include a cosmetically restored 1905 Atlantic Coastline Railroad 0-6-0 Baldwin Locomotive and Tender, and a cosmetically restored 1953 Seaboard Airline Railroad Caboose. They also operate a one-mile miniature train ride that winds through miniature villages. 7330 Gladiolus Dr; Fort Myers, FL 33966; Phone: (239) 267-1905; https://rrmsf.org/#home

Six Mile Cypress Slough Preserve is over 3500 acres of wetland with a boardwalk trail and an interpretative center. Admission is FREE but there is a charge for parking. 7751 Penzance Blvd; Fort Myers, FL 33966; Phone: (239) 533-7550; https://www.sloughpreserve.org/

Southwest Florida Military Museum & Library preserves and displays military artifacts and memorabilia ranging from the Revolutionary War through the Afghanistan conflict. FREE (with donations appreciated). Edison Mall; 4125 Cleveland Ave #1755; Fort Myers FL 33901; Phone: (239) 541-8704; https://www.swflmm.org/

Fort Myers Beach, FL (Estero Island, Lee County)

Lovers Key State Park, considered one of the most beautiful in the state, is dotted with canals and lagoons with almost five miles of trails. It is accessed by boardwalk and pedestrian ramps. The Discovery Center offers exhibits. 8700 Estero Blvd, Fort Myers Beach, FL 33931 Phone: (239) 463-4588; https://www.floridastateparks.org/Lovers-Key

Estero Island's oldest standing structure, the **Mound House**, is situated on top of a Calusa Indian site. The interior space is now a museum and education center. Nearby, an underground exhibit takes you inside the prehistoric mound to learn about its original construction and the story of life during that time period. It is currently closed for repairs. 451 Connecticut St; Fort Myers Beach, FL 33931; Phone: (239) 765-0865; https://moundhouse.org/

Ostego Bay Foundation Marine Science Center provides interactive exhibits, aquaria, and a touch tank. Call for feeding times to watch the marine creatures come out for lunch. Located on San Carlos Island, just before Estero Island. Currently closed for repairs. 718 Fishermans Wharf; Fort Myers Beach, FL 33931; Phone: (239) 765-8101; http://www.ostegobay.org/

North Fort Myers, FL (Lee County)

ECHO Global Farm develops and teaches small-scale, sustainable farming methods to individuals and communities. The farm has seven different areas featuring crops, techniques, and animals from around the world. ECHO is home to one of the largest collections of tropical food plants in the United States. Guided tours are available seasonally, generally May through November. NOTE: They strongly advise online reservations and payment. They also offer a separate tour of **Anderson Appropriate Technology Center** which is focused on simple technologies using local or recycled materials that can improve food, water, and shelter for millions of people. 17391 Durrance Rd; North Fort Myers, FL 33917; Phone: (239) 543-3246; https://echonet.org

Shell Factory and Nature Park has a little bit of everything – amusements, eateries, and lots of seashells. 2787 N Tamiami Trail; North Fort Myers, FL 33903; Phone: (239) 995-2141 ext. 117; https://www.shellfactory.com

Immokalee, FL (Collier County)

Originally home to cattleman Robert Roberts and his family, **Immokalee Pioneer Museum at Roberts Ranch** now provides visitors with daily working life on a Southwest Florida pioneer homestead from the early 1900s. Exhibits, programs, and fifteen carefully preserved original buildings relate the lives of cow hunters, ranchers, and pioneer-spirited families struggling on the edge of the Big Cypress Swamp. FREE. 1215 Roberts Ave W; Immokalee, FL 34142; Phone: (239) 252-2611; https://colliermuseums.com/locations/immokalee-pioneer-museum-at-roberts-ranch

LaBelle, FL (Hendry County)

LaBelle is home to one of the state's unusual festivals – the Swamp Cabbage Festival. The sabal palm, also called the palmetto palm and the cabbage palm, is the official state tree of Florida since 1953. The central core is called swamp cabbage with the consistency, tenderness, and texture of regular cabbage. It's often cut into thin slices and cooked with meat seasoning until tender. The festival is held in February. https://www.labelleswampcabbagefestival.org/

Harold P. Curtis Honey Co sells locally produced honey and related products. 335 N Bridge St; LaBelle, FL 33975; Phone: (863) 675-2187; http://www.curtishoney.com/

Lido Key, FL (Sarasota County) (SBMA)

Lido Key is part of the city of Sarasota and is connected to the mainland by John Ringling Causeway.

Marco Island, FL (Collier County)

Marco Island Center for the Arts features exhibits, artist receptions, and one-day workshops as well as multi-day classes. 1010 Winterberry Dr; Marco Island, FL 34145; Phone: (239) 394-4221; https://marcoislandart.org

This area has long been famous for its Key Marco Cat, a 6-inch statue that is half feline, half human. It is considered one of the most complete examples of pre-Columbian art in North America. Visitors can find the famous cat in the **Marco Island Historical Museum** which also explores the culture of Southwest Florida's Calusa Indians through displays, and a recreated village scene. Permanent and traveling exhibits trace the settlement of the island from a fishing village, pineapple plantation and clam cannery, through its growth in the 1960s. FREE. 180 S Heathwood Dr; Marco Island, FL 34145; Phone: (239) 252-1440; https://colliermuseums.com/locations/marco-island-historical-museum

Matlacha, FL (Lee County)

Matlacha (pronounced mat-la-*SHAY*) is its own tiny island along the bridge from the mainland to Pine Island. As you drive along the road, you'll also be going down the main street of the town. If you choose to stop (and can find parking), you might want to check out some of the quirky offerings. NOTE: Seriously damaged from Hurricane Ian, the town is working towards reopening.

Leoma Lovegrove's **Lovegrove Gallery & Gardens** is a mix of art, pop sculpture, and gift ideas with a garden out in back.

NOTE: Currently closed as a result of Hurricane Ian. Check the website for updates. 4637 Pine Island Rd NW; Matlacha, FL 33993; Phone: (239) 283-6453; https://www.leomalovegrove.com/

Myakka City, FL (Manatee County) (SBMA)

Bearadise Ranch Preserve, home to the Welde family bears, was established in 1926 to promote awareness for habitat preservation and conservation for all bear species. For visitors this means – come watch them in a natural habitat. 6908 245th St E; Myakka City, FL 34251; Phone: (941) 322-2462; https://bearadiseranch.com/; https://www.facebook.com/BearadiseRanch/

Herrmann's Royal Lipizzan Ranch opens its training sessions to the public. 32755 Singletary Rd; Myakka City, FL 34251; Phone: (941) 322-1501; https://www.herrmannsroyallipizzans.com/; https://www.facebook.com/HerrmannsRoyalLipizzanStallions

Myakka Elephant Ranch is non-profit conservation center offering elephant interactions as a method of education. Visits start with an educational seminar, and continue with helping the staff to care for these gentle behemoths. NOTE: Advanced reservations are required. Phone: (941) 702-0220; https://www.myakkaelephantranch.org/

Naples, FL (Collier County)

Known for its high-end shopping, golfing, and wealthy residents, the town’s name is said to have come from public relations stories in the 1870s and 1880s touting the area's mild climate and abundant fish, and describing the bay as *surpassing the bay in Naples, Italy.*

FOCUS ON: Swamp Buggies and Their Races

When you plan your visit to Naples you might want to add watching (or perhaps even experiencing) a swamp buggy race. The swamp buggy was invented in nearby Bonita Springs by Ed Frank somewhere between 1918 and 1920 to handle the muddy roads and swampy terrain. These rugged vehicles which can even cross moderately dense vegetation, logs, and stumps, became quite popular. What would be more logical than racing them? Starting in the 1940s owners begin to challenge each other's home-built buggies. On November 12, 1949, the first official Swamp Buggy Race took place. Races are still held three or four times a year. Learn more about the racing schedule at: https://www.swampbuggy.com/

Learn more about Ed Frank's history and invention of swamp buggies at: http://bonitaspringshistoricalsociety.org/Explore/swamp-buggies/index.html

Artis—Naples is home to the **Baker Museum** (once known as the Naples Museum of Art). Emphasizing modern and contemporary art, it creates time-limited exhibits drawn from its permanent collection and specializes in American and Mexican modern art. 5833 Pelican Bay Blvd; Naples, FL 34108; Phone: (239) 597-1900; https://artisnaples.org/

Collier Museum at Government Center is focused on local history. There are also native gardens, restored cottages, an archaeology lab, Seminole village, and Calusa Indian camp. FREE. 3331 Tamiami Trail E; Naples, FL 34112; Phone: (239) 252-8476; https://colliermuseums.com/locations/collier-museum-at-government-center

The 7,271-acre **Collier-Seminole State Park** lies partly

within the great mangrove swamp of South Florida, one of the largest mangrove swamps in the world. With an unusual blend of temperate and tropical native plant communities the park is home to a wide variety of wildlife. The park is also the site of a **National Historic Mechanical Engineering Landmark**, the last existing Bay City Walking Dredge. Built in 1924, the dredge was used to build the Tamiami Trail Highway (US 41) through the Everglades and Big Cypress Swamp. Check the website for updated information. 20200 Tamiami Trail E; Naples, FL 34114; Phone: (239) 394-3397; https://www.floridastateparks.org/parks-and-trails/collier-seminole-state-park

Conservancy of Southwest Florida offers the **Susan and William Dalton Discovery Center** as well as tours and walks. 1495 Smith Preserve Way; Goodlette-Frank Rd and 14th Ave N; Naples, FL 34102; Phone: (239) 262-0304; https://conservancy.org

Delnor-Wiggins Pass State Park is a barrier island and much of the area is either submerged or a swamp but that makes it a perfect home for dolphins, manatees, sea turtles, and other marine life. It's also known for its shelling. NOTE: The parking lot is often closed on weekends due to high visitation. 11135 Gulfshore Dr; Naples, FL 34108; Phone: (239) 597-6196; https://www.floridastateparks.org/parks-and-trails/delnor-wiggins-pass-state-park

Golisano Children's Museum of Naples adds art to STEM – science, technology, engineering, and math – to create STEAM. 15080 Livingston Rd; Naples, FL 34109; Phone: (239) 514-0084; https://cmon.org

The 140-acre **Gordon River Greenway Park** provides trails meandering through six different native plant communities. Visitors are invited to enjoy walking, jogging, biking, rollerblading, and skateboarding. The park is leashed-dog friendly and also contains fishing and look-out piers as well as wildlife viewing stations, and decorative bridges. 1596 Golden Gate Pkwy; Naples, FL 34105; Phone: (239) 252-4000; https://www.gordonrivergreenway.org/

Naples Art hosts a variety of exhibitions by established and emerging local artists, as well as outdoor shows, classes, workshops and events. FREE. 585 Park St; Naples, FL 34102; Phone: (239) 262-6517; https://naplesart.org/

Naples Botanical Garden features plants from around the world at a latitude of 26 degrees north and south of the Earth's equatorial plane, the latitude of the city of Naples. 4820 Bayshore Dr; Naples, FL 34112; Phone: (239) 643-7275; https://www.naplesgarden.org

The restored Seaboard Air Line Railway passenger station offers two places for visitors to explore. The **Naples Depot Museum** explains how technology and transportation took over the frontier. Seminole dugout canoes, a mule wagon, antique swamp buggy, restored rail cars, and interactive exhibits illuminate how trade and travel impacted the city. FREE. 1051 Fifth Ave S, Naples, FL 34102; Phone: (239) 252-8419; https://colliermuseums.com/locations/naples-depot-museum. The **Naples Train Museum** is a private museum featuring an interactive model layout and train ride for children. NOTE: Despite the different addresses, the two attractions are located adjacent one another. 401 10th St S; Naples, FL 34102; Phone: (239) 262-1776; http://www.naplestrainmuseum.org

Naples Museum of Military History has over 12,000 military artifacts from the Revolutionary War, War of 1812, Civil War, World War I, World War II, and the Korean, Vietnam, and Gulf wars. FREE. Located at the Naples

Municipal Airport. North Road Terminal; 500 Terminal Dr; Naples, FL 34104; Phone: (239) 241-1697

Located in the heart of the city, the tiny 9-acre **Naples Preserve** contains a wide variety of plants and wildlife associated with one of the oldest ecological communities in Florida. A boardwalk takes visitors through an ecosystem that once comprised most of early Naples Florida. FREE. 1690 Tamiami Trail N; Naples, FL 34102; Phone: (239) 213-7120; https://www.naplesgov.com/parksrec/page/naples-preserve

In addition to standard zoo offerings, **Naples Zoo at Caribbean Gardens** takes visitors on the Primate Expedition Cruise, a guided tour past islands inhabited by monkeys, lemurs, and gibbons. 1590 Goodlette-Frank Rd; Naples, FL 34102; Phone: (239) 262-5409; https://www.napleszoo.org/

Revs Institute is home to the Miles Collier Collections of over one hundred significant automobiles built between 1896 and 1995. The automobiles are fully operational and on display. NOTE: Tickets must be reserved in advance. Check the website for availability. 2500 Horseshoe Dr S; Naples, FL 34104; Phone: (239) 687-7387; https://revsinstitute.org

Rookery Bay National Estuarine Research Reserve is 110,000 acres of pristine mangrove forest, uplands, and protected waters. Rookery Bay Environmental Learning Center welcomes visitors and serves as a training facility with research laboratories. Large windows into the Reserve's laboratories allow visitors to observe ongoing research. A monitor displays film footage of local, and visiting scientists conducting research and monitoring programs in the reserve. 300 Tower Rd; Naples, FL 34113; Phone: 239-530-5972; https://rookerybay.org/

Guided kayak and boat tours are also available. These are extra fee-based tours (which include free admission to the Environmental Learning Center on day of the trip) and proceeds support the non-profit Friends of Rookery Bay. https://rookerybay.org/visit/explore-the-reserve/

Shy Wolf Sanctuary is a nonprofit sanctuary and refuge for wolves, foxes, and even the threatened Florida Gopher Tortoise. Reservations required to tour the facility and meet the animals. NOTE: They recommend planning ahead as spots fill up quickly. Phone: (855) 749-9653; https://shywolfsanctuary.org

North Port, FL (Sarasota County) (SBMA)

There's no shortage of springs in Florida. In fact, there's about 1,000 of them, mostly in the north and central parts of the state. The temperature of underground springs is usually around 70 degrees. **Warm Mineral Springs** is unusual because it is the only warm water mineral spring in the state, 85 F year-round. It started as a sink hole formed when the cavern roof collapsed about 30,000 years ago. Spa services are available. 12200 San Servando Ave; North Port, FL 34287; Phone: (941) 426-1692; https://www.cityofnorthport.com/visitors/visit-north-port/warm-mineral-springs-park

Ochopee, FL (Collier County)

Today, there are two ways to cross the bottom of the Florida peninsula, the more scenic is the two-lane Tamiami Trail, ccompleted in 1928 to connect Tampa on the west coast with Miami on the eastern side. Running 264 miles it spurred the creation of small towns along the way. One of the tiny south Florida towns is Ochopee, which is surrounded by Everglades National Park, Big Cypress National Preserve, Florida Panther

National Wildlife Refuge, the Sovereign Miccosukee Seminole Nation, and Turner River Indian Reservation. https://www.nps.gov/bicy/learn/historyculture/ochopee.htm

Big Cypress National Preserve safeguards over 729,000 acres of vast swamp home to a diversity of wildlife, including the elusive Florida panther. Both ranger-led and commercial programs offer walking tours, and an introduction to birding, as well as kayak tours, and swamp buggy excursions. You can also take a 27-mile drive through dwarf cypress forest, pine forests and deep strands, or a 17-mile drive along open prairies and wading bird feeding areas. There are two visitor centers with natural and cultural history exhibits, and an introductory film. Big Cypress National Preserve is a designated International Dark Sky Park. FREE. 33000 Tamiami Trail E; Ochopee, FL 34141; Phone: (239) 695-4758; https://www.nps.gov/bicy/index.htm

Ochopee Post Office is the smallest in the United States. According to the Postal Service, the building used to be a storage shed but was converted into a post office in 1953, after a fire destroyed a previous post office. You won't be able to go inside – there's only room for the postal clerk – but you can stop by and wave and even, perhaps, get your letter stamped. 38000 Tamiami Trail E; Ochopee, FL 34141; https://facts.usps.com/smallest-post-office/

The Florida version of Big Foot is just as elusive, but his or her stomping ground (quite literally) is much easier to visit. Dave Shealy's **Skunk-Ape Research Headquarters** celebrates this shy creature – you can decide if it's real or not. In addition, you can book a tour of the Everglades and Big Cypress Swamp. 40904 Tamiami Trail E; Ochopee, FL 34141 Phone: (239) 695-2275; https://www.skunkape.info/

Osprey, FL (Sarasota County) (SBMA)

Most bridges open up to allow marine vessels but **Blackburn Point Bridge** is unusual – it's a one-lane swing bridge that rotates horizontally to allow tall ships to pass. Blackburn Point Road at the Gulf Intracoastal Waterway.
https://en.wikipedia.org/wiki/Blackburn_Point_Bridge

Historic Spanish Point is a 30-acre museum complex within the **Marie Selby Botanical Gardens**. **Webb Packing House** showcases the citrus packing and shipping business. The fully restored two-story wooden home, **Guptill House**, is decorated in the style of the time. Visitors can stroll the grounds and learn about the earliest inhabitants. NOTE: The other Marie Selby Botanical campus is in Sarasota. 337 N Tamiami Trail; Osprey, FL 34229; Phone: (941) 966-5214;
https://selby.org/hsp/visit-historic-spanish-point/

Surrounded by the typical urban sprawl of highways and housing **Oscar Scherer State Park** provides a nature break with the only freshwater (human-created) swimming lake in the county. Eagles often nest there for the winter. Walks and tours are available. 1843 South Tamiami Trail; Osprey FL 34229; Phone: (941) 483-5956;
https://www.floridastateparks.org/parks-and-trails/oscar-scherer-state-park

Palmdale, FL (Glades County)

Gatorama is not your warm and fuzzy tourist attraction. It is truly a farm open to the public where alligators and crocodiles are raised for meat and skins. Perhaps their motto regarding their animal feedings best sums up their attitude... *Fast Hands or No Hands*. 10665 US-27; Palmdale, FL 33944; Phone: (863) 675-0623; https://www.gatorama.com

Palmetto, FL (Manatee County) (SBMA)

Agriculture has always been part of Manatee County's history and economy. At the **Manatee County Agricultural Museum** exhibits focus on the primary commodities including livestock, vegetables, citrus, horticulture, and commercial fishing. 1015 Sixth St W; Palmetto, FL 34221; Phone: (941) 721-2034; https://www.manateecountyagmuseum.com/

Palmetto Historical Park, located in the heart of Palmetto Historic District, invites exploration of the first post office, as well as a cottage museum, historical one room schoolhouse, small military museum, and a reproduction chapel representative of area churches. NOTE: They advise calling ahead as the site is frequently used for school trips. 515 10th Ave W; Palmetto, FL 34221; Phone: (941) 723-4991; https://palmettohistoricalpark.com/

Parrish, FL (Manatee County) (SBMA)

Florida Railroad Museum preserves over a dozen restored rolling stock and equipment. Visitors can also take a round-trip tourist excursion between the towns of Parrish and Willow. NOTE: The museum's exhibits and train rides are available on weekends only and the cars are not wheelchair accessible. 12210 83rd St E; Parrish, FL 34219; Phone: (941) 776-0906; http://www.frrm.org/

Pine Island, FL (Lee County)

Located just off Florida's Gulf Coast Pine Island is comprised of several towns. The largest are Bokeelia, and Pineland at the northern end. St James City sits at the southern tip.

Bokeelia, FL

Museum of the Islands features a large wall mural depicting a Calusa village based on the 1895 field notes of archaeologist Frank Cushing. There are also artifacts, pottery, shell tools, and other materials found in excavations of the Calusa mound. For quirk, there is a beaded tapestry of George Washington completed in 1874. NOTE: Currently open with limited hours, call and they will arrange a special visit. 5728 Sesame Dr; Bokeelia, FL 33922; Phone: (239) 283-1525; https://www.museumoftheislands.com/

Pineland, FL

Randell Research Center offers the almost one-mile Calusa Heritage Trail that leads visitors through the mounds, canals, and other features of the archaeological site which had been a Calusa Native American village. Interpretive signs provide detailed information, and observation platforms sit atop the site's tallest shell mound. Parking is available inside the main gate at the Randell Research Center. NOTE: The trail has been reopened although some parts may be temporarily closed. Check the website for updates. 13810 Waterfront Dr; Pineland, FL 33945; Phone: (239) 283-2062; https://www.floridamuseum.ufl.edu/rrc/visit/trail/

St. James City, FL

Galt Preserve provides 2 1/2 miles of hiking trails and boardwalks and is home to a variety of bird and animal species including bald eagles and bobcats. NOTE: Bathrooms and boardwalk are currently closed due to Hurricane Ian damage. Check the website for updates. 3661 Stringfellow Rd; St. James City, FL 33956; Phone: (239) 220-7243; https://www.leegov.com/parks/preserves/galt

Punta Gorda, FL (Charlotte County)

Located about an hour south of Sarasota, Punta Gorda (which

means Fat Tip because it protrudes into the harbor) is sometimes considered a suburb of that art-filled city, but it is also its own destination.

The Victorian **AC Freeman House,** listed on the National Register of Historic Landmarks, was moved to its present site in 2006. Owned by the City of Punta Gorda, it is currently closed for historical renovation. Check the website for updates. 311 W Retta Esplanade; Punta Gorda, FL 33950; Phone: (941) 639-2222; https://www.ci.punta-gorda.fl.us/Home/Components/FacilityDirectory/FacilityDirectory/16/743

Blanchard House Museum is a historic home, and an African American museum dedicated to the Black Americans who have played a significant role in Punta Gorda history. NOTE: Currently closed due to hurricane damage. Opening date is unavailable. 406 Dr Martin Luther King Jr Blvd; Punta Gorda, FL 33950; Phone: (941) 575-7518; http://www.blanchardhousemuseum.org/

At 46,000 acres, **Charlotte Harbor Preserve State Park** is the third largest park in the state. Most of the acreage is shallow water fringed by mangroves but hikers and birdwatchers can access the park's upland areas with pedestrian walk-throughs available in each section of the park. Charlotte Harbor Environmental Center provides interpretive guided hikes and six miles of marked trails. FREE. 12301 Burnt Store Rd; Punta Gorda, FL 33955; Phone: (941) 575-5816; https://www.floridastateparks.org/parks-and-trails/charlotte-harbor-preserve-state-park

Military Heritage Museum covers military history from the Revolutionary War through modern conflicts with gallery displays and exhibits, as well as simulations and virtual reality experiences. 900 W Marion Ave; Punta Gorda, FL 33950;

Phone: (941) 575-9002; https://militaryheritagemuseum.org/

Started by Roger and Linda Tetrault, **Peace River Botanical & Sculpture Gardens** stretches across 27 acres of preserved native habitats. Boardwalks provide views of aquatic and terrestrial species while sculptures, flowering trees, and plants dot the landscape. 5827 Riverside Dr; Punta Gorda, FL 33982; Phone: (941) 621-8299; https://peacerivergardens.org/

Peace River Wildlife Center rescues and releases injured wildlife. Critters that cannot be released become ambassadors as well as part of their volunteer-led and self-guided tours. FREE with donations gratefully accepted. 3400 Ponce de Leon Pkwy; Punta Gorda, FL 33950; Phone: (941) 637-3830; https://prwildlife.org/

Sanibel Island, FL (Lee County)

Sanibel Island is one of the Florida's most famous shell beaches. They have even designated June 21st as National Seashell Day. Sanibel was devastated by Hurricane Ian (September, 2020). Much was destroyed or damaged. Please check for updates at https://sanibel-captiva.org/

Bailey-Matthews National Shell Museum pays homage to Sanibel Island's shell-filled beaches with an aquarium, and 30 exhibits on everything shell-related. It is also the home of the annual Shell Festival held in March. NOTE: Currently closed due to damage from Hurricane Ian, the museum staff is working hard to reopen. 3075 Sanibel Captiva Rd; Sanibel, FL 33957; Phone: (239) 395-2233; https://www.shellmuseum.org

CROW (Clinic for the Rehabilitation of Wildlife) offers an educational center and an array of educational experiences. 3883 Sanibel Captiva Rd; Sanibel Island, FL 33957; Phone: (239) 472-3644; http://www.crowclinic.org/

The **J N "Ding" Darling National Wildlife Refuge** is part of a larger complex that encompasses several refuges. It was named for Pulitzer Prize winning cartoonist Jay Norwood Darling who was also an ardent conservationist. His nickname derives from first initial of his last name with the last three letters. Visitors to the refuge can enjoy beach walks, and trail hikes, as well as birding and bike tours. There is usually a tram tour available. Refuge's official concessionaire offers boat cruises to explore the Tarpon Bay area of the Refuge. One Wildlife Dr; Sanibel, FL 33957; Phone: (239) 472-1100; https://dingdarlingsociety.org/; https://www.fws.gov/refuge/JN_Ding_Darling/

Sanibel Shellcrafters is a group of artisans who meet at the Community House in Sanibel to create art from shells. They generously open it to visitors on Mondays from 10 AM to Noon. Pay for the shells and the classes are free. 2173 Periwinkle Way; Sanibel, FL 33957; Phone: (239) 472-2155; https://www.facebook.com/sanibelshellcrafters/

Sarasota, FL (Sarasota County) (SBMA)

The city of Sarasota is located on the mainland across from the barrier beaches, and it has one thing no other town in Florida provides... true circus history through its association with the Ringling Brothers circus. It began in 1927 when John Ringling moved the winter quarters of his Ringling Bros. and Barnum & Bailey Circus from Connecticut to Sarasota. Learn more at: https://www.visitsarasota.com/article/sarasota-county-and-american-clown-100-year-relationship

Architecture Sarasota is the joint venture of the Center for Architecture Sarasota and the Sarasota Architectural Foundation. They offer exhibits, lectures, tours, and special events. 265 S Orange Ave; Sarasota, FL 34236; Phone: (941) 350-5430; https://architecturesarasota.org/

Baltimore Orioles at Ed Smith Stadium is part of Florida's Grapefruit League – major league spring training locations across the state. Ed Smith Stadium; 2700 12th St; Sarasota, FL 34237; https://www.mlb.com/orioles/spring-training

Circus Arts Conservatory is a hub for performances, classes, shows, and more. It highlights dance, music, and circus arts. 2075 Bahia Vista St; Sarasota, FL 34239; Phone: (941) 355-9335; https://circusarts.org/

Focused on pioneer history and artifacts, the **Crowley Museum and Nature Center** includes a museum, pioneer cabin, blacksmith shop, and working sugar cane mill. A half-mile boardwalk takes visitors through five Florida habitats ending with a two-story observation tower overlooking the marsh and the Myakka River. 16405 Myakka Rd; Sarasota, FL 34240; Phone: (941) 322-1000; https://crowleyfl.org

Featuring a plethora of tropical plants, the **Marie Selby Botanical Gardens** has two campuses (the other location is in Ospry, FL). This campus highlights their mangrove walkway which hugs Sarasota Bay. The environments include a rainforest, desert, native Florida, and display gardens. The greenhouses include many of their gorgeous orchids and bromeliads. 1534 Mound St; Sarasota, FL 34236; Phone: (941) 366-5731; https://selby.org/

Myakka River State Park follows the river through 58 square miles of unspoiled wetlands, prairies, hammocks, and pinelands. Boat and tram tours are available. Myakka Canopy Walkway, 25 feet above the ground, provides easy access to observe life in the treetops of an oak and palm hammock. The 74-foot tower presents a view of treetops, wetlands and the prairie/hammock interface. 13208 SR 72; Sarasota FL 34241; Phone: (941) 361-6511;

https://www.floridastateparks.org/parks-and-trails/myakka-river-state-park

Marietta Museum of Art & Whimsy is filled with offbeat and contemporary paintings, sculpture, and other artwork. Open seasonally. 2121 N Tamiami Trail; Sarasota, FL 34234; Phone: (941) 364-3399; http://www.whimsymuseum.org/

Mote Marine Laboratory and Aquarium is in the process of a major expansion at a new location. Their upcoming Mote Science Education Aquarium (Mote SEA) will be in Nathan Benderson Park with three stories of hands-on teaching labs, onsite diving programs, scientific demonstrations, and interactive technology. https://moteoceansforall.org. Currently visitors can explore touch pools, hands-on exhibits, and peer through windows into the science and conservation of Mote Marine Laboratory. NOTE: Tickets must be purchased through their website. Mote Aquarium has two sections separated by an approximately 4-minute walk along Ken Thompson Parkway. 1600 Ken Thompson Pkwy; Sarasota, FL 34236; Phone: (941) 388-4441; https://mote.org/

Pinecraft is an Amish and Mennonite community within the city limits of Sarasota. Although it started out as their snow bird location the mild winters made it attractive for winter farming. You are unlikely to see Old Order Amish, many of whom see the Florida community as too worldly. For a taste of their lifestyle, Florida-style, locally owned Yoder's restaurant is a visitor favorite. Der Dutchman Restaurant is another popular spot. https://www.visitsarasota.com/article/pinecraft-amish-snowbird-community-sarasota

Now simply called **The Ringling** the campus includes the **Circus Museum, Museum of Art**, and **Bayfront Gardens** as well as **Ca' d'Zan** (the winter home of John Ringling and his wife Mable Ringling). 5401 Bay Shore Rd; Sarasota, FL

34243; Phone: (941) 359-5700; https://www.ringling.org

The **Circus Museum** contains performers' wardrobes, performing props, as well as all types of equipment, including carved parade wagons, and utility wagons. Explore the *Wisconsin*, the railroad car in which John and Mable Ringling traveled across the country. The centerpiece of the Circus Museum is the 3,800 square foot Howard Brothers Circus Model, a 44,000-piece re-creation of the Ringling Bros and Barnum & Bailey® Circus shows from 1919-1938. NOTE: Admission includes entry to the Museum of Art, Circus Museum, and Bayfront Gardens.

Ringling Museum of Art encompasses 31 galleries filled with the art from old masters to contemporary modernists. The 66 acres of Bayfront Gardens combines greenery, flowers, and sculpture, with the rose garden as a highlight. Dating from 1913, it is the oldest continually planted rose garden in the State of Florida. Ca' d'Zan (meaning House of John) was inspired by the palazzi of Venice. Its 36,000 square feet covers five stories. NOTE: The Museum of Art and Bayfront Gardens are free to the public on Mondays, but only those two attractions.

Sailor Circus Academy is America's oldest youth circus and provides public performances. Circus Arts partners with other organizations to present the Summer Circus Spectacular at the Historic Asolo Theater in August. 2075 Bahia Vista St; Sarasota, FL 34239; Phone: (941) 355-9335; https://circusarts.org/programs/sailor-circus-academy/; https://circusarts.org/calendar/

Sarasota Cuban Ballet trains dancers in the Cuban style of ballet, and offers performances that are open to the public. 501 N Beneva Rd (Town and Country Shopping Plaza); Sarasota, FL 34232; Phone: (941) 365-8400; http://srqcubanballet.com/

Sarasota Classic Car Museum housed about 100 vintage

cars in a rotating collection. The Italian Car Collection includes cars from Alfa Romeo, Ferrari, and Rivolta. NOTE: The museum is in the process of moving after the New College of Florida ended their lease. Check the website for updates. Phone: (941) 355-6228; https://www.sarasotacarmuseum.org

The **Sarasota Ski-A-Rees** encourages water skiing as both recreation and entertainment, and offers afternoon shows seasonally. FREE. 1602 Ken Thompson Pkwy; Sarasota, FL 34236; Phone: (941) 388-1666; https://www.skiarees.com/

Siesta Key, FL (Sarasota County) (SBMA)

Siesta Key is a barrier island in the Gulf of Mexico, off the coast of Sarasota, Florida. Some of Siesta Key lies within the boundary of Sarasota while the rest is its own census designated place. It is known for its beautiful beaches.

When you're ready to leave the beach... consider rum, the spirit that has come to define island paradise. **Siesta Key Rum** offers tours and tastings. FREE. 2212 Industrial Blvd; Sarasota, FL 34234; Phone: (941) 702-8143; https://www.siestakeyrum.com

Venice, FL (Sarasota County) (SBMA)

Venice is known for its offshore coral reef. But it's also famous for shark teeth, and calls itself the *Shark Tooth Capital of the World.* Their annual festival is generally held in April. https://www.visitvenicefl.org/shark-tooth-capital/

Caspersen Beach is noted for its shelling and prehistoric sharks' teeth. It also offers a nature trail through a coastal hammock. The southern two thirds of beachfront have been left in its natural state. 4100 Harbor Dr; Venice, FL 34285;

https://www.scgov.net/Home/Components/FacilityDirectory/FacilityDirectory/603/4283

Spring training for the Atlanta Braves takes place at **CoolToday Park,** in the master-planned community of West Villages. 18800 W Villages Pkwy; Venice, FL 34293; https://www.mlb.com/braves/braves-spring-training/faqs; https://www.mlb.com/braves/braves-spring-training

Venice Area Audubon Rookery is a convenient bird-watching location. Best time to visit is nesting season, December through May. Environmental programs are held at the Venice Audubon Center September through May. FREE. NOTE: Center is located behind the Anderson Sarasota County Administration Center off Annex Road. 4002 S Tamiami Trail; Venice, FL 34293; Phone: (941) 496-8984 https://www.veniceaudubon.org/rookery

Venice Art Center offers classes and exhibits in its Pat Buster Gallery and Altman-Vogt Gallery. 390 Nokomis Ave S; Venice, FL 34285; Phone: (941) 485-7136; https://www.veniceartcenter.com/

For fishing off a pier, head to the city-owned **Venice Fishing Pier**, open 24/7 with free admission and no fishing license required. NOTE: Dogs, glass containers, tobacco products, and tents are prohibited. 1600 S. Harbor Dr; Venice, FL 34285; https://www.venicegov.com/visiting/fishing-pier

Venice Museum & Archives (VMA) interprets historical and prehistorical material relating to the city of Venice and its neighboring communities. Located in the 1927 Triangle Inn building, the museum also offers tours of the historical structure. FREE. 351 Nassau St South; Venice, FL 34285; Phone: (941) 486-2487; https://www.venicemuseum.org/

Built in 1927, the **Venice Train Depot** hosts refurbished trains outside. Inside find displays and artifacts in the Depot's two waiting rooms. Lovers of the circus may recognize the statue of Gunther Gebel-Williams, famous animal trainer and star of the Ringling Bros and Barnum & Bailey Circus. Gebel-Williams lived in Venice with his family from 1969 until his death in 2001. FREE. Limited hours. 303 E Venice Ave; Venice FL 34285; Phone: (941) 412-0151; https://veniceareahistoricalsociety.org/

Region 8 South Central: Sebring, and Old Florida

Offering a bit of everything, this region is Old Florida with city amenities. Some of the counties hug the Gulf Coast and others border massive Lake Okeechobee, where the nationally recognized Florida National Scenic Trail includes a stretch on the Lake Okeechobee Scenic Trail.

Sebring is the largest city in Region Eight and its metropolitan area includes all of Highlands County. In Polk County the towns of **Lakeland** and **Winter Haven** form another smaller metropolitan area.

Arcadia, FL (DeSoto County)

Arcadia sits in the middle of Florida's cowboy country where the Old West meets the Old South. There's a much-loved Watermelon Festival in May but the town is most famous for its program of rodeos throughout the year. For more information visit: https://arcadiarodeo.com

Joshua Citrus Grove Stand has been family owned and operated for over 130 years. Stop by to tour the groves. Of course, there's also fresh squeezed juices, fresh citrus in season, soft serve ice cream, and the ever-popular Florida style gifts. NOTE: Open seasonally generally from October through mid-May. 4135 SE CR 760; Arcadia, FL 34266; Phone: (800) 749-8219; https://www.joshuacitrus.com/grovestand.asp

Avon Park, FL (Highlands County)

South Florida State College Museum of Florida Art & Culture highlights its Highwaymen Collection with selections generally on display. Their Florida Masters Collection is considered one of the finest collections of contemporary

Florida regional art and is displayed in buildings throughout the campus. The permanent displays include a timeline of Florida history, photographs, artwork, and objects. FREE. May close during school breaks. 600 W College Dr; Avon Park, FL 33825; Phone: (863) 784-7240; http://mofac.org

Bartow, FL (Polk County)

Designed and constructed in 1892 by a self-taught master carpenter, what makes the **L B Brown House** particularly noteworthy is that Mr. Brown was born into slavery in 1856. Although he had limited formal education Lawrence Brown became one of Polk County's most successful businessmen and community leaders. The house is listed on the National Register of Historic Places and may be the only house still in existence in Florida that was built and owned by a former enslaved person. Tours are available by appointment. 470 S LB Brown Ave; Bartow, FL 33830; Phone: (863) 944-6136; http://www.lbbrown.com

Polk County History Center displays local and regional history, as well as time-limited special exhibits. Located in the historic Old Polk County Courthouse. FREE. 100 E Main St; Bartow, FL 33830; Phone: (863) 534-4386; https://www.polk-county.net/history-center

Wonder House stands four stories above ground, but with two more stories below. Conrad Schuck built it with his own blend of concrete reinforced with steel, and then went on to decorate with inlaid glass, and tile mosaics. Although constructed in the 1920s, Schuck included delayed light switches, a laundry chute, and even a form of air conditioning. The Wonder House is a full-time private residence but is open for tours booked through the website. 1075 Mann Rd; Bartow, FL 33830; https://www.wonderhousebartow.com/

Bowling Green, FL (Hardee County)

Paynes Creek Historic State Park started out as a trading post built in 1849 during the Seminole Wars. When it was attacked and destroyed Fort Chokonikla was established nearby as the first outpost in a chain of forts. A museum at the visitor center depicts the lives of Florida's Seminole Indians, and the pioneers during the 19th century. NOTE: This is a different park from Paynes Prairie which is located in Micanopy. 888 Lake Branch Rd; Bowling Green, FL 33834; Phone: (863) 375-4717; https://www.floridastateparks.org/parks-and-trails/paynes-creek-historic-state-park

Davenport, FL (Polk County)

Central Florida Visitor Information Center highlights the **Florida Sports Hall of Fame** displaying memorabilia from some of the state's most noted athletes. It currently includes the USA Water Ski & Wake Sports Hall of Fame. 101 Adventure Ct; Davenport, FL 33837; Phone: (863) 420-2586; http://flasportshof.org

Dundee, FL (Polk County)

Known for its citrus-based jams, jellies, and candy available for sale throughout the state **Davidson of Dundee** has its flagship store in Dundee and welcomes visitors for samples and a factory tour. FREE. 28421 US-27; Dundee, FL 33838; Phone: (863) 439-1698; https://www.davidsonofdundee.com

Lakeland, FL (Polk County)

Circle B Bar Reserve is a former cattle ranch turned nature preserve. The Nature Discovery Center features interactive displays about the plants, animals, and ecosystems of the reserve. Alligator Alley leads you through an oak canopy to a long boardwalk through the swamp. The trail ends by the ranch's old cattle pens. NOTE: No pets are permitted. 4399 Winter Lake Rd; Lakeland, FL 33803; Phone: (863) 668-4673; https://polknature.com/explore/circle-b-bar-reserve

Florida Air Museum offers interactive aerospace and aviation-oriented displays and exhibits, as well as Florida Aviation Hall of Fame, and an A/F-18 Flight Simulator. 4175 Medulla Rd; Lakeland, FL 33811; Phone: (863) 904-6833; http://www.floridaairmuseum.org

Florida Polytechnic University delights with something unique in Florida – its very own Calatrava-designed building. The striking Innovation, Science and Technology (IST) building, designed by Santiago Calatrava, won the prestigious International Architectural Award in 2015. Located at Interstate 4 and Polk Parkway. 4700 Research Way; Lakeland, FL 33805; Phone: (863) 583-9050; https://floridapoly.edu

Florida Southern College is home to the world's largest collection of **Frank Lloyd Wright** architecture, boasting 13 Wright-designed structures. Highlights include Wright's largest water feature, his only constructed planetarium, his final commissioned work of stained glass, and his only theater-in-the-round. Start your Wright experience at the visitor center. 750 Frank Lloyd Wright Way; Lakeland, FL 33801; Phone: (863) 680-4597; https://www.flsouthern.edu/frank-lloyd-wright-home

Hollis Garden provides botanical displays amid an architectural environment complete with public art, and ornamental fountains. FREE. 614 E Orange St; Lakeland, FL 33801; Phone: (863) 834-2280; https://www.lakelandgov.net/departments/parks-recreation-and-cultural-arts/hollis-garden/

Drive-in movie theaters aren't plentiful. The **Silver Moon Drive-In,** established in 1948, is the last one in Polk County. And they offer double features. Ask about a tour of the projection equipment. 4100 New Tampa Hwy; Lakeland, FL 33815; Phone: (863) 682-0849; https://www.silvermoondrivein.com/

Oponay Farms is a commercial as well as a U-pick farm. Depending on the season you might be able to pick blueberries, blackberries, peaches, or strawberries. Seasonal hours. 5129 Hancock Lake Rd; Lakeland, FL 33812; Phone: (863) 698-7994; http://www.oponayfarmsllc.com/

Polk Museum of Art is part of Florida Southern College and highlights modern and contemporary art with a focus on Florida artists and themes. FREE. 800 East Palmetto St; Lakeland, FL 33801; Phone: (863) 688-7743; https://polkmuseumofart.org/

Safari Wilderness Ranch delivers guided tours through 260 acres of wilderness home to herds of exotic game. Visitors can ride a customized safari vehicle, an ATV, a camel, or paddle a kayak. Reservations are required. 10850 Moore Rd; Lakeland, FL 33809; Phone: (813) 382-2120; https://safariwilderness.com/

Lake Placid, FL (Highlands County)

A fun fact is that 98% of the world's caladium bulbs come from Lake Placid. They bloom from June until the end of October, with the Caladium Festival held the last full weekend in July as a highlight. https://www.caladiumfestival.org

The Lake Placid Mural Society was formed to beautify the town and tell its history. It does that with over 47 murals, 45 bird plaques, a life size bronze Florida black bear, and over 27 clown cut-outs. There's a reason for the clowns, but start your art walk at the **Chamber of Commerce Visitor's Center/Mural Art Gallery** with a 10-minute video describing the mural program. 18 N Oak Ave; Lake Placid, FL 33852; Phone: (863) 465-4335; http://www.muralsoflakeplacid.com/

Richard Archbold Research Center stretches over 10,000 acres and is home to 3,000 head of cattle. Visitors can learn about the ranch's ecological, economic, and cultural sustainability. There's a learning center and nature trails, but the ranch is only open to visitors with scheduled tours. 300 Buck Island Ranch Rd; Lake Placid, FL 33852; Phone: (863) 465-2571 x 233; https://archbold-station.org/visit/

Sugar Sand Distillery is open for drinking and music, but once a week they offer tours of the distillery. They also offer free tastings. 264 Henscratch Rd; Lake Placid, FL 33852; Phone: (863) 873-4725; https://sugarsanddistillery.com/

Toby the Clown Foundation and Museum is known for its significant collection of art prints and posters plus a miniature circus, costumes, and lots of clown-related materials. Do you want to become a clown? Clown School is offered periodically for both adults and children. 109 W Interlake Blvd; Lake Placid, FL 33852; Phone: (863) 465-2920; http://www.tobysclownfoundation.org/

Lake Wales, FL (Polk County)

This is another of the historic towns that dot the Florida landscape, with many buildings restored to their 1920s appearance.

Bok Tower Gardens is known for its 250-acre garden designed by Frederick Law Olmsted, Jr, (son of the man who designed New York City's famed Central Park), and the 205-

foot-tall Singing Tower with its carillon bells. Visitors can enjoy carillon concerts and regularly scheduled short programs. **El Retiro** (also called the Pinewood Estate) is a 20-room Mediterranean-style 1930s mansion that is open for tours. 1151 Tower Blvd; Lake Wales, FL 33853; Phone: (863) 676-1408; https://boktowergardens.org/

Grove House is the visitor center for the Florida Natural Growers cooperative. Organized in 1933, the co-op has over 1,100 grower members who own more than 60,000 acres of citrus groves. Visitors can explore exhibits about the area's history, and horticulture. The theater presents a virtual tour from grove to glass. Take a self-guided tour through the orange groves. NOTE: Open seasonally October through May. FREE. 20160 Highway 27; Lake Wales, FL 33853; Phone: (863) 679-4110; https://floridasnaturalgrovehouse.com/pages/visit

Lake Kissimmee State Park and Cow Camp is perfect for folks who want to learn more about Florida's unique Cracker cows. The site has living history demonstrations of the early Florida cow hunters living in an 1876-era cow camp. 14248 Camp Mack Rd; Lake Wales, FL 33898; Phone: (863) 696-1112; https://www.floridastateparks.org/parks-and-trails/lake-kissimmee-state-park

Lake Wales History Museum offers permanent and temporary exhibits as well as three train cars: 1926 Seaboard Air Line Railroad caboose; the 1916 Pullman passenger car; and 1944 US Army locomotive engine. 325 S Scenic Hwy; Lake Wales, FL 33853; Phone: (863) 676-1759; https://lakewaleshistory.org/

Saint Anne Shrine was a rural stone shrine erected about 1920 by French-speaking Catholics. It included the church, and statuary stations of the cross on a set of trails. A statue of

St. Anne stood in the lake itself on a raised stone platform. The shrine was de-sanctified by the Diocese of St. Augustine in the 1960s, and most of the shrine was removed to prevent vandalism. Some historical traces remain. 1207 St Anne Shrine Rd; Lake Wales, FL 33898; https://en.wikipedia.org/wiki/Ste_Anne_des_Lacs

Spook Hill derives its name from the optical illusion that makes visitors think they are driving uphill when they are truly going downhill. There is (of course) a spooky legend. 600 N Wales Dr; Lake Wales, FL 33853; https://www.nps.gov/places/spook-hill.htm

Mulberry, FL (Polk County)

Mulberry started as a phosphate mining boom town. Although a form of phosphate is used in everything from industrial and institutional detergents to toothpaste and mouthwash Mulberry phosphate is most commonly used in fertilizers. Phosphate mining was welcomed for its economic importance, but it is not without disadvantages – in the form of a toxic (and slightly radioactive) waste material called phosphogypsum. Located in the city's original railroad depot, the **Mulberry Phosphate Museum** exhibits fossils, memorabilia, and exhibits about the phosphate mining industry and the history of the town. 101 SE First St; Mulberry, FL 33860; Phone: (863) 425-2823; http://www.mulberryphosphatemuseum.org/home.html

Okeechobee, FL (Okeechobee County)

Kissimmee Prairie Preserve State Park is one of the largest parks in the Florida State Parks System and one of the state's few Dark Sky Parks. The park closes at sunset, so to enjoy the dark sky you'll need to reserve an astronomy pad online or call (800) 326-3521. Want to go horse camping? The park has equestrian camping with 50-amp electrical service and water at each of the 10 available sites. One paddock is provided for each campsite. Horses are not provided. Take a ranger-led prairie buggy tour and see the remote areas of the park on weekends, and state holidays from November through March. Reservations are strongly suggested. 33104 NW 192nd Ave; Okeechobee, FL 34972; Phone: (863) 462-5360; https://www.floridastateparks.org/parks-and-trails/kissimmee-prairie-preserve-state-park

Okeechobee Battlefield Historic State Park was the site of one of Florida's significant battles during the Second Seminole War (1835-1842). Fought on Christmas Day, 1837 the battle ended with the Seminole and Miccosukee going deep into the Everglades. FREE. 3500 SE 38th Ave; Okeechobee FL 34974; Phone: (863) 462-5360; https://www.floridastateparks.org/parks-and-trails/okeechobee-battlefield-historic-state-park

Port Mayaca Polo Club welcomes visitors to watch practices and tournament games. Polo season runs from December to April. FREE (with the exception of Molly's House Charity Match). NOTE: There is no food available. 12499 SW Conners; Okeechobee, FL 34974; Phone: (772) 228-0115; https://www.pmpolo.com/

Ona, FL (Hardee County)

Solomon's Castle started in 1974 when Howard Solomon began building his castle out of discarded aluminum printing plates. It just kept growing from there, now with 80 interpretive stained-glass windows and countless metal sculptures. He even built his Boat-in-the-Moat restaurant if you're feeling a bit hungry. NOTE: Credit cards are NOT accepted. 4533 Solomon Rd; Ona, FL 33865; Phone: (863) 494-6077; http://solomonscastle.com/

Polk City, FL (Polk County)

Fantasy of Flight invites visitors to see the private and personal aircraft collection of Kermit Weeks. The main building is now a restoration center but there is a smaller hanger with 20 to 25 aircraft on display. Hours are limited and highly seasonal. Visitors are advised to check the website and calendar before visiting. 1400 Broadway Blvd SE; Polk City, FL 33868; Phone: (863) 984-3500; https://www.fantasyofflight.com

River Ranch, FL (Polk County)

Is River Ranch a town? A resort? A bit of both? At the far eastern end of Polk County, much of the community is occupied by the cowboy-themed Westgate River Ranch Resort. Their **Westgate River Ranch Resort & Rodeo** is included here because it offers a weekly rodeo that is open to the public. 3200 River Ranch Blvd; River Ranch, FL 33867; Phone: (863) 692-1321; https://www.westgateresorts.com/hotels/florida/river-ranch/westgate-river-ranch-resort/activities/rodeo

Sebring, FL (Highlands County)

Nicknamed *The City on the Circle* because of the unusual circular plan, the 1912 historic district spreads along Circle Drive. The city is most famous for its **12 Hours of Sebring** held in March and in former years attracting drivers such as A.J. Foyt, and Mario Andretti. Sebring Hall of Fame inductee and famed actor (and lover of race cars) Paul Newman had also been a driver. https://www.sebringraceway.com/ For quirky, don't miss Sebring Soda Festival held yearly in April featuring more than 200 craft sodas. https://www.sebringsodafest.com/

Sebring occupies the southern end of the Lake Wales Ridge, a

100-mile-long range of sand hills, scrub, and freshwater lakes. Once a group of prehistoric islands, the area is home to dozens of rare species of plants and animals. **Highlands Hammock State Park** enables visitors to traverse a cypress swamp on an elevated boardwalk with an historic catwalk (currently closed for repairs). Or, take the park tram tour (fully accessible) to observe alligators, turtles, wading birds, deer, and other wildlife relatively close up. Learn about the Great Depression, and the work and legacy of the CCC at the Civilian Conservation Corps Museum (seasonal hours). 5931 Hammock Rd; Sebring, Fl 33872; Phone: (863) 386-6094; https://www.floridastateparks.org/parks-and-trails/highlands-hammock-state-park

Highlands Museum of the Arts offers time-limited themed exhibits. FREE. 351 W Center Ave; Sebring, FL 33870; Phone: (863)385-5312; https://www.highlandsartleague.org/home/about-2/mota/

Military Sea Services Museum preserves and maintains the customs and traditions of the three military sea services. FREE. 1402 Roseland Ave; Sebring, FL 33870; Phone: (863) 840-3359; http://www.milseasvcmuseum.org/

Sebring Soda & Ice Cream Works offers over 200 different flavors of sodas from all over the world and over 38 flavors of ice cream. 201 Circle Park Dr; Sebring, FL 33870; Phone: (863) 417-8813; https://www.sebringsoda.com

Venus, FL (Highlands County)

The **Archbold Biological Station** is a research institute on a 5,192-acre estate known for its Florida scrub, a scientifically interesting and highly threatened ecosystem. 123 Main Dr; Venus, FL 33960; Phone: (863) 465-2571; https://archbold-station.org/visit/

Self-described as an "organization that proposes a feasible plan of action for social change, one that works towards a peaceful and sustainable global civilization." **The Venus Project** will introduce visitors to their vision through a seminar and guided tours available every other Saturday. The current cost is $130 per person OR household (defined as sharing the same address). 21 Valley La; Venus, FL 33960; Phone: (863) 465-0321; http://www.thevenusproject.com/the-venus-project/

Winter Haven, FL (Polk County)

Auburndale Speedway holds weekend stock car competitions. Open seasonally. 5640 E County Rd 542, Winter Haven, FL 33880 Phone: (863) 551-1131; https://www.auburndalespeedway.net/

Cypress Gardens was one of Florida's beloved early attractions. Although it featured beautiful gardens, it was best known for the water-skiing shows. Bought in 2010, the site became Legoland. The gardens are still there, but only available to Legoland's paying guests. 6000 Cypress Gardens Boulevard, Winter Haven FL 33884; Phone: (855) 753-8888; https://www.legoland.com/florida/

Zolfo Springs, FL (Hardee County)

Cracker Trail Museum and Village features a wide variety of Florida memorabilia. 2822 Museum Dr; Zolfo Springs, FL 33890; Phone: (863) 473-5076; https://www.hardeecountyfl.gov/departments/museum

Hardee County Wildlife Refuge provides a home to native Florida wildlife in natural-type habitats. Guests are encouraged to stroll the elevated boardwalk and learn about the animals that live in the refuge. 650 Animal Way; Zolfo Springs, FL 33890; Phone: (863) 473-4890; https://www.hardeecountyfl.gov/departments/wildlife-refuge

Region 9 East Florida: Port St. Lucie, Sebastian, Vero Beach, and Palm Beach

Self-named the **Treasure Coast** for the Spanish treasure fleet lost in a 1715 hurricane, the name also has connotations of pirates and booty, and separates itself from Miami's Gold Coast further south.

Port St. Lucie (PSL) metro area encompasses both St. Lucie, and Martin counties. **Sebastian–Vero Beach metropolitan area** includes all the towns in Indian River County. **Palm Beach** is another of its own metropolitan areas. Created in 1909 from a portion of Dade County, Palm Beach is sometimes lumped into the Miami metro area, but it is actually about 90 minutes north of the city of Miami and is its own metro area.

FOCUS ON: Barefoot Mailman

The Barefoot Mailman is a legendary figure across southeast Florida. The Barefoot Mailman movie (based on a book of the same name) was set in late 19th century Florida. According to its description, Jerome Courtland portrays a mailman who delivers mail along a 100-mile stretch of coast from present day Palm Beach to Miami. There's misadventures and bad guys and a town that's saved. https://museumoffloridahistory.com/explore/collections/florida-movie-posters/the-barefoot-mailman/

The true story of these intrepid men has a tragic element. One man, James "Ed" Hamilton, disappeared on October 11, 1887 while trying to cross the Hillsboro Inlet on his way to Miami. No one ever determined what happened to him.

In 1939 the Treasury Department's Section of Fine Arts contracted with Stevan Dohanos to paint six murals depicting the *Legend of James Edward Hamilton, Mail Carrier* for the West Palm Beach, Florida Post Office. Charles W. Pierce, who had been one of the carriers on the barefoot route, was Postmaster in Boynton Beach, Florida at the time, and corresponded with Dohanos, providing photos of James Hamilton in the clothes he wore on his route. Dohanos later recalled that Pierce first used the term *barefoot mailman* in their conversations, and that the term thereafter was applied to the murals. In other tellings of the history, Theodore Pratt was said to have created the name for his book *The Barefoot Mailman* published in 1943.
https://en.wikipedia.org/wiki/Barefoot_mailman

Art honoring these legendary postal carriers spans the route they traversed through the two counties of Palm Beach and Miami-Dade. Both Region 9 and Region 10 have sites dedicated to these undaunted men. These can be found in Hypoluxo, Pompano Beach, and West Palm Beach.

Read more at:
https://web.archive.org/web/20120218185102/;
http://www.lwpa.org/barefoot_mail_route.html

Boca Raton, FL (Palm Beach County)

The meaning and source of the name of this popular tourist destination is under a bit of dispute. It was reportedly first seen on maps in Spanish as *Boca de Ratones* which could be translated as *Estuary of Reef*, or *Mouth of Reef* referring to the rocky seafloors. Another translation story is that it means *Rat's Mouth* from the hidden sharp-pointed rocks that gnawed or fretted ships' cables. Or, perhaps it was a navigational term referring to a rocky or jagged inlet. Some say that the maps actually put it further south, closer to Miami. Regardless, the name stuck even if interpretations vary as to its meaning.

Avron B. Fogelman Sports History Museum is considered one of the largest private sports libraries amassed by an individual. It was donated by former Kansas City Royals owner and longtime Boca Raton resident Avron B. Fogelman and can be found at the Schmidt Family Complex for Academic and Athletic Excellence at Florida Atlantic University. FREE, although there is a charge for parking. 777 Glades Rd; Boca Raton, FL 33431; Phone: (561) 297-2595; https://www.fau.edu/artsandletters/fogelman-sports-museum/

The Schmidt Boca Raton History Museum is in historic Town Hall and owned by Boca Raton Historical Society. It features both permanent and temporary exhibits covering the history of the area. 71 N Federal Hwy; Boca Raton, FL 33432; Phone: (561) 395-6766; https://www.bocahistory.org/

Boca Raton Museum of Art highlights large-scale exhibits, and a sculpture garden. On display are paintings, sculpture, and photography. Special themed exhibits rotate regularly. 501 Plaza Real; Boca Raton, FL 33432; Phone: (561) 392-2500; https://bocamuseum.org/

Childrens Science Explorium provides interactive exhibits and programs for children on a range of science-based topics. FREE. 300 S Military Trail; Boca Raton, FL 33486; Phone: (561) 347-3912; http://sugarsandpark.org/science-explorium

Daggerwing Nature Center in Burt Aaronson South County Regional Park features an exhibit hall with live animals and interactive features. FREE. 11435 Park Access Rd; Boca Raton, FL 33498; Phone: (561) 629-8760; https://discover.pbcgov.org/parks/Pages/Daggerwing.aspx

Gumbo Limbo Nature Center provides a half-mile round-trip boardwalk through a coastal hammock, gopher tortoises, aquariums, butterfly garden, and exhibits. 1801 N Ocean Blvd (A1A); Boca Raton, FL 33432; Phone: (561) 544-8605; https://www.gumbolimbo.org

A local Boca Raton favorite may be the destination mall of **Mizner Park**, designed by architect Addison Mizner to reflect his love of Mediterranean architecture. Beyond shopping opportunities, it is also home to the **Boca Raton Museum of Art (see above)**, an outdoor amphitheater, and a movie theater complex. 327 Plaza Real; Boca Raton, FL 33432; Phone: (561) 362-0606; https://www.miznerpark.com/en.html

Sports Immortals Museum features an extensive collection of memorabilia from auto racing to tennis. 6830 N Federal Hwy; Boca Raton, FL 33487; Phone: (561) 997-2575; http://sportsimmortals.com/

The **Wick Theatre and Costume Museum** describes itself as the only museum of its kind, with the finest costumes ever brought to the Broadway stage. But the Wick Theatre also produces plays and creates special performances. Visits to the museum are currently combined with other experiences. 7901 N Federal Hwy; Boca Raton, FL 33487; Phone: (561) 995-2333; https://thewick.org

Boynton Beach, FL (Palm Beach County)

Green Cay Wetlands is part of the south section of the Great Florida Birding Trail. Stroll the elevated boardwalk through various habitats, discover a Seminole Chickee hut, and several gazebos. Green Cay is more than just a pretty site. Each day, the Southern Region Water Reclamation Facility pumps approximately two million gallons of highly treated wastewater into the Green Cay Wetlands, which in turn acts as a percolation pond, returning billions of gallons of fresh water back into the water table. FREE. 12800 Hagen Ranch Rd; Boynton Beach, FL 33437; https://discover.pbcgov.org/waterutilities/Pages/Wetlands.aspx

Delray Beach, FL (Palm Beach County)

Arts Garage is a visual and performing arts center offering gallery shows, musical performances, live theater, and arts education. 94 NE Second Ave; Delray Beach, FL 33444; Phone: (561) 450-6357; https://artsgarage.org/

Cornell Art Museum at Old School Square highlights contemporary artists who create innovative and provocative works of art. 51 N Swinton Ave; Delray Beach, FL 33444; Phone: (561) 243-7922; https://oldschoolsquare.org/cornell-museum/

Discover shady hardwood forests with a canopy of live oak, cabbage palm, and strangler fig towering over wild coffee, American beautyberry, and several species of ferns all at **Delray Oaks**. Walk the trails or stand at the observation platform. It's part of the great Florida Birding and Wildlife Trail. 2021 SW 29th St; Delray Beach, FL 33445; Phone: (561) 233-2400; https://discover.pbcgov.org/erm/NaturalAreas/Delray-Oaks.aspx

If Japanese culture, gardening, or anything botanical calls to you, explore **Morikami Museum and Japanese Gardens**, named after George Morikami, a native of Miyazu, Japan. In the early 1900s a group of Japanese farmers came to Florida to start an agricultural colony they called Yamato, an ancient name for Japan. The crops did poorly and the hopeful growers eventually left the area. Today, the Morikami Collections holds more than 7,000 Japanese art objects and artifacts, including a 500-piece collection of tea ceremony items, more than 200 textile pieces and fine art acquisitions. But the expansive Japanese gardens with strolling paths, a world-class bonsai collection, and lakes teeming with koi and other wildlife beguiles visitors. This is one of Florida's underknown gems. 4000 Morikami Park Rd; Delray Beach, FL 33446; Phone: (561) 495-0233; https://morikami.org/

Sandoway Discovery Center in a 1936 beachfront house features exhibits on coastal ecosystems and marine life. 142 S Ocean Blvd; Delray Beach, FL 33483; Phone: (561) 274-7263; https://sandoway.org/

Silverball Retro Arcade is a game arcade starring classic pinball machines from the 1930s through to today. 19 NE Third Ave; Delray Beach, FL 33483; Phone: (561) 266-3294; https://silverballmuseum.com/delray-beach/

Spady Museum is in the former home of the late Solomon David Spady, a prominent Black educator and community leader in Delray Beach from 1922 to 1957. The museum collects, and shares the African-American history and heritage of Palm Beach County. It also offers a historical tour of Delray Beach. 170 NW Fifth Ave; Delray Beach, FL 33444; Phone: (561) 279-8883; https://www.spadymuseum.com

Constructed on 50 acres of previous wastewater utility property **Wakodahatchee Wetlands** features a three-quarter mile boardwalk that crosses between open water ponds and islands landscaped to attract nesting birds. Over 178 bird species have been identified, along with turtles, alligators, rabbits, fish, frogs, and raccoons. FREE. 13270 Jog Rd; Delray Beach, FL 33446; https://discover.pbcgov.org/waterutilities/Pages/Wetlands.aspx

Fellsmere, FL (Indian River County)

Fellsmere is the self-proclaimed Frog Leg Capital of the World. The town holds two Guinness Book World Records for the most frog legs served in one day, and for the largest frog leg festival in the world, which is held at the end of January. https://www.froglegfestival.com/

Fort Pierce, FL (St. Lucie County) (PSL)

Fort Pierce is an access point to Hutchinson Island (see below). But this town is far better known for two very different creative forces. It commemorates the Florida Highwaymen, and the life of Zora Neale Hurston (See Eatonville, FL for more about Hurston's life and her legacy).

The **Dust Tracks Heritage Trail** honors Hurston, a Harlem Renaissance author, anthropologist, storyteller, and dramatist who lived in Fort Pierce during the final years of her life. The trail starts at the Zora Neale Hurston Branch Library which is also home of Ade Rossman's *Zora Art Series*, a cycle of paintings commissioned in 2006 by the St. Lucie County Cultural Affairs Department. The town of Eatonville, Florida was Hurston's home town and has other sites honoring her. Learn more about the trail at: https://www.cityoffortpierce.com/386/Zora-Neale-Hurston-Dust-Tracks-Heritage-

The town is also proud of the **Florida Highwaymen**, 26 storied, world-renown Black American landscape artists who originated in the city of Fort Pierce. Start your explorations at the **Fort Pierce Visitor Center** in the historic Seven Gables House at the beginning of **The Highwaymen Heritage Trail**. 482 N Indian River Dr; Fort Pierce, FL 34950; Phone: (772) 468-9152; https://www.cityoffortpierce.com/534/About-the-Highwaymen-Heritage-Trail

FOCUS ON: The Florida Highwaymen

Visitors in and around central Florida, especially Fort Pierce, may come across exhibits of the art of the Florida Highwaymen, a group of 26 Black artists from the Indian River area who began painting the state's natural landscapes in the late 1950s.

Their story begins with A. E. Backus (1906 -- 1990), also known as Beanie Backus, born in Fort Pierce and famous for his vibrant paintings of Florida landscapes. In an era of Jim Crow, Backus famously ignored skin color, throwing parties and musical jam sessions open to everyone. The community seemed to shrug and attribute it to his artistic temperament.

Backus mentored artists, including Alfred Hair, who was brought to him by Black art instructor Zanobia Jefferson. Meanwhile Harold Newton, a young Black painter, already had a list of clients when he met Backus who encouraged him to paint Florida landscapes. They were joined by Roy McLendon Sr. another of the core members. Although always called the Highwaymen, Mary Ann Carroll was one of the earliest artists in the group and the only woman. In 2011, she presented a painting to Michelle Obama at the First Lady's Luncheon in Washington, DC.

Largely self-taught and unable to gain entrance into museums and art galleries, they sold their art door-to-door to businesses and individuals as well as from the trunks of their cars along the popular tourist routes of A1A and US1.

By the 1980s sales began to languish, but that changed in the mid 1990s when several newspaper

articles about this unusual group of artists were published. Jim Fitch, a Florida art historian, referred to them as *The Florida Highwaymen* for their business of selling art along Florida's Highways. Their careers were re-ignited. All 26 Florida Highwaymen were inducted into the Florida Artists Hall of Fame in 2004. The paintings have escalated in value and are now prized by collectors. Many of the members, and A. E. Backus have died but their legacy continues.
https://www.floridahighwaymenpaintings.com/
https://en.wikipedia.org/wiki/The_Highwaymen_(landscape_artists)
https://highwaymenajbrown.com/

A.E. Backus Museum & Gallery highlights landscapes by Fort Pierce native, A. E. "Bean" Backus (1906-1990). He is also known for his mentorship of many of the Florida Highwaymen. The museum also includes changing displays of the works of the Florida Highwaymen. Backus was inducted into the Florida Artists Hall of Fame in 1984. The museum screens an excellent documentary about his life and work. 500 N Indian River Dr; Fort Pierce, FL 34950; Phone: (772) 465-0630; https://backusmuseum.org/

Al's Family Farm Tours are offered seasonally generally from January through Easter. Any time of year, visit this three-generation family-owned business where they offer "more local citrus varieties than anyone in the Indian River growing region." 2001 N Kings Hwy; Fort Pierce, FL 34951; Phone: (772) 460-0556; https://www.alsfamilyfarms.com/

Heathcote Botanical Garden offers specialty gardens including a Japanese Garden, Reflection Garden, Herb Garden, Rainforest Display, Native Plants Garden, and a Palm & Cycad Walk. Their Pioneer House, or Florida Cracker

House, is a replica of the style settlers used about two hundred years ago. NOTE: Wheelchairs are available. 210 Savannah Rd; Fort Pierce, FL 34982; Phone: (772) 464-4672; https://www.heathcotebotanicalgardens.org/

Highwaymen Trail Obelisk features mosaic duplicates of Highwaymen paintings. It was created by Florida artist Stephanie Jaffe Werner. Located at Avenue D and 15th Street. https://stephaniejaffeart.com/florida-highwaymen-obelisk

Manatee Education and Observation Center combines education with wildlife viewing. It's located in the same marina as the Backus Museum. Visitors can learn about manatees, and Florida's diverse habitats, but the reason to visit is the potential for manatee sightings. Stand along the covered observation walkway or climb the second story observation tower for a view of the manatees. FREE. 480 N Indian River Dr; Fort Pierce, FL 34950; Phone: (772) 429-6266; http://www.manateecenter.com/

National Navy UDT-SEAL Museum, also known as the Navy SEAL Museum, features exhibits to inform and educate on the role of Navy Underwater Demolition Teams, and the Sea, Air, Land teams. It is the only museum dedicated to preserving the history of the Navy SEALs and their predecessors. Excellent video presentations add depth to this fitting tribute and illumination of their bravery and skill. NOTE: The same parking lot provides access to Pepper Park Beach. 3300 N Hwy A1A; Fort Pierce, FL 34949; Phone: (772) 595-5845; https://www.navysealmuseum.org/

Ocean Discovery Visitor Center at Florida Atlantic University Harbor Branch showcases the cutting-edge technology used in oceanographic research. Visitors can also study displays of marine environments along with over 80 species of marine and plant life. Guided tours are available.

Both admission and tours are FREE (donations encouraged). 5600 N US 1; Fort Pierce, FL 34946; Phone: (772) 242-2400; https://www.fau.edu/hboi/discover-fau-harbor-branch/

Urca De Lima is part of the fabled Spanish treasure fleet that sank off the coast of present-day Fort Pierce in 1715 during a hurricane. Rediscovered in 1928 the Urca de Lima became Florida's first Underwater Archaeological Preserve in 1987. It's 200 yards offshore in 10-15 feet of water about 1,000 yards north of Pepper Beach Park near Fort Pierce. http://www.museumsinthesea.com/_docs/urcadelima_brochure.pdf

St. Lucie County Aquarium offers daily feeding tours as well as weekly behind-the-scenes tours. At any time, visitors can view the underwater worlds of the Indian River Lagoon, and Atlantic Ocean. 420 Seaway Dr; Fort Pierce, FL 34949; Phone: (772) 462-3474; https://www.stlucieco.gov/departments-services/a-z/parks-recreation-department/aquarium-smithsonian

St. Lucie County Regional History Center, just down the road from the aquarium, begins with the Native Americans, continues to the rise of the fishing industry, and the efforts at pineapple farming. Explore Cobb's General Store, take a walk down Main Street past the doctor's office and the printing press, or tour of the fully furnished 1900s Gardner House. 414 Seaway Dr; Fort Pierce, FL 34949; Phone: (772) 462-1795; https://www.stlucieco.gov/departments-services/a-z/parks-recreation-and-facilities-department/st-lucie-county-regional-history-center

Hobe Sound, FL (Martin County)

Blowing Rocks Preserve gets its name from the action of waves on the rocks when the ocean is rough and the tide is high. During these extreme conditions the waters break against the rocks and its force sends plumes of water up to 50 feet skyward. These conditions are most common in winter. Though the dark, jagged rocks have been compared to a lava flow, they are a sedimentary rock called Anastasia limestone. Blowing Rocks Preserve harbors the largest outcropping on the US Atlantic Coast. FREE with a $2 donation requested. 574 S Beach Rd; Hobe Sound, FL 33455; Phone: (561) 744-6668; https://www.nature.org/en-us/get-involved/how-to-help/places-we-protect/blowing-rocks-preserve/

Hobe Sound National Wildlife Refuge and Nature Center offers family-friendly free programs including Night Explorers, Beach Dynamics, and weekly naturalist hikes along the trails. FREE. 13640 SE Federal Hwy; Hobe Sound, FL 33455; Phone: (772) 546-2067; http://www.hobesoundnaturecenter.com/

Jonathan Dickinson State Park, the largest state park in Southeast Florida, combines nature and history. Nature lovers can explore coastal sand hills, upland lakes, and scrub forests as well as the pristine Loxahatchee River. History lovers will want to learn about a secret World War II training camp, the story of the shipwrecked Quaker merchant who is the park's namesake, and Trapper Nelson -- the legendary Wild Man of the Loxahatchee. Ranger-guided tours of Trapper Nelson's 1930s pioneer homestead are available year-round. 16450 SE Federal Hwy; Hobe Sound, FL 33455; Phone: (772) 546-2771; https://www.floridastateparks.org/parks-and-trails/jonathan-dickinson-state-park

Hutchinson Island, FL (Martin, St. Lucie, and Indian River Counties) (PSL)

Hutchinson Island lies off the coast of Martin, St. Lucie, and Indian River counties. Its two barrier islands are separated by the Fort Pierce Inlet and are known as North Hutchinson Island and South Hutchinson Island. They stretch from Fort Pierce to Stuart, Florida. Three highways lead to Hutchinson Island from Fort Pierce, Jensen Beach, and Stuart.

The Houses of Refuge were havens for shipwrecked sailors and travelers along the sparsely populated Atlantic coastline of Florida. *Keepers* patrolled the beach to rescue sailors who fell victim to Florida's treacherous reefs and shoals. **Gilbert's Bar House of Refuge Museum** is the only remaining House of Refuge. The museum provides their stories. 301 SE MacArthur Blvd; Stuart, FL 34996; Phone: (772) 225-1875; https://hsmc-fl.com/house-of-refuge/

One hundred yards offshore lies the **wreck of Georges Valentine**, an iron-hulled screw steamer originally built in 1869. After being sold and resold, it eventually found its way to Florida in the early 1900s. It's now a popular snorkeling and scuba-diving site located about 100 yards off the House of Refuge in relatively shallow water.
http://www.museumsinthesea.com/_docs/georges_brochure.pdf

Hypoluxo, FL (Palm Beach County)

This small town is self-named *Home of the Barefoot Mailman*, and still honors that legacy.

Hypoluxo Scrub Natural Area is a remnant of pre-development Florida. Entrance to the trail system is located under the observation structure. This was part of the route traveled by the trail-blazing Barefoot Mailmen and plaques on the main level between the towers explain the area's history. Learn more about this section of the route at: https://www.hypoluxo.org/community/page/history. 150 Hypoluxo Rd; Hypoluxo, FL 33462; Phone: (561) 233-2400;

https://discover.pbcgov.org/erm/NaturalAreas/Hypoluxo-Scrub.aspx

Jensen Beach, FL (Martin County) (PSL)

This town is one of the access points to Hutchinson Island. Visitors will find three of the town's best attractions (listed below) conveniently located in **Indian Riverside Park.** The park also features a 3/4-mile walking path, and a mangrove boardwalk, along with a fishing pier, interactive play fountain, beach access, and gardens. https://www.martin.fl.us/IRSP

Captain Henry Sewall's House, built in 1889, was the home of local pioneer and developer Henry E. Sewall. Owned by the county, free tours are held every first and third Wednesday of the month from October through May. 1707 NE Indian River Dr; Jensen Beach, FL 34957; Phone: (772) 463-3201; https://www.martin.fl.us/SewallsHouse

Children's Museum of the Treasure Coast includes a grocery store, a traditional Cracker house, a wellness center, and a beach themed toddler play area. 1707 NE Indian River Dr; Jensen Beach, FL 34957; Phone (772) 225-7575; https://www.childrensmuseumtc.org/

Mansion at Tuckahoe (also known as the Leach Mansion) was once the home of Coca-Cola heiress Anne Bates Leach. The county offers free seasonal tours by reservation only. 1707 NE Indian River Dr; Jensen Beach, FL 34957; Phone: (772) 463-3201; https://www.martin.fl.us/Mansion

Juno Beach, FL (Palm Beach County)

The 569-acre **Juno Dunes Natural Area** links the Atlantic Ocean to the Intracoastal Waterway. The ocean-front tract offers views of the surrounding area from atop an ancient sand dune. The Intracoastal or west tract has several miles of trails and floating docks. Intracoastal entrance: 14501 South US Hwy 1; Juno Beach, FL 33408. Ocean entrance: 14200 South US Hwy 1; Juno Beach; Phone: (561) 233-2400; https://discover.pbcgov.org/erm/NaturalAreas/Juno-Dunes.aspx

Loggerhead Marinelife Center focuses on ocean and sea turtle conservation and provides visitors with a mix of free and fee-based activities. Admission is FREE as are the talks on sea turtle biology, ecology, and conservation as well as interactive shows. Fee-based tours and special seasonal experiences are available. Advanced registration is advised. 14200 US 1; Juno Beach, FL 33408; Phone: (561) 627-8280; https://marinelife.org

Jupiter, FL (Palm Beach County)

If you're a fan of Burt Reynolds then the town of Jupiter may sound familiar, over and above its tourism possibilities. Scenes from several of the popular actor's movies were filmed in and around Jupiter and he donated generously to various local projects. A town park bears his name.

Busch Wildlife Sanctuary (not to be confused with Busch Gardens in Tampa) combines a nature center with a wildlife rehabilitation hospital. There are nature trails with exhibits of native animals, and a center with interactive displays and multimedia productions. 17855 Rocky Pines Rd; Jupiter, FL 33458; Phone: (561) 575-3399; https://www.buschwildlife.org/

Dubois Park contains the remains of a village occupied by the Jobe Native Americans (also known as Jaega) and their predecessors who lived in the area well before the Spanish colonization. The **DuBois Pioneer Home** was built in 1898 on

an ancient midden (mound of ancient domestic waste) dating back 1,000 years ago. NOTE: There is no wheelchair access and visitor must climb stairs to enter the house. Docent-led tours are available. 19075 Dubois Rd; Jupiter, FL 33477; Phone: (561) 966-6609;
https://discover.pbcgov.org/parks/Locations/DuBoisPioneer.aspx

Jupiter Inlet Lighthouse & Museum is open for visitors to enjoy the 105-foot-tall structure, with its first-order Fresnel lens. The accompanying museum features 5,000 years of regional history. 500 Captain Armour's Way; Jupiter, FL 33469; Phone: (561) 747-8380 x101;
https://www.jupiterlighthouse.org

River Center features aquatic tanks, interactive exhibits, and a touch tank that represents the Loxahatchee River system. The River Center is located in Burt Reynolds Park. 805 US 1; Jupiter, FL 33477; Phone: (561) 743-7123;
https://lrdrivercenter.org

Roger Dean Chevrolet Stadium is one of only two stadiums in Florida to host two Major League Baseball teams annually for Spring Training: Miami Marlins, and St. Louis Cardinals.
https://rogerdeanchevroletstadium.com;
https://rogerdeanchevroletstadium.com/tickets-events/

Lake Worth Beach, FL (Palm Beach County)

Lake Worth and Lake Worth Beach are not two separate towns, as is the case for several other places in Florida. Instead, it was a name change with voters (barely) agreeing to rename Lake Worth as Lake Worth Beach to make their town sound beachier. Regardless of the name, the town has a vibrant art focus with listings of art, music, theater, and more:
https://www.lakewortharts.com/

Cottages of Lake Worth Beach are said to number over 1,000 and be the largest concentration of these historic tiny houses anywhere in Florida. You can create your own self-guided tour with the map at:
http://www.cottagesoflakeworth.com/tours/
There's also a Facebook page at:
https://www.facebook.com/CottagesofLakeWorth/

Although only a half-mile in length, the **Custard Apple Trail** is a true piece of old Florida history. In the excellent historical novel, *A Land Remembered* by Patrick D. Smith, Tobias MacIvey buys a swath of land to protect the custard apple forest that he loved. Of course, he didn't succeed because almost nothing stops development, especially in Florida's earliest years. Unique to the Americas, when fully ripe and soft the fruit is sweet and scooped out of the skin to enjoy. It is said to taste like custard and is related to the pawpaw. The pond apple trees can be found at the wetland portion of this trail. Entrance to the trail is at: 4759 S. Congress Ave. The trail is part of **John Prince Memorial Park**. 2700 Sixth Ave S; Lake Worth Beach, FL 33461; Phone: (561) 966-6600; https://discover.pbcgov.org/parks/Locations/John-Prince.aspx; https://discover.pbcgov.org/parks/pages/naturetrails.aspx

Loxahatchee, FL (Palm Beach County)

Lion Country Safari, opened in 1967, could be the grandparent of drive-through safari parks. On over 600 acres visitors to the park can enjoy a walk-through safari, animal encounters, take a boat ride, and play in the splash pad. 2003 Lion Country Safari Rd; Loxahatchee, FL 33470; Phone: (561) 793-1084; https://www.lioncountrysafari.com/

Panther Ridge Conservation Center houses cheetahs, jaguars, leopards, and other endangered cat species. Visitors can take a guided tour, go behind the scenes with the head keeper tour, and even be keeper-for-a-day. 2143 D Rd; Loxahatchee, FL 33470; Phone: (561) 795-8914; https://pantherridge.org/

Manalapan, FL (Palm Beach County)

The **Lofthus wreck** is the remains of an iron-hulled sailing vessel from the late 1900s. Divers and snorkelers can find it in 15-20 feet of water, less than a mile north of Boynton Inlet and 175 yards off-shore of Manalapan.
http://www.museumsinthesea.com/_docs/Lofthus_brochure.pdf

Palm Beaches, FL (Palm Beach County)

Several towns make up the Palm Beaches: Palm Beach; North Palm Beach; and West Palm Beach. The county also has an abundance of free-to-visit nature areas -- more than 31,000 acres open sunrise to sunset. Learn more here:
https://discover.pbcgov.org/erm/Pages/Natural-Areas.aspx

Want to combine a DIY tour and selfies? Take their **Selfie Trail** described as: "easy-to-follow Selfie Trail pinpoints a suggested starter list of popular attractions and hidden gems of where to capture the most buzz-worthy selfies."
https://www.thepalmbeaches.com/selfie-trail-palm-beaches

Palm Beach, FL

The much-loved **Giant Kapok tree** is rumored to be a transplant from the Amazon rainforest, brought here as an experimental crop tree in Palm Beach's earliest days, making it over 180 years old. It's on the popular Palm Beach Lake Trail and part of the grounds of the Royal Poinciana Chapel. 60 Cocoanut Row; Palm Beach, FL 33480; Phone: (561) 655-

4212; https://royalpoincianachapel.org/about/buildings-and-grounds/

Henry Morrison Flagler Museum recreates the opulent lifestyle that Henry Morrison Flagler and his third wife Mary Lily Kenan shared as part of Florida's history and America's legendary Gilded Age. Completed in 1902, it is considered one of the few Gilded Age mansions in the state and is an important example of neoclassical Beaux Arts architecture. Two other Gilded Age mansions are Stetson House in Deland, and Vizcaya in Miami. One Whitehall Way; Palm Beach, FL 33480; Phone: (561) 655-2833; https://www.flaglermuseum.us

Society of the Four Arts is home to two libraries, a performance hall, and an art gallery, as well as the Four Arts Botanical Garden, and the Philip Hulitar Sculpture Garden with 20 sculptures set among bougainvillea-laden pergolas. 100 Four Arts Plaza; Palm Beach, FL 33480; Phone: (561) 655-7227; https://www.fourarts.org/

North Palm Beach, FL

A unique mixture of coastal and tropical hammock and mangrove forest, **John D. MacArthur Beach State Park** provides a haven for several rare or endangered native tropical and coastal plant species. There's a nature center, beach, and fishing. At Lake Worth Beach entrance visitors will also find the Custard Apple Trail (See Lake Worth Beach). 10900 Jack Nicklaus Dr; North Palm Beach, FL 33408; Phone: (561) 624-6950; https://www.floridastateparks.org/parks-and-trails/john-d-macarthur-beach-state-park

West Palm Beach, FL

Ann Norton Sculpture Gardens are part of the former residence of sculptor Ann Weaver Norton (1905-1982). Throughout the house, studio, and gardens are more than one hundred of Norton's sculptures. Special exhibitions also take place on the grounds. 253 Barcelona Rd; West Palm Beach, FL 33401; Phone: (561) 832-5328; https://www.ansg.org/

Bulk Candy Store Museum offers guided fee-based tours and video presentations describing the history of candy and how favorite candies are made and packaged. 235 N Jog Rd; West Palm Beach, FL 33413; Phone: (561) 540-1600; https://www.bulkcandystore.com/tours/

Power plants and manatees have an unusual relationship. During the winter months these marine mammals seek the warmer temperatures near natural springs, as well as the warm-water outflows of coastal power plants. Florida Power & Light (FPL) has created **Manatee Lagoon** for the public to enjoy. **FPL Eco-Discovery Center** has a dedicated area for viewing manatees up close, plus exhibits about manatees. FREE. 6000 N Flagler Dr; West Palm Beach, FL 33407; Phone: (561) 626-2833; https://www.visitmanateelagoon.com/

McCarthys Wildlife Sanctuary provides sanctuary for over 170 animals. Reservations required. 12943 61st St N; West Palm Beach, FL 33412; Phone: (561)-790-2116; https://www.mccarthyswildlife.com/

Over 2,000 species of tropical and subtropical plants from six continents are spread over 14 acres at **Mounts Botanical Garden**. 531 N Military Trail; West Palm Beach, FL 33415; Phone: (561) 233-1757; https://www.mounts.org/

Palm Beach Photographic Centre Museum features rotating exhibits exploring the entire spectrum of photography, from the historic to the cutting-edge. FREE. 415 Clematis St; West Palm Beach, FL 33401; Phone: (561) 253-2600; https://www.workshop.org/museum/

South Florida Science Center and Aquarium offers a one-stop science experience from the human brain to astronomy, plus outdoor trails, and marine science. 4801 Dreher Trail N; West Palm Beach, FL 33405; Phone: (561) 832-1988; https://www.sfsciencecenter.org/

The 1,094-acre protected **Sweetbay Natural Area** provides sanctuary for wading birds, red-shouldered hawks, bobcats, eastern lubber grasshoppers, and Florida box turtles. There's a short, paved trail and boardwalk trails to an observation platform overlooking its wetlands. It is part of the Great Florida Bird and Wildlife Trail. FREE. 12560 Aviation Rd; West Palm Beach, FL 33412; Phone: (561) 233-2400; https://discover.pbcgov.org/erm/NaturalAreas/Sweetbay.aspx

West Palm Beach Post Office is home to six murals depicting the *Legend of James Edward Hamilton, Mail Carrier* painted by Stevan Dohanos (1907-1994). In 1939 the Treasury Department's Section of Fine Arts hired Dohanos to paint the panels for display at the West Palm Beach, Florida Post Office. They hang there today (up near the ceiling) for all to appreciate. 3200 Summit Blvd, West Palm Beach, FL 33416

Port St. Lucie, FL (St. Lucie County) (PSL)

Clover Park is home to the New York Mets Spring Training, the St. Lucie Mets Minor League Team, and all the New York Mets Minor League operations. 525 NW Peacock Blvd; Port St. Lucie, FL 34986; Phone: (772) 871-2115; https://floridagrapefruitleague.com/teams/new-york-mets/

Situated on 225-acres along the North Fork of the St Lucie River, the **Oxbow Eco-Center** is both a nature preserve, and an environmental learning center with boardwalks, pedestrian trails and observation towers. 5400 NE St James Dr; Port St. Lucie, FL 34983; Phone: (772) 785-5833;

https://www.stlucieco.gov/departments-services/a-z/oxbow-eco-center

Port St. Lucie Botanical Gardens offers specialized gardens from bamboo and bromeliads to orchids and roses. Sculptures are sited throughout the grounds. 2140 SE Westmoreland Blvd; Port St. Lucie, FL 34952; Phone: (772) 337-1959; https://www.pslbg.org/

Riviera Beach, FL (Palm Beach County)

Peanut Island Park is an 80-acre oasis can only be reached by boat, but there are water taxis available. One unusual historical tidbit is that the island is the site of President John F. Kennedy's Cold War-era bunker (which is currently closed to visitors). Phone: (561) 845-4445; https://discover.pbcgov.org/parks/Pages/PeanutIsland.aspx

The **Blue Heron Bridge** area is recognized for its abundance of unique marine life but **Phil Foster Park** goes a bit further with a snorkel trail made of limestone boulders and prefabricated reef modules. It spans a two-acre area in six to ten feet of water off Blue Heron Blvd by the bridge. https://discover.pbcgov.org/parks/PDF/philfostersnorkeltrail.pdf

Sebastian, FL (Indian River County)

Mel Fisher's Treasures displays some of the riches found in ships sunk off the coast of Florida. Included are salvages from the 1715 Fleet, and Nuestra Señora de Atocha. See also Key West for Mel Fisher's other museum. There's usually a $5 off coupon available at:
https://www.melfisher.com/TreasureSales/Sebastian.asp
1322 US 1; Sebastian, FL 32958; Phone: (772) 589-9875; https://www.melfisher.com/Sebastian.asp

FOCUS ON: Who Was Mel Fisher?

Famous among those who love treasure hunting, Mel Fisher (1922 – 1998) achieved fame (and fortune) for finding the 1622 wreck of the *Nuestra Señora de Atocha* in Florida waters. Side note: his wife Dolores Horton was one of the first women to learn how to dive and set a women's record by staying underwater for 50 hours.

But that discovery came later on. He started his career in 1963, in Vero Beach, salvaging the 1715 Fleet, ships filled with treasure that sank off the coast near Vero Beach and which also gave that area its name of *Florida's Treasure Coast.*

He eventually moved his activities to the Florida Keys discovering the treasure-laden galleon the *Nuestra Señora de Atocha.* But that discovery was not without tragedy. Fisher found silver bars from the wrecked galleon in 1973, two years later his son Dirk found five bronze cannons whose markings would prove to be that of the *Atocha.* Sadly Dirk, his wife Angel, and diver Rick Gage died days later when their boat sank.

An estimated $450 million cache was eventually recovered from the Atocha including 40 tons of gold and silver and priceless emeralds. And that is only part of what was reported to be on the ship.

The discovery also sparked a bit of financial envy. The state of Florida claimed title to the wreck and forced Fisher's company, Treasure Salvors, Inc., to give up 25% of the found treasure. Fisher's company fought the state, and after eight years of litigation, in 1982, the U.S. Supreme Court ruled in Fisher's favor and his Treasure Salvors, Inc. was awarded all rights to the treasure.

Fisher and Treasure Salvors found the remains of several other shipwrecks in Florida waters, including the *Atocha's* sister galleon the *Santa Margarita*, lost in the same year, and the remains of a slave ship known as the *Henrietta Marie*, lost in 1700.
https://en.wikipedia.org/wiki/Mel_Fisher
https://www.melfisher.com/sebastian.html

Sebastian Area Historical Museum in the 1927 Historic Sebastian Public School includes exhibits on the Ais Indians, Pelican Island, and historical items from the area. 1235 Main St; Sebastian, FL 32958; Phone: (772) 581-1380; https://verobeach.com/explore-vero-beach/sebastian-area-historical-museum

Stuart, FL (Martin County) (PSL)

Stuart is located on the eastern point of the 54-mile-long Okeechobee Waterway, Florida's only cross-state canal, extending from the Atlantic Ocean in Stuart to the Gulf of Mexico in Ft. Myers.
https://www.saj.usace.army.mil/Missions/Civil-Works/Lake-Okeechobee/Okeechobee-Waterway-OWW/

Designed in Art Deco style and built in 1937, **Court House Cultural Center Gallery** hosts fine art exhibitions. FREE with donations appreciated. 80 E Ocean Blvd; Stuart, FL 34996; Phone: (772) 287-6676; https://www.martinarts.org/

The **Elliott Museum** offers a variety of collections, from vintage cars and baseball artifacts to a miniature circus, plus rotating exhibits. 825 NE Ocean Blvd; Stuart, FL 34996; Phone: (772) 225-1961; https://hsmc-fl.com/elliott-museum/

Stuart Heritage Museum presents the history of the people, businesses, and agriculture of the town. FREE. 161 SW Flagler Ave; Stuart, FL 34994; Phone: (772) 220-4600; http://www.stuartheritagemuseum.com/

Vero Beach, FL (Indian River County)

Florida is famous for its citrus fruits and the **Indian River Citrus Museum** explains the history of the industry in Indian River County from its beginnings in the late 1800s. FREE. 2140 14th Ave; Vero Beach, FL 32960; Phone: (772) 770-2263; https://www.veroheritage.org/citrus-museum/

Considered to be one of the oldest botanical gardens in Florida, **McKee Botanical Garden** is an 18-acre subtropical jungle hammock. The Royal Palm Grove was created to resemble the original 1937 garden. A highlight is a Stickwork installation called *Grand Central* by Patrick and Sam Dougherty in which volunteers wove, bent, trimmed, and shaped willow saplings into an intricate structural sculpture. 350 US 1; Vero Beach, FL 32962; Phone: (772) 794-0601; https://mckeegarden.org/

Region 10 South Florida: Fort Lauderdale, Miami, and more

Greater Miami metropolitan area dominates south Florida. For travel planning Greater Miami covers Miami-Dade and Broward counties, making all of Region 10 the Greater Miami metro area and offering some of the state's most sophisticated pleasures.

FOCUS ON: Jai-Alai

A favorite in Latin American countries and in Spain, jai-alai was once wildly popular throughout Florida. Over nine of the three-sided frontons once offered live viewing of the fast-paced and exciting sport where players leapt up walls and flung balls at speeds too quick to follow.

Betting on the outcome was a major factor in its popularity, and its decline. When other gambling options became widely available, the sport began to lose its audience. Today, only one year-round location remains. Magic City Casino offers live jai-alai most of the year. 450 NW 37th Ave; Miami, FL 33125; Phone: (305) 649-3000; https://jaialaiworld.com/pelota; https://jaialaiworld.com/

A second location has recently re-opened for a special invitational event, but hopes are high that it will continue. The Annual Dania Beach Invitational starts in December but will run only a few weeks. 301 E Dania Beach Blvd; Dania Beach, FL 33004; Phone: (954) 920-1511; https://www.casinodaniabeach.com/jai-alai/

Finally, there is one more jai-alai focused attraction in Florida. The J Laca Museum is filled with the collection of sports and jai-alai memorabilia of Jeff "Laca" Conway and is located in his home. http://pelotapress.com/museum/ Contact him to set up a time to visit. JeffConway1955@gmail.com

For everything jai-alai visit http://pelotapress.com/

Coconut Creek, FL (Broward County)

Butterfly World encompasses three acres of butterfly aviaries, botanical gardens, and a research center. But the most unusual aspect is the butterfly farm. There is a market for purchasing butterflies, and this attraction meets that need. The public is invited to learn more about it, and their efforts to save endangered species. There are also aviaries for tropical birds, and an interactive lorikeet encounter. 600 W Sample Rd; Coconut Creek, FL 33073; Phone: (954) 977-4434; https://www.butterflyworld.com/

As its name suggests **Fern Forest** shelters over 30 species of ferns, some of which are considered endangered. The nature center includes information and interactive exhibits. FREE. 201 S Lyons Rd; Coconut Creek, FL 33063; Phone: (954) 357-5198;
https://www.broward.org/Parks/Pages/park.aspx?park=14

Coral Gables, FL (Miami-Dade County)

Coral Gables Museum is in the Coral Gables Police and Fire Station, a historic building completed in 1939 as a Works Progress Administration (WPA) project. Visitors can see the former jail cells, and courtroom. Additional outdoor spaces and galleries have been added and the museum curates a full program of time-limited exhibits. NOTE: It is a fully accessible facility. 285 Aragon Ave; Coral Gables, FL 33134; Phone: (305) 603-8067; https://coralgablesmuseum.org/

Fairchild Tropical Botanical Garden invites visitors to enjoy their grounds featuring 11 lakes and seven pools, and a tropical fruit pavilion filled with some of the tropical world's most exotic fruit. There's also a 12-acre display of 740 species of tropical flowering trees, shrubs and vines collected from all tropical regions of the world, and hundreds of spectacular butterflies. 10901 Old Cutler Rd; Phone: (305) 667-1651; http://www.fairchildgarden.org

The **Gifford Arboretum**, part of the University of Miami, is a collection of trees and plants important for research and education. FREE. 1301 Memorial Dr; Coral Gables, FL 33146; Phone: (305) 284-1302; https://arboretum.as.miami.edu/

Lowe Art Museum on University of Miami's Coral Gables campus has a permanent collection of culturally significant archaeological/ethnographic artifacts as well as fine art. Two dozen sculptures by local, national, and international artists have been added to key focal points around campus. 1301 Stanford Dr; Coral Gables, FL 33124; Phone: (305) 284-3603; https://www.lowe.miami.edu/index.html

Merrick House was the home of the George Merrick who founded Coral Gables. Docents lead tours of the 14 rooms, while the grounds are open for self-guided tours. 907 Coral Way; Coral Gables, FL 33134; Phone: (305) 774-0155; https://www.coralgables.com/coral-gables-merrick-house

Completed in 1924, **Venetian Pool** is a historic public pool fed with spring water from an underground aquifer. 2701 De Soto Blvd; Coral Gables, FL 33134; Phone: (305) 460-5306; https://www.coralgables.com/venetianpool

Dania and Dania Beach, FL (Broward County)

Dania Beach is quasi famous for its monkey population. Deborah "Missy" Williams, PhD, of Florida Atlantic University leads the Dania Beach Vervet Project and has traced the free-roaming monkeys to an escape from a Dania research facility in the 1940s. https://vervetproject.org/

The **Holocaust Documentation and Education Center** has collected over 2400 oral histories to add depth to the stories of the Holocaust. 303 N Federal Hwy; Dania Beach, FL 33004; Phone: (954) 929-5690; https://hdec.org/

Davie, FL (Broward County)

Flamingo Gardens and Wildlife Sanctuary is 60 acres of rare and native plants, some of Florida's largest and oldest trees, and over 90 species of Florida native animals. The historic Wray Home Museum depicts Florida life in the 1930s. 3750 S Flamingo Rd; Davie, FL 33330; Phone: (954) 473-2955; https://www.flamingogardens.org/

Long Key Natural Area and Nature Center highlights ecology, nature, and history. The centerpiece of the exhibit hall is an actual archaeological dig, but there's also hands-on exhibits of native vegetation and birds. The area was the home of the Tequesta, and Seminole Native Americans. 3501 SW 130th Ave; Davie, FL 33330; Phone: (954) 357-8797; https://www.broward.org/Parks/Pages/Park.aspx?=22

Dating back to 1918, the **Old Davie School Historical Museum** offers the oldest existing school building in Broward County, plus two original homes built in 1912, a replica of a 1909 early settler's shack, and an authentic Chickee hut. Exhibits and special events are also scheduled. 6650 Griffin Rd; Davie, FL 33314; Phone: (954) 797-1044; http://www.olddavieschool.org/

Tree Tops Park is another nature oasis with trails, horseback riding, boating, and fishing. A 28-foot observation tower provides views of the surrounding area. The visitor center features exhibits on area history including the Battle of Pine Island Ridge during the Second Seminole War. 3900 SW 100th Ave, Davie, FL 33328; Phone: (954) 357-5130; https://www.broward.org/Parks/Pages/park.aspx?=40

Deerfield Beach, FL (Broward County)

James D. and Alice Butler House is both the headquarters of the Deerfield Beach Historical Society and their museum. The house contains many of the original furnishings. NOTE: Open only on Saturdays. FREE with donations gratefully accepted. 380 E Hillsboro Blvd; Deerfield Beach, FL 33441; Phone: (954) 429-0378; http://www.deerfieldbeachhistoricalsociety.com/guided-tours/

Fort Lauderdale, FL (Broward County)

There can be a bit of confusion between Fort Lauderdale and Lauderdale-by-the-Sea. They are two different towns, located about 20 minutes apart. The former is more inland and the latter, as its name implies, is on the water.

Nothing remains of the fort for which the city was named, and today Fort Lauderdale is far more famous for its recreational opportunities, and its attractions.

Built in 1920 by Frederic Clay Bonnet, **Bonnet House Museum & Gardens** includes the main house and a courtyard highlighted with carousel animals. Guided tours are available. 900 N Birch Rd; Fort Lauderdale, FL 33304; Phone: (954) 563-5393; http://www.bonnethouse.org

Fire and Safety Museum details nearly 100 years of the history of the Fort Lauderdale Fire Department through photos, videos, as well as historic uniforms and equipment. 1022 W Las Olas Blvd; Fort Lauderdale, FL 33316; Phone: (954) 290-6901; https://fortlauderdalefiremuseum.com/

History Fort Lauderdale is a destination with multiple places to learn about history. The **New River Inn** uses displays and recorded recreated pioneer voices to trace the history and development of the greater Fort Lauderdale area from pre-historic First Nation People to the present day. Rotating visual arts exhibits are in its first-floor galleries. The **New River Artists' Co-op** offers studio tours and live demonstrations on the third floor. The **Pioneer House Museum** is set as if the family will return at any moment for their 1907 Sunday supper. There's also extensive antique furniture, as well as kitchen, doll, and toy collections. The **Schoolhouse Museum** provides the 1899 school experience complete with period wooden desks and McGuffey readers. 219 SW Second Ave; Fort Lauderdale, FL 33301; Phone: (954) 463-4431; https://historyfortlauderdale.org/museum/

International Swimming Hall of Fame and Museum has 40 exhibits and displays to illustrate the history of aquatic sports including swimming, diving, water polo, and synchronized swimming. One Hall of Fame Dr; Fort Lauderdale, FL 33316; Phone: (954) 462-6536; https://www.ishof.org/museum/

Museum of Discovery and Science is a comprehensive children's science museum with hands-on experiences, demonstrations, and simulations. 401 SW Second St; Fort Lauderdale, FL 33312; Phone: (954) 467-6637; https://mods.org/

Naval Air Station Fort Lauderdale Museum is filled with displays on naval aviation. Perhaps the most intriguing exhibit focuses the enigma of Flight 19. On December 5, 1945 Flight 19 left the air station… and vanished into the Bermuda Triangle. 4000 W Perimeter Rd; Fort Lauderdale, FL 333215; Phone: (954) 359-4400; https://www.nasflmuseum.com/

NSU Art Museum Fort Lauderdale at Nova Southeastern University has the largest holding in America of the post WWII, avant-garde European artists of the CoBrA movement. The name is derived from the initials of the members' home capital cities – Copenhagen, Brussels, and Amsterdam. It also has a significant collection of the works and archival materials by American painter William J. Glackens and his peers. One E Las Olas Blvd; Fort Lauderdale, FL 33301; Phone: (954) 525-5500; https://nsuartmuseum.org/

Old Dillard was the Fort Lauderdale’s first school for Black students when it opened in 1907. Today the building houses the **Old Dillard Museum** with guided tours of its exhibits, as well as films and lectures. 1009 NW Fourth St; Fort Lauderdale, FL 33311; Phone: (754) 322-8828; https://www.browardschools.com/Page/35769

A prime area to explore is the 22-block **Riverwalk Arts and Entertainment District**. Located along the New River it encompasses famed Las Olas Boulevard, and many of the most popular places to visit. Phone: (954) 522-5334; https://www.goriverwalk.com/

Stranahan House was the home of Fort Lauderdale pioneers Frank and Ivy Stranahan. Built in 1901 as a trading post it was converted into a residence for the Stranahans in 1906. It is the city’s oldest surviving structure. Currently admission is by guided tour only. 335 SE Sixth Ave, Fort Lauderdale, FL 33301; Phone: (954) 524-4736; https://stranahanhouse.org/

Hallandale Beach, FL (Broward County)

Gulfstream Park is one of the state's well-known horse racing tracks and offers live racing. Check the website for the racing schedule. Gulfstream Park Village encompasses restaurants, bars, and shopping. General Admission to the racetrack is free on regular race days. 901 S Federal Hwy; Hallandale Beach, FL 33009; Phone: (954) 454-7000; https://www.gulfstreampark.com

Hialeah, FL (Miami-Dade County)

Hialeah Race Track was considered one of the most beautiful racetracks in the world when it opened in 1932. It became famous for its flamingo flocks and was once officially designated as a sanctuary. It stopped hosting racing in 2001 when a new state law prohibited Hialeah from having exclusive race dates separate from competing tracks of Gulfstream and Calder. It now simulcasts racing and is more a casino and entertainment center. 100 E 32nd St; Hialeah, FL 33013; Phone: (305) 885-8000; https://hialeahparkcasino.com

Hollywood, FL (Broward County)

Anne Kolb Nature Center is the largest park in the Broward system and offers a five-story nature observation tower amid the mangrove eco-system. FREE. 751 Sheridan St; Hollywood, FL 33019; Phone: (954) 357-5161; https://www.broward.org/Parks/Pages/Park.aspx?=1

The **Art and Culture Center/Hollywood** is in the Kagey mansion, built in 1924 in the Mediterranean Revival style of architecture. The center curates contemporary visual and performing arts shows in the gallery spaces. 1650 Harrison St; Hollywood, FL 33020; Phone: (954) 921-3274; https://www.artandculturecenter.org

Wiener Museum of Decorative Arts celebrates the art of fire with exhibits of studio glass featuring Chihuly and Lalique. There's also a collection of British and European pottery, and porcelain from the 19th and 20th centuries created by Wedgwood and Royal Doulton. 3250 N 29th Ave; Hollywood, FL 33020; Phone: (954) 376-6690; https://www.wmoda.com/

Homestead, FL (Miami-Dade County)

For an array of wildlife, including hundreds of species of colorful fish and plants found nowhere else in the United States, as well as pelicans, manatees, and sea turtles head to **Biscayne National Park**.

Dante Fascell Visitor Center, located at Convoy Point nine miles east of the city, provides a virtual journey through the park's four ecosystems. Use the park's website to make arrangements for commercial tours and adventures. Admission to the park is FREE, adventures will incur a fee. 9700 SW 328th St; Sir Lancelot Jones Way; Homestead, FL 33033; Phone: (305) 230-1144; https://www.nps.gov/bisc/index.htm.

Stiltsville, now part of Biscayne National Park, has an intriguing history. Started in the1930s, when "Crawfish Eddie Walker" built the first shack on stilts above the water, over the years more buildings were constructed. Accessible only by water, the area was the place to see and be seen when visiting the winter resorts on nearby Miami Beach. Stories of illegal alcohol and gambling led to several police raids. At its peak in 1960, there were 27 buildings, but hurricanes, fires and the ravages of being in such an exposed place made them relatively short-lived. You can see the remnants of these structures from the water. It is possible to arrange for a special permit to visit, but it is pricey. Check http://stiltsvilletrust.org/

Coral Castle is an oolite limestone structure created by the Latvian-American vernacular artist Edward Leedskalnin. From 1923 to 1951, he carved over 1,100 tons of coral rock to create the Coral Castle. This form of sedimentary rock is made of ooids, egg-like pieces of calcium carbonate. 28655 S Dixie Hwy; Homestead, FL 33033; Phone: (305) 248-6345; https://coralcastle.com/

Everglades National Park has its main entrance in the town of Homestead (the other two entrances are in Miami, and Everglades City). The sprawling 1,509,000 acres spans Miami-Dade County, Monroe County, and Collier County with three visitor centers. The different sections offer trails and ranger-led programs as well as sites specific to the location. https://www.nps.gov/ever/index.htm. This part of the Everglades encompasses the historic Nike Missile Site, HM69 with an actual missile, and many of the original support buildings. Temporarily closed. Check with the Ernest F. Coe Visitor Center for updates. Everglades Institute offers several guided tours of the park as a part of their programming, visit http://evernpi.org for more information.

Ernest F. Coe entrance provides visitors with information about the Everglades, an informational movie, and an interactive gallery. A series of walking trails begin a short drive from the visitor center. 40001 SR 9336; Homestead, FL 33034; Phone: (305) 242-7237; https://www.nps.gov/ever/planyourvisit/coedirections.htm

Flamingo Visitor Center provides visitors with educational displays, informational brochures, a public boat ramp, a marina store, and hiking and canoeing trails. There are currently several fee-based boat tours available. One Flamingo Lodge Hwy; Homestead, FL 33034; Phone: (239) 695-2945; https://www.nps.gov/ever/planyourvisit/gbvc.htm

Royal Palm is located a little over a mile away from the Homestead park entrance. Ranger-led walks and talks are available. The visitor center includes a small bookstore, restrooms and vending machines. Phone: (305) 242-7237; https://www.nps.gov/ever/planyourvisit/royal-palm.htm

The **Fruit & Spice Park** has a climate that can be found nowhere else in the continental USA. Its botanic gardens host over 500 varieties of fruits, vegetables, spices, herbs, nuts, and other commercially important plant specimens from around the world. In their words: *You are welcome to indulge in some fallen fruit along the way if you know what the fruit is – not everything we have is edible! If you are not sure it is safe to eat, bring it with you to the Welcome Center or ask one of our helpful staff. Please don't pick from the trees—the fruit may not be ripe – and besides that will leave some for everyone. Also, don't be afraid to go off the path and explore.* Guided tours are available. 24801 SW 187th Ave; Homestead, FL 33031; Phone: (305) 247-5727; https://redlandfruitandspice.com/

Key Biscayne, FL (Miami-Dade County)

Bill Baggs Cape Florida State Park derives its name from Cape Florida, or *the Cape of Florida*, named by Ponce de Leon during the first Spanish expedition to Florida in 1513. Visitors can delve into history on guided tours through the lighthouse and keeper's cottage, or explore the park on foot, on a bicycle, by boat, or kayak. Also on the grounds is the 1825 **Cape Florida Lighthouse** that guided mariners off the Florida Reef. 1200 South Crandon Blvd; Key Biscayne FL 33149; Phone: (786) 582-2673; https://www.floridastateparks.org/parks-and-trails/bill-baggs-cape-florida-state-park; https://www.floridastateparks.org/parks-and-trails/bill-baggs-cape-florida-state-park/cape-florida-light

The German two-masted, 366-ton steel schooner-yacht, originally christened Germania, was built in 1908. Fast in the water, it was a racing yacht before being seized as a prize of war in 1914. Renamed **Half Moon** it was used as a floating cabaret until it sank in the early 1930s. Located on a shoal off of Key Biscayne near Miami, it rests in eight to ten feet of water about three feet below the surface. The shipwreck is located within a Florida Underwater Archaeological Preserve. A laminated underwater guide is available from local dive shops. The preserve is open to the public year-round. FREE. http://www.museumsinthesea.com/_docs/Halfmoon_brochure.pdf

Neptune Memorial Reef™ is a cremation site transforming over 16 acres of ocean floor into an artistic representation of the Lost City of Atlantis, located 40 feet under the sea. These structures promote coral and marine organism's growth. Visits are possible by boat and for divers. Phone: (954) 630-3279; https://nmreef.com/visit-memorial-reef/

Lauderdale-By-The-Sea, FL (Broward County)

This waterside town is smaller than the more famous Fort Lauderdale and about 20 minutes away. A bit more Old Florida, the town describes itself as *Florida's Beach Diving Capital* with a coral reef within a swim from the shore. **SS Copenhagen** is a shipwreck off the coast. The single screw steamer was built in Sunderland, England in 1898, sunk in 1900, and used for target practice by the military during WWII. Today it's an artificial reef resting in 16 to 31 feet of water about ¾ of a nautical mile off Lauderdale-by-the-Sea. It's within a Florida Underwater Archaeological Preserve. FREE. https://www.nps.gov/articles/sscopenhagen.htm; https://www.lauderdalebythesea-fl.gov/232/SS-Copenhagen

Miami, FL (Miami-Dade County)

Miami is a huge, cosmopolitan city that has reinvented itself with stunning architecture, sophisticated restaurants, and urban pleasures. Miami Beach is oceanside for nightclubs, partying, and sandy shores. North Miami Beach is actually a

separate town, despite the name.
https://www.miamiandbeaches.com/neighborhoods

Miami, FL

The **American Museum of the Cuban Diaspora** documents the history, culture, and contributions of the Cuban exile community. 1200 Coral Way; Miami, FL 33145; Phone: (305) 529-5400; https://thecuban.org/

Built in 1891, the **Barnacle Historic State Park** was the home of Ralph Middleton Munroe and showcases frontier life when all travel to and from Miami was by sea. Left in its natural state, the park appears much as it did in Munroe's day, but with replicas of two of his sailboats. 3485 Main Hwy; Miami, FL 33133; Phone: (305) 442-6866; https://www.floridastateparks.org/parks-and-trails/barnacle-historic-state-park

Cubaocho Museum and Performing Arts Center & Tower Theater mixes music, art, discussions, and rum. It features one of the largest privately-owned Cuban art collections in the world, to be enjoyed with cocktails. *Art lovers can gaze at the museum's large collection of 19th century and early- to mid-20th century Cuban art as they sip on a cocktail.* Who could resist? 1465 SW Eighth St; Suite 106; Miami, FL 33135; Phone: (305) 285-5880; https://www.cubaocho.com/

The **Deering Estate** preserves the 1920s era Miami estate of Charles Deering, a Chicago industrialist and first chairman of the International Harvester Company. Take a self-guided tour of the house, and a staff-guided tour of the preserve. 16701 SW 72nd Ave; Miami, FL 33157; Phone: (305) 235-1668; https://deeringestate.org/

Everglades National Park has three entrances in three different cities across southern Florida. In addition to Miami the park can be accessed at Homestead, FL, and Everglades City, FL. **Shark Valley Visitor Center**, the entrance closest to Greater Miami, has educational displays, a park video, guided tram tours, short walking trails, as well as ranger-led, and commercial tours. 36000 SW Eighth St; Miami, FL 33194; Phone: (305) 221-8776;
https://www.nps.gov/ever/planyourvisit/svdirections.htm

Sometimes considered the *Ellis Island of the South* for services provided to Cuban refugees from 1962 through 1974, the **Freedom Tower** conveys the story of the Cuban exodus to the United States. Now owned by Miami Dade College, it is home to the **Museum of Art and Design** (MOAD), and MDC Special Collections which include the Cuban Legacy Gallery, the Kislak Center, and the Exile Experience. MOAD offers exhibitions and programs that aim to foster a reimagined Miami. It is currently undergoing renovation. 600 Biscayne Blvd; Miami, FL 33132; Phone: (305) 237-7700;
https://moadmdc.org/freedom-tower/about-the-freedom-tower

Gold Coast Railroad Museum offers a collection of historic railroad cars and memorabilia. On permanent exhibit is the presidential Pullman car Ferdinand Magellan, used by former presidents Roosevelt, Truman, Eisenhower, and Reagan plus over 40 historic rail cars. It is one of Florida's official railroad museums. NOTE: Located next to Zoo Miami. 12450 SW 152nd St; Miami, FL 33177; Phone: (305)253-0063;
https://www.goldcoastrailroadmuseum.org/

If you're flying into or out of Miami, with some time before (or after) your flight, consider the **Hall of Aviation** located within Miami International Airport (MIA). It explores flight and the history of aviation, with an emphasis on Miami and Miami International Airport. South Terminal J, International

Arrivals, Mezzanine level; https://www.miami-airport.com/miami_from_the_sky.asp

During segregation, **Hampton House** was part of the Green Book, a listing of places where Blacks could safely stay when traveling or vacationing. Hotel guests included Dr. Martin Luther King Jr., Sammy Davis Jr., Duke Ellington, Nancy Wilson, Louis Armstrong, LaVern Baker, Malcolm X, and Muhammad Ali. Its permanent exhibit is a virtual reality film on the challenges of traveling as a person of color in the United States. As lodging, it was featured in the 2021 film *One Night in Miami* where boxing legend Cassius Clay (later Muhammad Ali), civil rights activist Malcolm X, football star Jim Brown, and singer Sam Cooke met after Clay had just won his first heavy weight title. Although the movie is a fictionalized account, the meeting and the setting were real. NOTE: Currently all reservations and payments must be made online. Tours are available. 4200 NW 27th Ave; Miami, FL 33142; Phone: (305) 635-5800; https://historichamptonhouse.org

A visit to **HistoryMiami** covers a lot of ground, from archaeology and culture to technology and home furnishing. For aviation enthusiasts there's one of the largest collections of Pan American Airways material in the US. The Folklife Gallery features an interactive exhibition showcasing artifacts and archival items from the museum's collection. 101 W Flagler St; Miami, FL 33130; Phone: (305) 375-1492; http://www.historymiami.org/

The **Kampong National Tropical Botanical Garden**, named for the Malay or Javanese word for a village or cluster of houses, offers collections from Southeast Asia, Central and South Americas, the Caribbean, and other tropical locales. Highlights include an 80-year-old baobab tree from Tanzania that weighs almost 50 tons, and flowering plants prized by the perfume industry. NOTE: Advance online registration currently required. 4013 Douglas Rd; Miami, FL 33133; Phone: (305) 442-7169; https://ntbg.org/gardens/kampong/

Miccosukee Indians were originally part of the Creek Nation who migrated to Florida before it became part of the United States. During the Seminole Wars of the 1800s most of the Miccosukee were forced to move to the West. However, some of both the Miccosukee and the Seminole nations never surrendered and remained in the Everglades. **Miccosukee Indian Village** highlights the Miccosukee way of life. US-41 at Mile Marker 36; Miami, FL 33194; Phone: (305) 552-8365; https://www.facebook.com/MiccosukeeIndianVillage/; https://miccosukee.com/news/

Patricia & Phillip Frost Art Museum, part of Florida International University, creates special exhibitions in addition to its permanent collection specializing in Haitian and Cuban art, with additional focus on non-western art. FREE. 10975 SW 17th St; Miami, FL 33199; Phone: (305) 348-2890; https://frost.fiu.edu

Phillip and Patricia Frost Museum of Science welcomes families to explore the planetarium, aquarium, ancient reptiles, and the science of flying. 1101 Biscayne Blvd; Miami, FL 33132; Phone: (305) 434-9600; https://www.frostscience.org/

Rubell Museum displays contemporary art in a repurposed DEA (Drug Enforcement Administration) facility. Don and Mera Rubell amassed over 7,200 works by more than 1,000 artists, and their museum is open to the public. Advanced ticket purchase is recommended. 1100 NW 23rd St; Miami, FL 33127; Phone: (305) 573-6090; https://rubellmuseum.org

Superblue is an immersive art experience, described as mind-bending use of color, light, animation, and sound. 1101 NW

23rd St; Miami, FL 33127; Phone: (786) 697-3414; https://www.superblue.com/miami/

Wings Over Miami displays and flies military and classic aircraft. Miami Executive Airport; 14710 SW 128th St; Miami, FL 33196; Phone: (305) 233-5197; http://www.wingsovermiami.com

Miami Beach, FL

Miami Beach has had a varied architectural history. Part of that legacy is the **Art Deco Historic District** with the nation's largest concentration of Art Deco architecture. It features historic buildings mainly from the 1920s and 1930s. The South Beach section covers Fifth Street to 23rd Street along Ocean Drive, Collins Avenue, and Washington Avenue. The other dominant architectural style is **MiMo** – Miami Modern which developed around the end of World War II.

The Miami Design Preservation League offers guided and self-guided walking tours. Visit their **Art Deco Museum** for context and special exhibits. NOTE: They recommend parking garages as on street parking is limited. 1001 Ocean Dr; Miami Beach, FL 33139; Phone: (305) 672-2014; https://mdpl.org/

For contemporary art, head to **The Bass** which has expanded the definition of contemporary art to include design, fashion, and architecture. 2100 Collins Ave; Miami Beach, FL 33139; Phone: (305) 673-7530; https://thebass.org/

Holocaust Memorial Miami Beach pays tribute to the six million Jews killed during the Nazi regime. Around the monument are more than 100 sculptures. The street address matches the years of the holocaust. FREE. 1933-1945 Meridian Ave; Miami Beach, FL 33139; Phone: (305) 538-1663; http://holocaustmemorialmiamibeach.org/

Two restored historic buildings that were formerly synagogues now host the **Jewish Museum of Florida**. The core exhibit is Jewish Life in Florida with 500 photos and artifacts that depict the Jewish experience in Florida since 1763. Currently admission is free on Saturdays, but check the website for any changes. Walking tours of the area are available at an additional cost. This museum is part of Florida International University. 301 Washington Ave; Miami Beach, FL 33139; Phone: (305) 672-5044; https://jmof.fiu.edu/

For a stroll down a walking street, **Lincoln Road Mall** is a pedestrian road between 16th Street and 17th Street. It's known for its shops, restaurants, and galleries. https://lincolnroadmall.com/

Miami Beach Botanical Garden is a small urban oasis with a koi pond, fountains, and specialized gardens plus special events. General admission is FREE. 2000 Convention Center Dr; Miami Beach, FL 33139; Phone: (305) 673-7256; https://mbgarden.org/

Museum of Illusions Miami describes itself as using interactive 3D illusions and their *Smash It!* exhibit to transport you to a world of fantasy and imagination. Visitors can look forward to flying on a magic carpet, walking on the edge of a sky-scraper, and surviving a lava bridge. NOTE: Photography is encouraged. 536 Lincoln Rd; Miami Beach, FL 33139; Phone: (305) 604-5000; https://miaillusions.com/

Oolite Arts offers gallery shows and workshops. 924 Lincoln Rd; Miami Beach, FL 33139; Phone: (305) 674-8278; https://oolitearts.org/

Wolfsonian is another of the museums of Florida International University. It traces the cultural development of the nation for the hundred years spanning 1850 to 1950 through its collection of over 200,000 objects. FREE. 1001 Washington Ave; Miami Beach, FL 33139; Phone: (305) 531-1001; https://wolfsonian.org

Wilzig Erotic Art Museum (formerly called the World Erotic Art Museum) uses its collection to illustrate the history of erotic art. It contains the 4000-piece collection of Naomi Wilzig. Located in the **Wilzig Museum Building** visitors can also explore the **George Daniell Museum** with the photography of George Daniell. 1205 Washington Ave; Miami Beach, FL 33139; Phone: (305) 532-9336; https://www.wilzigmuseumbuilding.com/

Vizcaya Museum & Gardens sits on 10 acres of lushly landscaped Italianate gardens. The museum is the first floor of the former villa and estate of businessman James Deering, of the Deering McCormick-International Harvester fortune. A planned expansion will include Vizcaya Village – 11 architecturally significant buildings on 12 acres. Built in 1916 to make Vizcaya self-sufficient, the Village included staff quarters, a garage and workshops, barns, greenhouses, and fields that supplied fresh flowers, fruits and vegetables. 3251 S Miami Ave; Miami, FL 33129; Phone: (305) 250-9133; https://vizcaya.org/

North Miami Beach, FL (Miami-Dade County)

Despite its name, North Miami Beach is a separate city from Miami. Originally named Fulford-by-the-Sea in 1926, it was renamed North Miami Beach in 1931. It's about a half-hour north of Miami.

Arch Creek Park & Nature Center offers a half-mile trail winding through hardwood hammocks beneath a canopy of gumbo limbo trees, live oaks, and strangler figs. As the name implies, several types of figs tend to slowly choke their host trees to death. Along the creek, you're likely to spot kingfisher, egrets, and other wading birds. Start or end your exploration inside the nature center with its exhibits on the Tequestas, and Miami's early pioneers. 1855 NE 135th St; North Miami Beach, FL 33181; Phone: (305) 944-6111; https://www.miamidade.gov/parks/arch-creek.asp

St. Bernard de Clairvaux Church, also known as the Ancient Spanish Monastery, is a true medieval Spanish monastery cloister. Built in Segovia, Spain in the 12th century, William Randolph Hearst purchased the Cloisters and the Monastery's outbuildings in 1925, had them dismantled and shipped to the United States. His intention was to make it part of Hearst Castle in San Simeon, California. But financial difficulties stopped Hearst's plans and the crates languished in a warehouse in Brooklyn, New York. In 1964, Colonel Robert Pentland, Jr purchased the Cloisters and presented it to the Bishop of Florida where it is now an Episcopal church in North Miami Beach. The public is invited to attend activities, worship, and enjoy a tour, or a concert. 16711 W Dixie Hwy; North Miami Beach, FL 33160; Phone: (305) 945-1461; https://www.spanishmonastery.com/

Pinecrest, FL (Miami-Dade County)

Set on the grounds of what was once the beloved Parrot Jungle, **Pinecrest Gardens** preserves the area's historical landscaping, and remaining structures. Stroll the paths that wind through the botanical garden, and a lake viewing area (Swan Lake) with resident wildlife. There are art exhibits as well as contemporary sculptures installed throughout the gardens. 11000 Red Rd; Pinecrest, FL 33156; Phone: (305) 669-6990; https://www.pinecrestgardens.org/

Plantation, FL (Broward County)

Learn about the different Caribbean communities and their cultures at the **Island SPACE Caribbean Museum**. 8000 W Broward Blvd; Plantation, FL 33388; Phone: (954) 999-0989; https://islandspacefl.org/

Plantation Historical Museum is focused on history of the city, but it also showcases fire department memorabilia. FREE. NOTE: Limited hours. 511 N Fig Tree Ln; Plantation, FL 33317; Phone: (954) 797-2722; https://www.plantation.org/government/departments/historical-museum

Pompano Beach, FL (Broward County)

Blanche Ely House is a cultural hub offering curated exhibits, special events, and gallery shows. 1500 NW Sixth Ave; Pompano Beach, FL 33060; Phone: (954) 786-7877; https://www.pompanobeacharts.org/ely

Sample-McDougald House, built in 1916, is open for guided tours as a house museum of pioneer South Florida life. It is located in Centennial Park. 450 NE 10th St; Pompano Beach, FL 33060; Phone: (754) 307-5446; https://www.samplemcdougald.org/

Hillsboro Inlet Lighthouse began operating in 1907, was electrified in 1932, and automated in 1974. Tours are held monthly. The museum is open Wednesday through Sunday with limited hours. Also on the grounds is a bronze statue honoring James E. Hamilton, the Barefoot Mailman who disappeared while delivering mail along the treacherous path. NOTE: Private company tours are also available: https://www.lighthousescenictours.com. 2700 N Ocean Blvd; Pompano Beach, FL 33061; Phone: (954) 942-2102; http://www.hillsborolighthouse.org/

Southwest Ranches, FL (Broward County)

The town is truly named Southwest Ranches, and describes itself as a *rural environment, filled with grazing animals, nurseries, farms, exquisite and unique scenery and an abundance of wildlife.*

South Florida Hindu Temple invites visitors to witness the Arti ceremony. It is an ancient Hindu offering made by moving lighted wicks before the sacred images to the accompaniment of a musical prayer. NOTE: Men and women sit separately during Arti. Shoulders to knees must be covered. 13010 Griffin Rd; Southwest Ranches, FL 33330; Phone: (954) 252-8802; https://sfht.org/visitor-information/

Sunrise, FL (Broward County)

Dauer Museum of Classic Cars is home to 70 vehicles, most of which are fully restored classic cars. Previously only by invitation the collection has recently been open to the public. 10801 NW 50th St; Sunrise, FL 33351; Phone: (954) 739-0978; https://dauercars.com

Hockey fans can indulge their passion at a **Florida Panthers** game at the FLA Live arena. The arena also hosts concerts and special events. One Panther Pkwy; Sunrise, FL 33323; Phone: (954) 835-8000; https://www.flalivearena.com/

Tamarac, FL (Broward County)

At 21 acres, **Woodmont Natural Area** is the largest remaining natural habitat in the town. It consists of pine flatwoods and a cypress/red maple wetland. It is a designated Urban Wilderness Area. FREE. 7250 NW 80th Ave; Tamarac, FL 33321; Phone: (954) 357-8109; https://www.broward.org/Parks/Pages/park.aspx?park=45

Weston, FL (Broward County)

Fox Astronomical Observatory is operated by the South Florida Amateur Astronomers Association. Located in Markham Park, the observatory is open to the public on Saturday evenings from sunset until midnight. 16001 SR 84; Sunrise, FL 33326; Phone: (954) 384-0442; http://www.sfaaa.com/

Region 11 The Keys: From Key Largo to Key West

Often lumped with Miami into a south Florida region, the Keys are their own special destination. Starting about 15 miles south of Miami, these tiny islands extend in a gentle arc towards Key West, ending a bit further in the uninhabited Dry Tortugas. These keys are all part of Monroe County. The only exception is Totten Key, in Biscayne National Park in Miami-Dade County in Region 10.

The water surrounding the Keys is protected by the Florida Keys National Marine Sanctuary. It includes the Florida Reef, the only barrier coral reef in North America. A highlight is their Shipwreck Trail that guides divers to several of the area's sunken ships. https://floridakeys.noaa.gov/visitor_information/

FOCUS ON: From Swamp to Cool

The Keys were initially not a popular destination. They were hard to reach and had an abundance of bugs, and humidity. But there was a deep-water port and Henry Flagler, who was building railroads and plush hotels further north, wanted to extend his already constructed railway down into these scaled-down islands. He would open the Keys to visitors from Miami, and to trade with other parts of the area.

Originally called the Florida East Coast Railway Key West Extension, it was more popularly known as the Florida Keys Over-Sea Railroad for its audacious plan to be built over miles of open water. Completed in 1912, Flagler lived just long enough to see its completion. But his dream didn't last. Severely damaged in the 1935 hurricane, the bridge was not rebuilt.

Eventually bits and pieces of roads and railway beds became woven into the roughly 110-mile Florida Keys Scenic Highway stretching across over 40 separate islands and becoming the southernmost segment of US 1. The Keys highway is the only All-American Road in Florida, and it is truly one of the country's rare road jewels. https://www.scenichighwayflkeys.com/

Beauty is plentiful in the Keys, but gorgeous sugar-sand beaches are in short supply. The Florida Keys are coral islands. Pockets of sandy beaches can be found, but mainly around resort communities.

FOCUS ON: Mile Markers of the Florida Keys

Mile Markers (MM) in the Florida Keys indicate location relative to the number of miles north of Key West, the most southern point in the continental United States.

Generally, addresses along the Overseas Highway, the name given to this section of Route 1, are expressed using MM with a four-, five-, or six-digit number. For example, the address of Laura Quinn Wild Bird Sanctuary (listed below) is at 93600 Overseas Hwy. Decoding that sequence tells drivers that it is at about MM 93.6. If the extreme right digit is an even number, it is on the west or Bay/Gulf side. An odd number would indicate it is on the east or ocean side. Subtracting two MMs gives the approximate number of miles between two known locations. However, exceptions certainly exist and this is only a guide.

NOTE: The Federal Highway Administration begins mileage numbering at the state's southern-most border. Thus, if the MMs are getting lower, you're traveling south. However, if you're traveling through the Keys, you've likely started by driving south from Miami, so the Keys in this section are listed going from north to south, starting with the highest mile markers.

Key Largo

This popular Key is the furthest north and extends from MM 107 down to MM 91 and includes several small towns.

Dolphin Plus offers more than a swim with dolphins, each participant attends an educational briefing about dolphin natural history, anatomy, social behavior, reproductive biology, echolocation, and conservation, as well as what to expect during your swim. Special shallow encounters are also available. 101900 Overseas Hwy; Key Largo, FL 33037; Phone: (305) 451-1993; http://www.dolphinsplus.com

The **Florida Keys Wild Bird Rehabilitation Center** rescues, rehabilitates, and releases native and migratory wild birds. It has two locations open to visitors. **Laura Quinn Wild Bird Sanctuary** invites the public to see their non-releasable birds, watch a pelican feeding, and stroll the boardwalk. 93600 Overseas Hwy; Tavernier, FL 33070; Phone: (305) 852-4486; https://www.missionwildbird.com. **Mission Wild Bird Hospital** has a visitor center open to the public. 82080 Overseas Hwy; Tavernier, FL 33070; Phone: (305) 852-4486; https://www.missionwildbird.com/

The first undersea park in the United States, **John**

Pennekamp Coral Reef State Park encompasses approximately 70 nautical square miles and offers the famous Christ of the Abyss underwater statue (a casting of the Italian original). In addition, there's hiking, kayaking, and boat tours. NOTE: All tour boats have at least one vessel that can accommodate wheelchairs. 102601 Overseas Hwy; Key Largo, FL 33037; Phone: (305) 451-6300; http://pennekamppark.com

At the time of its sinking, the 510-foot **USS Spiegel Grove** was the largest ship ever intentionally sunk to create a new reef for divers, and it remains one of the largest ships ever scuttled for that purpose. Location: 25° 04.00' N; 80° 18.65' W (6 miles off Key Largo). https://fla-keys.com/diving/spiegel-grove/

Islamorada

Calling itself the *Sport Fishing Capital of the World*, Islamorada goes from MM 90 to MM 74 and is itself composed of smaller keys including Tea Table, Upper and Lower Matecumbe, Windley, and Plantation Key.

History of Diving Museum invites visitors to sit in a replica diving bell, try on a helmet, and learn about 4,000 years of diving history. 82990 Overseas Hwy; Islamorada, FL 33036; Phone: (305) 664-9737; http://www.divingmuseum.org

Just off the coast is the **Indian Key State Historic Park,** the site of a 19th century ghost town whose economy was based on salvaging cargo from shipwrecks. NOTE: It is accessible only by kayak. Phone: (305) 664-2540; https://www.floridastateparks.org/IndianKey; https://www.floridastateparks.org/sites/default/files/media/file/Indian%20Key-1218.pdf

Lignumvitae Key Botanical State Park is on an offshore island named after the native lignumvitae tree. Meaning *the wood of life* in Latin, it is among the densest and heaviest woods on earth and the Keys is one of the few places in Florida where the tree has survived destructive harvesting. NOTE: The island is only accessible by boat. Phone: (305) 664-2540; http://www.floridastateparks.org/parks-and-trails/lignumvitae-key-botanical-state-park

Robbie's Marina definitely has rentals and tours, as well as an eatery, but visitors can also feed a tarpon. A school of tarpon come daily, likely because they know they'll be getting an easy meal. Admission to the dock is fee-based and there is a charge for each bucket of fish you toss to the tarpon. 77522 Overseas Hwy; Islamorada, FL 33036; Phone: (305) 664-8070; https://www.robbies.com/tarpon.htm

In 1733 the **Spanish galleon San Pedro** sunk in a hurricane near Islamorada. It was part of a fleet of ships heavy with treasures from the New World. Today it is one of Florida's oldest artificial reefs, and home to a variety of sea creatures. Little remains of the San Pedro but the underwater site has been enhanced with seven replica cannons, an anchor, and an information plaque. 77200 Overseas Hwy; Islamorada, Fl 33001; Location: 24° 51.802'N 80° 40.780'W; Phone: (305) 664-2540; https://www.floridastateparks.org/SanPedro

Windley Key Fossil Reef Geological State Park is formed of fossilized coral called Key Largo limestone. In the early 1900s Florida East Coast Railroad used the stone in building Henry Flagler's Overseas Railroad. After the railroad was built, the quarry was used to produce pieces of decorative stone called Keystone. Today, visitors can walk along eight-foot-high quarry walls to see cross sections of the ancient coral and learn about the quarry and its operation. Samples of the quarry machinery have been preserved at the park. The visitor center features educational exhibits. 84900 Overseas Hwy; Islamorada, FL 33036; Phone: (305) 664-2540; https://www.floridastateparks.org/WindleyKey

Going further south is Fiesta Key (MM 70), Long Key (MM 67.5), and Duck Key (MM 61).

Grassy Key

Going from MM 60 to MM 58, Grassy Key is small, but it has one of the best places in the state to appreciate dolphins. The resident dolphins and sea lions of the **Dolphin Research Center** live in natural, seawater lagoons in the bay side of the Grassy Key. What makes this center different is encapsulated in their caution... *Dolphins and sea lions choose to participate in sessions, including interactive programs from the docks or in the water. None are ever forced. Therefore, on any given day, program availability and times may vary based on the needs of the animals.* 58901 Overseas Hwy; Grassy Key FL 33050; Phone: (305) 289-1121; https://dolphins.org/

Marathon Key

About an hour from Key West in the south and Key Largo in the north, Marathon is in the center of the Florida Keys stretching from MM 60 to MM 47. It encompasses a historic bridge and several islands. According to their website: *The name Marathon came about by the railroad workers who were working night and day to complete the railway. Due to the unrelenting pace and struggle to complete the project the popular exclamation, "This is getting to be a real Marathon", is how the name originated.* https://www.ci.marathon.fl.us/community/page/residential-and-visitor-information

The **Turtle Hospital** is a small non-profit organization

dedicated to the rehabilitation of endangered sea turtles. The only way to visit the hospital is through a guided tour with a presentation on sea turtles which includes a behind-the-scenes look at the hospital facilities and rehabilitation area. 2396 Overseas Hwy; Marathon, FL 33050; Phone: (305) 743-2552; https://www.turtlehospital.org/

Florida Keys Aquarium Encounters provides several aquarium tours. The Coral Reef Encounters provide a snorkeling experience as swimmers witness an actual ecosystem. You can also choose to interact with a shark – the relatively small and docile nurse shark – or go into a tank with a stingray. 11710 Overseas Hwy; Marathon, FL 33050; Phone: (305) 407-3262;
http://www.floridakeysaquariumencounters.com

The **Seven Mile Bridge** covers the seven miles from MM 47 to MM 40. There is both an old and a new Seven Mile Bridge. Visitors today travel over the new bridge. However, a section of the **Old Seven Mile Bridge** has been reopened as a two-mile pedestrian walkway and a gateway to historic Pigeon Key, tucked beneath the original bridge. The ramp to Pigeon Key is open 9 AM to 5 PM.
https://www.ci.marathon.fl.us/community/page/old-seven-mile-bridge

Pigeon Key Historic District on **Pigeon Key at MM 45** is a U S Historic District with 11 buildings and three structures all nestled beneath the Old Seven Mile Bridge. In the early 1900s, the five-acre island was a base camp for workers during construction of the original Seven Mile Bridge, the centerpiece of Henry Flagler's Key West Extension of the Florida East Coast Railroad. The museum chronicles its construction. In addition to walking or biking to the island, a ferry is available from the Pigeon Key Gift Shop. The Foundation offers historical tours, including a train ride, from their visitor center. NOTE: NO pets are permitted on Pigeon Key. 2010 Overseas

Hwy; Marathon, FL 33050; Phone: (305) 743-5999; https://pigeonkey.net/; https://fla-keys.com/marathon/pigeon-key

Bahia Honda Key

Located near MM 36 to 38 this uninhabited key is known for the 524-acre **Bahia Honda State Park**. It's just north of Big Pine Key. The channel at the island's west end is one of the deepest natural channels in the Florida Keys and provides the key's Spanish name which means Deep Bay. It has a natural white sand beach, a nature trail, biking, fishing, and snorkeling as well as camping and mooring facilities. NOTE: The park closes to visitors when it reaches maximum capacity. 36850 Overseas Hwy; Big Pine Key, FL 33043; Phone: (305) 872-2353; https://www.floridastateparks.org/BahiaHonda

Big Pine Key

Covering only two miles, from MM 32 to MM 30, Big Pine Key is home to several popular attractions spread out across several smaller keys.

A highlight of this section is the **Key Deer Refuge**. The much-loved deer are the smallest subspecies of the North American white-tailed deer. The tiny Key Deer roam only through the Lower Keys. Within the Refuge a prime viewing location is the Blue Hole (MM 31) a few miles north of the visitor center. The **Blue Hole Observation Platform** was originally a limestone quarry, now filled with freshwater, and shaded by native plants. A short, paved trail leads to the observation platform. There are also interpretive trails just north of Blue Hole on Key Deer Blvd. NOTE: There is little shade on these trails so dress appropriately and always bring water. 30587 Overseas Hwy; Big Pine Key, FL 33043; Phone: (305) 872-0774; https://www.fws.gov/refuge/national-key-deer.

The **Great White Heron National Wildlife Refuge** is known for fishing, boating, and birding. The visitor center is the same one as the Key Deer Refuge.
https://www.fws.gov/refuge/great-white-heron

No Name Pub is famous for its unusual ceiling decor. Started in 1931 as general store, and bait and tackle shop, the owners added a tavern room in 1936. At one time the tavern/restaurant was estimated to have over $90,000 in dollar bills pinned to its ceiling and walls. NOTE: The pub is on Big Pine Key which is different from the tiny No Name Key. 30813 Watson Blvd; Big Pine Key, FL 33043; Phone: (305) 872-9115; https://nonamepub.com

Key West

Finally, at the very end of the Overseas Highway is Key West. It is the ultimate vacation state of mind and everyone seems quite pleased about that. As expected, there are definitely quirky festivals held in Key West. Hemingway Days are held in July. Fantasy Fest is Halloween fun at the end of October. April brings Conch Republic Independence Celebration. Whenever you visit there's likely something being held. https://fla-keys.com/calendar/key-west/. If somehow there's nothing official, head to Mallory Square for the daily Sunset Celebration. In fact, head there anyway. It's part of the exuberant life of Key West.

FOCUS ON: The Conch Republic

For quirky history, nothing beats 1982 when Key West famously declared itself the Conch Republic. The story behind this act of rebellion begins in March of that year when the federal government placed a Border Patrol roadblock at the Last Chance Saloon in

Florida City, located at the northern end of the Overseas Highway.

Allegedly searching for illegal drugs and people, the blockade effectively stopped cars from leaving and entering the Keys. Traffic was snarled and both residents and tourists were upset. The mayor of Key West was beyond annoyed and declared that the city would secede; on April 23rd the Conch Republic was born.

A secession must have a battle, and the *Great Battle of the Conch Republic* occurred when a locally-owned schooner reportedly attacked a Coast Guard cutter with water balloons, conch fritters, and stale bread. The attack was met with fire hoses (which ended the battle), whereupon the mayor surrendered and demanded foreign aid. The road block was quietly removed and Key West has called itself the *Conch Republic* ever since, with a yearly celebration of its birth. Learn more at: https://conchrepublic.com

But why the Conch Republic? Conch started as slang for Bahamians of European descent. When the American Revolution ended in 1783, the Floridas were handed back to Spain. Spain's hold on Florida was tenuous in the years after American independence and British Loyalists needed a refuge. Thousands went to the Bahamas which was still British territory.

But the British had just lost an expensive war (that would be the American Revolution) and needed money, so they began taxing the Bahamians on their food. One story goes that the Bahamians said they'd rather eat the local conch (pronounced *conk*) than pay taxes, and they did just that. Another less colorful story traces the term back to the use of a shell on a flag. Regardless, the term Conch started to be applied to the descendants of Bahamian immigrants. Eventually many of those who made the island their home were proudly nicknamed Key West Conchs.

Visitors to Key West are often entranced by its vernacular Conch architecture. Houses are built of wood raised above the ground to allow air to circulate. Large windows, high ceilings, and louvered shutters further encourage cooler interiors.

Bahama Village is a dozen-block neighborhood between Whitehead and Fort, and Angela and Catherine Streets. Settled by Black Bahamian residents in the 1800s it now offers restaurants, bars, market stalls, and shops. Look for the decorative arch spanning Petronia Street where it intersects with Duval Street.

The **Dry Tortugas National Park and Fort Jefferson** is located roughly 70 miles west of Key West. It is actually made up of seven Keys (Garden, Loggerhead, Bush, Long, East, Hospital, and Middle) which are collectively known as the Dry Tortugas. Transportation to and from the park can be made through local ferry and seaplane service. A historical highlight of the Dry Tortugas is the 19th century fort, with its Civil War history. Its most famous prisoner was Dr. Samuel Mudd, who was imprisoned for his involvement in providing medical care and a refuge to John Wilkes Boothe after the assassination of President Abraham Lincoln. Mudd was given a life sentence. However, his work saving lives during the Yellow Fever epidemic prompted a presidential pardon in 1869. Phone: (305) 242-7700; https://www.nps.gov/drto/index.htm

Florida Keys Eco-Discovery Center covers the plants and

animals of the Florida Keys National Marine Sanctuary. 35 Quay Rd; Key West, FL 33040; Phone: (305) 809-4750; https://floridakeys.noaa.gov/eco_discovery.html

In 1822, the US Navy surveyed sites to determine effective places for a fort whose guns could command Key West harbor. The original plans were considered too expensive and the revision led to **Fort Zachary Taylor** and two batteries – the **East and West Martello Towers**. They were never armed or involved in a battle and today both are museums and exhibition spaces known as Fort East Martello and the West Martello Tower. These are located several miles apart and are not contiguous.

Fort Zachary Taylor Historic State Park, on the southern edge of Key West, is the southernmost state park in the continental United States. Built to guard the harbor of Key West, Fort Taylor was used in the Civil War, Spanish American War, WWI, WWII, and the Cuban Missile Crisis. It is said to contain the largest cache of Civil War armament in the world. Guided tours and scheduled historic demonstrations are available. A beach at the southern end is open for swimming and picnicking. 601 Howard England Way; Key West, FL 33040; Phone: (305) 292-6713; https://www.floridastateparks.org/parks-and-trails/fort-zachary-taylor-historic-state-park

East Martello offers exhibits on the island's history, and the important industries of sponging, wrecking, and cigar manufacturing that drove Key West's economy. Visitors can also enjoy the work of Stanley Papio – Junkyard Rebel. 3501 S Roosevelt Blvd; Key West, FL 33040; Phone: (305) 296-3913; https://www.kwahs.org/museums/fort-east-martello/visit

West Martello Gardens and Fort is a tropical garden maintained by member-volunteers of the Key West Garden Club. FREE. 1100 Atlantic Blvd; Key West, FL 33040; Phone: (305) 294-3210; https://keywestgardenclub.com/

Harry S. Truman Little White House has been described as Florida's only Presidential Museum – and it is an unusual one, which also provides a fascinating portrait of one of America's most loved, and unconventional presidents. 111 Front St; Key West, FL 33040; Phone: (305) 671-9199; https://www.trumanlittlewhitehouse.com/

Hemingway Home and Museum honors one of the island's most famous residents. Ernest Hemingway lived in the 1851 Spanish Colonial style home and a visit provides an intimate look at the writer's life and life style. 907 Whitehead St; Key West, FL 33040; Phone: (305) 294-1136; https://www.hemingwayhome.com/

Hemingway Rum Company makes Papa's Pilar Rum, named after Hemingway's beloved boat. The distillery is open for a variety of tours and tastings. 201 Simonton St; Key West, FL 33040; Phone: (305) 414-8754; https://www.papaspilar.com/

Key West Lighthouse Museum & Keeper's Quarters is considered one of the prime spots for watching the sunset, but the lighthouse has feminist history as well. It opened in 1848 with a woman as its keeper, which was nearly unheard of during the 19th century. No longer a working lighthouse, visitors can walk up the 88 steps to the top of the light as well as explore the belongings, photographs, and words of the lighthouse keepers and their families. 938 Whitehead St; Key West, FL 33040; Phone: (305) 294-0012; https://www.kwahs.org/museums/lighthouse-keepers-quarters/visit

Key West Museum of Art & History at the Custom House is an example of Richardsonian Romanesque architecture, typical for Federal building projects near the end of the 19th century. It is currently leased to the Key West Art & Historical Society for use as a museum with two floors of exhibitions that weave together two centuries of history, art, people, and events. 281 Front St; Key West, FL 33040; Phone: (305) 295-6616; https://www.kwahs.org/museums/custom-house/visit

Key West Wildlife Center cares for injured wildlife but is open to the public and offers a nature trail overlooking a pond and two aviaries. The center is inside **Sonny McCoy Indigenous Park**, a native tree and bird park. 1801 White St; Key West, FL 33040; Phone: (305) 292-1008; http://keywestwildlifecenter.org/

One of the most famous (and free) activities in Key West is a visit to **Mallory Square** for its **Sunset Celebration**. It's a nightly party watching the sun set over the Gulf of Mexico. The square fills hours ahead of sunset with magicians, jugglers, clowns, psychics, local musicians, artists, and food. The square itself also hosts shops, galleries, and restaurants. 400 Wall St; Key West, FL 33040; https://www.mallorysquare.com/

Named after its founder, the late Mel Fisher, the **Mel Fisher Maritime Museum** displays some of the artifacts from his famous wreck-finding career. An unusual highlight is the fully operating Conservation and Archaeology Laboratory, and an exhibit on the trading of enslaved people. For more on Mel Fisher and his other museum see Sebastian, FL. 200 Greene St; Key West, FL 33040; Phone: (305) 294-2633; https://www.melfisher.org/

Nancy Forrester's Secret Garden is a haven for rescued and adopted parrots. NOTE: Hours may be limited. 518 Elizabeth St; Key West, FL 33040; Phone: (305) 294-0015; https://www.keywestparrots.com/

The **Old Town Literary Walking Tour** is offered by Key West Literary Seminar. The tour features homes and haunts of some of the literary greats of Key West. Available seasonally. https://www.kwls.org/tour/

Oldest House in South Florida features family portraits and original furnishings, as well as other period pieces, and documents telling the story of old Key West. 322 Duval St; Key West, FL 33040; Phone: (305) 294-9501; https://oirf.org/

Founded in 1871 by Cuban exiles **San Carlos Institute** is considered to be the cradle of Cuba's independence movement. Exhibits primarily focus on Cuba's history and the history of the Cuban-American community in Florida. A highlight is the exhibit on José Martí, Cuba's legendary patriot and poet. FREE. 516 Duval St; Key West, FL 33040; Phone: (305) 294-3887; https://www.institutosancarlos.org/

Southernmost Point in the Continental USA is definitely a selfie and tourist spot, but fun nonetheless. Whitehead St at South St; Key West, FL 33040.

Studios of Key West presents free exhibitions in the galleries, and fee-based performances and theater. 533 Eaton St; Key West, FL 33040; Phone: (305) 296-0458; http://www.tskw.org

Tennessee Williams Museum honors one of America's foremost playwrights who called Key West home for over thirty years. Peruse their collection of photographs, first edition plays and books, videos, and his typewriter as well as other artifacts. 513 Truman Ave; Key West, Florida 33040; Phone: (305) 204-4527; https://www.kwahs.org/museums/tennessee-williams/visit

Further Resources

Destination Archaeology Resource Center describes the Florida archaeological sites that you can visit, both on land and underwater. Phone: (850) 595-0050, Ext 108; https://destinationarchaeology.org/sites-to-visit

Florida Antique Tackle Collectors, Inc (FATC) sponsors three exhibitions each year. Club members bring historical displays from their collections as well as old tackle to trade. Open to the public, and visitors are even encouraged to bring their own old tackle for free appraisals. http://www.fatc.net/index.htm

Florida's Underwater Archaeological Preserves offers information on the remains of ships throughout the state. Some of the more accessible wrecks are included in this book but the website includes all the protected ships. http://www.museumsinthesea.com

With over 1.2 million acres of public land, the **National Forests of Florida** have many special places within their boundaries, including wilderness areas, botanical areas, freshwater springs, and scenic waterways. Learn more about them here: https://www.fs.usda.gov/main/florida/specialplaces

Scenic Trails

It's not the famed Appalachian Trail but the **Florida National Scenic Trail**, better known as the Florida Trail, is a federally-designated, non-motorized recreation trail that meanders approximately 1,300 miles across some of the landscapes unique to Florida. It's one of 11 national scenic trails in the United States. https://www.fs.usda.gov/florida/;

https://www.fs.usda.gov/main/fnst/home;
https://floridatrail.org/

Florida Paddling Trails Association provides information on most water trails in the state including the longest paddling trail in the continental United States.
https://www.floridapaddlingtrails.com

Florida State Parks website provides information on trails both within and outside the parks. It includes hiking, biking, and paddling opportunities.
https://www.floridastateparks.org/learn/trails-florida-state-parks

The Rails-to-Trails Conservancy offers **Florida Trails and Map**, a comprehensive interactive map of Florida trails.
https://www.traillink.com/state/fl-trails/

Great Florida Birding and Wildlife Trail is a network of 510 premier wildlife viewing sites across the state.
https://floridabirdingtrail.com/

Indian River Lagoon National Scenic Byway rambles along the Space Coast through state parks, preserves, small towns and lagoons. http://www.indianriverlagoonbyway.com/

Made in the USA
Columbia, SC
23 February 2024